The Mojer Mafia

Not that mafia, but my family

SHERRY LYNNE

First Edition

NEWMAN SPRINGS PUBLISHING
320 Broad Street
Red Bank, NJ 07701

First originally published by Newman Springs Publishing 2024

ISBN 979-8-89061-926-6 (Paperback)
ISBN 979-8-89308-355-2 (Hardcover)
ISBN 979-8-89061-927-3 (Digital)

Printed in the United States of America

To my mother, Sherrill. This book simply wouldn't have happened without her.

CONTENTS

ACKNOWLEDGMENTS

I would like to acknowledge my mother and father and Uncle Dan for their absolutely essential contributions to this book. I would also like to acknowledge the support I received from my husband and family over many years to write this book.

CHAPTER 1

"Ring of Fire"

(Johnny Cash)

"What in the world is he doing?" my grandmother, Helen, asked my aunt Bell.

"Well, I guess he's pretty mad," answered Bell.

"What made him so mad to do *this*?" my grandmother asked. "That brother of yours is dangerous, Nan," my grandmother said, using the nickname that she had for my aunt, whose name was actually Nannie Bell.

My Aunt Bell and my grandmother, Helen, were neighbors, and were the best of friends. They worked in the box department together at the Bata Shoe Factory in nearby Belcamp, Maryland. Helen ran the box machine, and Bell was the first one on the conveyor belt after Helen's machine. They had already been pretty good friends before Helen moved to the Edgewood Heights to be Bell's neighbor, just a few houses down. When they began to ride back and forth to work together, they became even closer. Neither of them knew how to drive, but they had a coworker nearby who drove them for many years.

Both women were good, hard-working, conservative women, about whom nobody could say a bad word. Bell was married, and Helen was divorced, which could, of course, have been scandalous in those days, but Helen's behavior was above reproach. Bell had her four boys, and Helen had four young children living at home at the time, so they were both very busy during the day, and worked at Bata all night. My mother, Sherrill, lived with my grandmother as well, although she was actually married. The women never really visited each other socially; but they were always borrowing sugar, or coffee, or whatever, or Helen would use Bell's phone because she didn't have one. That was about all the relationship they had time for outside of work. Years later, after Helen passed away, Bell told my mom that she felt so bad that she'd let so much time go by without seeing her friend after Helen moved away from Edgewood, and she never told Helen how much their friendship had helped her. Bell said she always drew strength from Helen, and when she thought she couldn't go on, she would look at Helen's strength, and she would get energized all over again.

Bell's brother, Thomas or Tom or my dad, did have a reputation for being a little crazy. He was a former Marine, where he had some success at boxing, and he was considered a badass. There were many stories circulating around the Edgewood Heights neighborhood, also known as the Projects, that he didn't take crap from anyone, fought a lot, and never lost. His reputation was deserved, at least in part. He never started a fight but didn't pass up many either. Dad had recently come from West Virginia to stay with his older sister after his stints in the military didn't end well. He was sleeping on her couch and trying to get his life together.

There were a lot of soldiers available for him to fight within the local area from the Edgewood Arsenal and the Aberdeen Proving Ground, both located northeast of Baltimore, Maryland, near the top of the Chesapeake Bay. Each Army installation had been established in 1917, Aberdeen to test field artillery and Edgewood to test, research, and develop chemical weapons. Musician Frank Zappa famously lived in Edgewood as a child in the 1940s while his father worked with chemicals like mustard gas and DDT as a meteorologist at the Edgewood Arsenal. It was currently 1962, and the two bases would later join as one in 1971.

There's no denying that Dad was a fighter with a lot of built-up anger inside, which came out sideways on anyone who messed with him. He was also, however, a really good guy who was willing to work hard and would help his family and friends with whatever they needed. Kids always loved him, maybe because he had a way of making us feel like we were valuable and precious, but would also hold us to the high standard of which he knew we were capable. While staying with Aunt Bell, he got close to her four young boys and spent a good deal of time with them.

Right now, he was on a mission. He was driving his big, black 1953 Chevy, as fast as he possibly could through the Projects, finding all of the big metal dumpsters in the vicinity, and pushing them with his car to line them up as best he could in front of Helen's house on Starr Street. The noise created by the metal dumpsters scraping across the road was extremely loud and annoying, and got everyone's attention. "He's not hurting anybody; he's just blowing off steam," Aunt Bell said to Helen, trying to defend her brother. "So, what IS he so mad at then?" Helen asked. "Someone's going to call the police!" she exclaimed. "He's mad because he found out that Sherrill is out on a date right now with one of his buddies," Aunt Bell answered. "*My* Sherry?" Helen asked with great surprise and confusion. Sherry was her nickname for my mom, Sherrill. When Bell answered, "Yes", Helen stated, "She's married, Nan." To which Bell replied, "Well, so is Thomas."

CHAPTER 2

"Take Me Home, Country Roads"

(John Denver)

My dad was born Thomas Edward Stanley on December 7, 1936, in Big Creek, West Virginia. Big Creek was way up in the mountains, about fifteen miles off the main highway. He was one of thirteen children, with one being stillborn and one dying of worms when he was three years old. Dad was right in the middle—having three older brothers, Earl, Ernest, and Emmett; two older sisters, Bell and Jean; one younger brother, Ellis; and four younger sisters, Ruth, Helen, Juanita, and Judy. My grandfather, Lawrence, worked in the coal mines, but money was always tight. The family was very poor, with their only advantage being the large garden they grew to provide their family with enough to eat. Because raising the crops was so essential to the family's survival, they had to be taken care of at all costs. My grandfather once bought a mule for $5 to help out in the garden, but it died as soon as he got it home. That money for the mule had been hard to come by, and he didn't get a refund for the mule, which was purchased "as is," just like a used car. Whenever they did have a mule for the farm, they did whatever it took to keep it working. My grandfather would attach a board across the front of the mule and hang an apple from it down at the end, tied on with a string, so the mule would keep walking, trying but never succeeding to get to that apple. It sounds like something you would see in a cartoon, but it worked. Another time, they had a mule that wandered down to the river and lay down, refusing to get up and go when it was time to work. My grandfather literally built a fire under the mule's butt to make him get up. That worked too.

Dad's father was from the Coalwood/Coretta area of West Virginia, and his family were all coal miners. My dad's mother, Ida, was born somewhere around the Roanoke/Salem area of Virginia, and her family probably came to West Virginia, seeking work in the coal mines. Her family lived in Yukon, West Virginia, when Dad was growing up. Dad remembers all his grandparents, and he said his paternal grandparents were very nice, but his mother's parents were just as evil as his mother would turn out to be, and he received more beatings from them than from his own parents. He doesn't know anything else about his family's histories or how his parents met. As was the custom of the time, parents didn't have those types of conversations with their children. His mother and father were affectionate and cordial with each other, and they appeared to have been a love match.

Dad's first memory was at five years old, and he was arguing with his parents about a bag of wheat puff cereal. The family had just moved to a different house, and Dad couldn't find the bag of cereal, so he thought they had left it at the old house. It turned out that his siblings had already eaten it. Knowing how Dad would later be treated by his parents, I couldn't believe that he would be arguing with them and getting away with it when I heard this story, but I would get my explanation later.

My grandfather had been a home preacher since before Dad was born, but during the Depression, he wasn't making enough money in the coal mines to care for his family, so he ran moonshine for a little while to make ends meet. After that experience, he stayed away from religion until about a year before his death. My dad thinks that his father felt guilty for committing such illegal acts during the Depression and didn't feel worthy of having a relationship with God for a long time. His father's relationship with religion might have had something to do with why Dad also turned his back on religion, and even God, for many years. Growing up, however, my grandmother and the children attended church every Sunday at an old-time Baptist church, where they spoke in tongues and danced around when they felt the spirit. Dad says the first time he ever saw a woman's vagina was when a woman was "feeling the spirit" in church. She was writhing on the floor with her dress coming up and wasn't wearing any underpants.

My grandfather was a hardworking, honest man, who wouldn't take anything from anyone and would rather give you something than sell it to you or take it from you. He started working in the coal mines some time before my dad was born. He was given an easy job because he played on a baseball farm team for the Cincinnati Reds, but the mining work was needed to subsidize his pay. His job was to run a tram of coal out of the mountains, with his eldest son as his brakeman. The family had the typical West Virginia mining town experience, with company-owned property, company store, company doctor, etc. Before Dad was five years old and the family moved away from Big Creek, Dad said my grandfather was getting too old to play baseball any longer. My aunt Judy says he stopped playing baseball because he injured his fingers in the mine. She said he would have had a chance at a major league career.

At the same time that my grandfather stopped playing minor league baseball, he left the coal mines and started working for the State Road Commission (SRC) as a road grader operator. A coworker rented my grandfather a house in an unincorporated community called Rift about ninety miles down the mountain from Big Creek, between the towns of War and Cucumber. The family lived in this house until my grandfather finished building their own three-bedroom house, with lumber that was provided by the SRC. My grandfather was a good carpenter and was quite capable of building his own home, but he liked to joke with my dad that he "cut that board off three times, and it's still too short." He had other skills too. Dad said he could peel an apple or a potato or anything else so thin that he might as well have left the peeling on. The house that my grandfather built was on about ten acres of land next to the Tug Fork River, across from a sawmill, but it all belonged to the state of West Virginia, not my grandfather. The family lived there for some time until my grandfather went back to work in the coal mines. Then they moved into a bigger home, back across the other side of the river, where they stayed for about fourteen years. The house was very unusual, having once been a roller-skating rink that was then converted into a very large duplex.

Dad said it was "pure hell" growing up in West Virginia because of the poverty and very hard work he had to endure as a child. Most of the community was as poor as Dad's family was, but his family had it worse because they had so many children to feed. In Dad's family, you were a baby until you were six years old and started school. While you were a baby, you didn't have any chores, and you weren't punished harshly for your behavior. This would explain how Dad got away with arguing with his parents at the age of five about the wheat puff cereal. Once you started school, however, you were given a job to do, and you got the belt when you misbehaved. Dad and his siblings had a tough childhood, which they agreed most children today wouldn't have survived. They spent a lot of time in the woods, traveling up and down the mountains. There were mountain lions, bears, poisonous snakes, and all manner of critters in those mountains. My aunt Helen said they were told a tale as kids that a panther lived in the mountains, up in a particular tree. She said the kids were scared when they had to pass under the tree to get to the well for water, and they would put their coats over their heads, like that would save them from the panther! Dad said the mountains weren't nearly as high as he remembered when he went back after leaving home. He joked that they must have leveled them off after he was gone. He said, "The mountains became hills, and the cliffs became big rocks." I'm sure the houses that he lived in were much smaller than he remembered as well.

Dad didn't like school at first, but then it became a haven away from home for him. A typical day for Dad growing up was to get on the school bus, usually with no breakfast, because my grandmother didn't like to get up and cook for the children. One time, he didn't get on the bus because his stomach was cramping very badly. He went back home, and his mom had made biscuits and gravy for his father's breakfast, so Dad got to eat breakfast too that morning. Afterward, he walked to school. His mother also didn't care for housekeeping at all and gave as many of the chores to her daughters as she could. The conditions in the house could be pretty bad. Dad never mentioned this, but one of my aunts tells of the kids sleeping on bare mattresses with giant holes in the center, apparently eaten away from bed-wetting, for which Dad and his siblings were punished. She said that there were shelves of canning in the house that had gotten old, and the jars had exploded and oozed out their contents, with nobody bothering to clean up the mess. This could be one reason Dad always appreciated what a wonderful housekeeper my mother was.

My dad believed that my grandmother was a hateful and selfish woman, and I saw that for myself when I was growing up. Others in my dad's family claim to have had a different experience with her, giving her more adoration and respect than I thought she deserved. Dad said she was nicer when he was younger but became meaner and meaner as he grew up. Maybe she learned it from her own family. When her children were growing up, she would eat candy right in front of them and not allow them to have any. It fascinates and confuses me that when she died, she had an entire room full of items she had bought over the years, still in boxes, that she never used or gave to anyone else. Dad said he never blamed himself for her behavior, like many abused children do; he learned from observing other mothers that his mother shouldn't have treated her children the way she did. Dad considered himself the black sheep of the family, although I don't remember any of his siblings referring to him as such. It is a peculiar fact, however, that he was called Thomas rather than Edward. Each of his four brothers were called by the *E* name they had been given, whether it was their first or middle name, but not my father.

Dad said that growing up, he always managed to do something wrong or mostly to make his mother angry about something. When his father arrived home from the coal mines in the middle of the night, he would get Dad out of bed and beat him for his transgressions that his mom had reported from that day. One of Dad's biggest sources of punishment was that he got into an argument nearly every day with his brother, Ellis, who was younger by eighteen months. Ellis would pick at Dad until he would lose his temper, and it would turn physical, for which Dad would be punished. The rule in the family was supposed to be that if you fought a sibling, you both got a beating. My grandmother, however, would change that rule, partly because Ellis was younger and smaller than Dad and partly because she just didn't seem to care for my dad. So rather than both boys being punished for the fight, usually only my dad would get the beating. Ellis would also do bad things and blame them on Dad to get him into trouble. This occurred all throughout Dad's childhood, from the time he started school. He was beaten sometimes up to five days a week. He said he knew that if his father went to work that day, he was probably getting a beating that night. Some old-school folks might say that these were merely spankings, but my grandfather used a leather mining belt that was full of metal fastenings to hold different tools, and the bruises from that metal would last for days. My dad said the worst part, though, was the waiting. From bedtime until his father finally came home, he would lie in bed waiting in the dark for the beating he knew was coming, unable to sleep from the fear and anxiety.

Ellis said that Dad would beat his ass every time they fought as he was bigger and stronger. One time, however, Ellis was able to get the best of Dad. They were fighting in the bed at bedtime, as they often did, when Ellis grabbed the terrible ingrown toenail that Dad had at the time. Dad was in awful pain and kept threatening to kill Ellis if he didn't let go, but Ellis would just squeeze harder. He said he was afraid to let go in fear that Dad would really hurt him once he did. Finally, Dad promised he wouldn't hurt Ellis if he would just let go, so they came to a truce, which each of them honored.

When Dad got home from school each day, he changed into his other of two outfits, one that was clean and one that was dirty. Then he went to work in the family's large garden, except in the wintertime when they would just sit around inside the house, where Dad loved to read. When the kids actually had time to play, they didn't have any toys except what little they could salvage from the riverbanks after a flood. He thought that was the good Lord's way of taking care of them. They would sometimes find little toy trucks and even a wagon once. Dad was so enamored of that wagon that he later made it a family tradition to buy his children, nieces and nephews, and grandchildren a little red wagon. They also salvaged bicycle parts. Once, when Dad was about thirteen years old, his older brother, Ernest, had a motorized bicycle whose motor no longer functioned, so he gave it to his younger brothers. They were pretty handy at putting parts together to create something they could ride. They managed to get spare paint sometimes and would paint the toys and bikes to make them look nicer. Once in a while, my grandfather would play baseball with his children when there wasn't work to be done. Dad loved that. He would continue to play the game for many years and enjoy it for the rest of his life.

Dad and his siblings had dogs as pets growing up, and Dad's favorite was Jack. They got him when a neighbor's dog had puppies, and he was a cross between a Collie and a German Shepherd. He was fearless at protecting the children from poisonous copperhead snakes when they were out in the yard and was bitten about a dozen times, as indicated by his coming home with a huge, swollen head, but he would always recover. Dad's favorite story about Jack was when he and another dog were fed boiled okra, which was so slimy and slippery in this form that it was possible for one of the dogs to slurp down his share from his bowl so fast that he thought the other dog had eaten it, and one hell of a fight commenced.

Once, Jack had been gone for fourteen days when the family got word that a neighbor had found him caught in a trap. When Dad's older brother Emmett got to the scene, the neighbor was trying to free the dog from the trap, but Jack was so afraid and traumatized that he kept trying to bite him. The neighbor raised a large stick in the air to bash the dog in the head and kill him, putting him out of his misery since he wouldn't allow the man to free him. Just as he was about to swing the stick, he heard the sound of a shotgun rack and turned to see Emmett standing there with a shotgun pointed at him. Emmett told him that if he hit the dog, it would be the last thing he ever did. The neighbor put the stick down, and Jack let Emmett free him from the trap. True to form, Jack made a complete recovery from his injuries.

Once, when Jack got distemper, they were told that it would cost $1 a day for the medicine to treat him. This was very expensive at the time, especially for a dog, so Dad thought that Jack would have to be put down. However, his older brother Emmett again stepped in to save the dog and took him to the home he shared with his wife, where he bought his medicine and cared for him until he was well, including feeding the dog pork chops every day because he had gotten down to skin and bones. Emmett kept Jack at his house from then on, and he appreciated Jack's protection of his young daughter in their yard. He taught Jack to be a great squirrel and rabbit retriever. Jack lived to age fourteen when he walked off into the woods to die alone.

Dad's happiest childhood memory was when his older brothers Emmett and Earl bought him and brother Ellis some Roy Rogers and Gene Autry cap guns and holster sets for Christmas when they were around eleven and twelve years old. It was the only Christmas present Dad ever got growing up. Dad read stories about Rogers and Autry and listened to their programs on the radio. He also liked *The Lone Ranger*, *Tales of the Texas Rangers*, and *Hopalong Cassidy* shows. Although he enjoyed the stories of these characters, Dad said his older brother Emmett was his real hero, and he never did look up to any famous people either. He said they were just real people like him but who had gotten lucky. The family would also gather around on Saturday nights to listen to the Grand Ole Opry together. They wouldn't have a television until 1956, by which time Dad had already left home.

Dad did well in school and was very proud of the fact that he was third highest in his class in the ninth grade and had perfect attendance at school for five years in a row. He would even walk to school when the snow or ice kept the bus from coming, just so he wouldn't miss a day. He did get into trouble in school a couple of times. The first time was in the second grade for hitting another boy with a rock at the bus stop before school. The boy had been picking relentlessly at Dad, as was his regular habit, and Dad was just trying to defend himself. After the incident, he got on the bus, went to school, and was sitting in class when he was called to the principal's office, where a state trooper was waiting for him along with the other boy and the boy's father. Dad was in big trouble for the wound he had inflicted on the boy's head with the rock, but once he and other witnesses had a chance to tell Dad's side of the story, the other boy was admonished by the trooper, and his father was told that his son was a troublemaker, so my dad was vindicated.

Another time, when Dad was still in elementary school, he and his friend, nicknamed Pecker Head, were playing tag on the playground after school, where they had to wait for forty-five minutes every afternoon for the bus to pick them up on its second trip. Pecker Head got the idea to go outside the schoolyard fence to keep from being tagged, and soon Dad tried it as well. Just as Dad got outside the fence to join his friend, the principal drove by in his car, leaving for the day, and told the two boys to report to his office the next morning to answer for their transgression. The principal was nicknamed Razor Face behind his back by his students, due to the razor strap he wielded for punishment. That next morning, he told the two boys that he was going to whip them until they cried. Each boy ended up with fifty licks with the razor strap because they refused to cry. Years later, when Dad came back from the Marine Corps, he went to the school to pay back Razor Face for the cruel whipping he had received as a small boy. He literally chased the man around the campus trying to catch him for about an hour, with Razor Face continuing to hide from and outrun Dad. Dad's friends finally convinced him to give up the chase and go home. Ironically, it wasn't even against the rules for the boys to have been outside the schoolyard fence, so there was never a reason for them to be punished in the first place.

Dad had decided at a very early age that he would not treat his loved ones with the same cruel, evil behavior that he saw from his mother and her family. He was very peaceful as a young child and didn't fight back with his siblings or schoolmates, but at some point, he said he couldn't take it anymore, and he did start fighting back. He became rebellious because he hated his surroundings. He tried to change the things that he thought were unfair but found that he had little control over them, and that made him very angry. He did manage to get back at his mom for some of her unjust behavior. She played card and board games with her children and would get very upset when they beat her, so they would all let her win, except for my dad. He wasn't going to let her win if he could beat her fair and square. At some point while Dad was growing up, his mother began to sell chocolate candy bars for money on the side. She kept the candy bars in a locked suitcase under her bed, and the children dreamed of all that candy sitting under there, with not one bite for them. My dad didn't like candy or any sweets until much later in his life, but he would use a bobby pin to open the suitcase and sneak a bar every now and then for his brothers and sisters to share. Nobody ever told that secret.

Dad did have a few pleasures in life growing up. He had his first crush on a girl in the seventh grade, and they became sweethearts two years later. They remained so until Dad left school, and she was a great comfort to him. His family lived about three and a half miles from the town of War, so they wouldn't go there very often, but Dad got to go to the theater in town around six times a year to see movies, always Westerns. Dad was sometimes allowed to earn fifty cents cutting a neighbor's grass, which gave him twenty-five cents for the show and twenty-five cents for popcorn and a coke. In spite of these fleeting happy moments, Dad was becoming more and more unhappy with his life. He was very intelligent and had a love for learning that he later passed on to his children, but he dropped out of school at age sixteen because he was made fun of for the way he dressed in dirty, ill-fitting coveralls and overalls, often with no shoes. He and his siblings were each provided with one pair of shoes at the beginning of the school year, and when they became too worn or painful to wear any longer, they had none. Dad's sister, my aunt Helen, played softball on a church team and never wore shoes because her one pair of shoes for the year had long worn or grown out by the time softball season started. After playing barefoot for over twenty years, the league finally required her to wear shoes to be able to play. By this time, she could afford the shoes; she was just accustomed to playing without them. Growing up, Dad's shoes were ordered from the Sears catalog. They were Brogans that laced up ankle high. They had metal taps on the toe and heel to protect from wear, so they tapped when he walked. This caused one teacher to always say, "Come in, Wild Bill, but leave your horse outside." Sounds like a funny comment, but as a self-conscious young boy, my dad didn't appreciate the attention.

Dad wanted to get a steady job after school to help pay for a better wardrobe, but his father wouldn't allow it because he required Dad to work on the family farm. If there wasn't work to do on the farm, his father found other work for the children to do to keep them out of trouble, he said. Often, they had enough surplus crops to sell some for extra money, but his father didn't believe in selling anything even if it would help provide in some small way for his very large family. He would give away the crops, mostly corn, instead. This really upset my dad because those surplus crops could have made his life just a little bit easier. My grandfather did allow my aunt Helen to get a job washing a lady's canning jars for one penny per jar, probably because she was a girl and couldn't work as hard on the farm as the boys. She thought she was making big money at the time and was just happy to have any job at all.

When I was growing up, both my parents were adamant that we always dressed well because they had each struggled with clothing as children. We weren't allowed to wear overalls, even when they were in fashion, because Dad was made to wear them growing up and was made fun of for it. We also weren't allowed to have a hole in our clothing, and if Dad saw one, he would put his finger in it and tear the garment from our bodies. We always thought this was really funny until one time when I was about twenty-seven years old and wearing a pair of ripped-up jeans, as was the fashion at the time. Dad always complained about my jeans, not understanding how people would pay money for jeans that already had holes in them when you bought them. One day, he managed to get his hands on a small hole on the side of my jeans and tear them all the way across the back. He thought he had done a proper job of destroying them so I wouldn't wear them again, but I just wore black tights underneath instead. Sorry, Dad, but I loved those jeans!

It was in the tenth grade that Dad finally quit school in spite of his love of learning and the good grades that he earned. He got a job helping a man who serviced jukeboxes, but it only paid $2 a day. He found better work on a gas pipeline digging ditches for $8 an hour and was promoted to welder's helper. He really wanted to get out of West Virginia, however, and make a better and different life for himself than the one he had growing up, so once he turned seventeen, he convinced his parents to sign for him to join the Marine Corps. Dad said that it was his father and the Marine Corps who made him the man he became, one who had discipline, respect for others, and a demand for respect for himself. He was very proud of his service in the Marines, and we heard a lot about it growing up, especially in our early years. When he left home to join the Marines, he intended to make something of his life and to never return to West Virginia again. He said that if some things hadn't happened to him, he would have been a much better man, but he didn't think he did too bad. He said he didn't learn about love or kindness or generosity growing up at home but started to learn about those things after he joined the Marines. He talked to people a lot about their families, how they grew up, and where they were from. Other people's positive experiences had a big effect on him and gave him hope for his future.

Dad was stationed in Korea in 1954, one year after the Korean war ended. He was in charge of the supply room on his post and liked his job. He was also a good marksman and enjoyed that as well. He was very proud of how he had advanced so quickly and easily in his career and loved being away from his oppressive and poverty-stricken life in West Virginia. He was respectful of and interested in the Korean culture. He learned to count to ten and to sing a little children's song, which he taught to us kids when we were little. One thing he didn't like, however, was the food. He said he practically lived off pizza that he got from the mess hall, and he ate so much of it that he never wanted it again, so we weren't allowed to have it when he was home while I was growing up. He liked exploring the countryside on a motorcycle that he had purchased there. Once, however, he was driving the bike on a winding road and took a curve too fast, which caused him and the bike to fly off the road and into a house. The house was not very sturdy, so he ran all the way through it on the bike, luckily not hitting anyone or hurting himself seriously but doing considerable damage to the house. He ended up giving the family his motorcycle to help pay for the repair of the house, so that was the end of that hobby.

Dad was able to go home to West Virginia on leave once and was sleeping on his parents' couch during the visit. One night, Dad went out drinking with his buddies and returned home sometime after midnight. He was trying to sleep on the couch, and his mother's pet parakeet wouldn't stop squawking and was keeping him awake. His mother discovered that the bird was dead the next morning, lying in the bottom of the cage. She thought that it must have frozen to death in the night. My dad agreed that it was very cold that night. He had actually silenced the bird, permanently, but never told his mother the truth.

Dad was boxing for the Marines and doing really well at it, as he was naturally a good fighter. He was very strong with a large body and large hands that packed one hell of a punch. He looked like he might have a future as a fighter, but then he started getting nosebleeds. The Marines assumed it was caused by the boxing, but even after stopping the activity, the nosebleeds continued. Because they couldn't find a cure for his malady, Dad was medically discharged from the Marines. One of his sisters, who was known for her embellishments, just like my mom, would later tell a story that my dad had gotten into a bar fight in Korea, had damaged his skull, and had a metal plate placed in his head. She said this horrible injury was the reason he left the Marines and returned home and was also the reason why he would later become violent when he drank alcohol. Dad said he loved his brothers and sisters growing up, but as they got older, he began to dislike some of their behavior, namely spreading rumors or telling lies about him or others, like the one about the metal plate. It wasn't always his siblings that did this; it was sometimes their spouses. Dad never participated in this type of behavior, and he hated it later when my mom did, so Mom tried to keep it away from him as much as she could, although that didn't stop her from participating. Dad said you should keep your mouth shut and leave people alone. He shared confidences with a few people in his life, but not many. It was true, however, that Dad would often become violent when he drank, but it wasn't because of a fictional metal plate in his head. It was much more complicated than that. He would also continue to fight for many years, although not in the ring.

Dad returned home from the Marine Corps to live with his parents again and began receiving unemployment benefits from the Marines. He helped provide for the family all he could as they were barely scraping by. My grandfather had been laid off from his job at the mine, and he and my grandmother were subsisting on welfare. By then, all but maybe the youngest child had left home. My grandfather was eligible to receive Social Security Disability due to his health but was denied the benefits. Dad did something remarkable for his background and upbringing at the time. He wrote a letter to a West Virginia congresswoman asking for help with getting his father's disability benefits approved. The letter was a success, and my grandfather received a lump sum of retroactive benefits along with his regular monthly checks. He hated owing people money and was very happy to pay the entire grocery bill he owed of about $100 as soon as he received his check.

Dad wasn't able to find work, hated being back home in West Virginia, and had loved the military, so he decided to join the Army. By now his nosebleeds had stopped, so that was no longer a problem, but he neglected to tell the Army recruiter about his Marine Corps service, which was a problem. While still in basic training, his marksmanship was so exemplary that the Army suspected he had prior military experience and did some research. When they discovered his records from the Marines, they discharged him with less than honorable service. With his second military career over, he headed for Edgewood, Maryland, to stay with his sister Bell and hopefully start a new life.

CHAPTER 3

"Broken Girl"

(Matthew West)

My mother also grew up poor but for different reasons. She was born Sherrill Jean Smith in Bel Air, Maryland, on August 19, 1945. She was one of nine children. Her father, Wade, was a civil service worker who made good wages but refused to share them with his family. He was not just hateful and cruel; he was evil. I have nothing good to say about him, and by the time I finally saw or heard of him offering a kindness to anyone, I was fourteen years old. The kindness was directed at me, and I turned it down.

Wade was born in 1920 to Joseph Jasper Smith and Viola Walthall on an Indian reservation in Pawhuska, Oklahoma. His parents had met on a ship to the US from England and were married after they got here. They were working on the reservation as missionaries and were not Native American, as Wade led everyone to believe all the way up until my aunt traced the family lineage through the Mormon church about ten years ago. He certainly looked Native American with his dark-red skin and chiseled face. He was very tall and very slim. He was not handsome but not unattractive and was very charming and funny. When Wade's father was bitten by a snake and died on the reservation, Viola's sister Lula, who lived in Pennsylvania, sent her husband, only known as PopPop, to pick up the family in Oklahoma. He was to take Viola, known to my mom as Gammy, along with her children to live with them on their farm, where they raised cattle, horses, and crops. He packed Viola, Wade and his three brothers, and Wade's sister Jean, known to my mom as Aunt Jeannie, into the car and was heading out of town when they crossed some railroad tracks, and the car was struck by a train. Wade's three brothers were killed, but Wade, Gammy, PopPop, and Aunt Jeannie survived.

In Pennsylvania, PopPop was horribly abusive to Wade, whom he would beat with a horse whip and once hit him in the head with a hammer for shoeing a horse incorrectly. He worked Wade like a dog along with his own three sons. The four boys were very strong and were able to pick up a car and move it, which they often did for fun. Mom always said that Aunt Jeannie was sent to Boston to a finishing school, but she actually attended the Eastern Nazarene College, a Christian liberal arts college located in Quincy, Massachusetts, a suburb of Boston. Whatever the school, she certainly had a very different life than her brother, with refinement and education rather than hard work and abuse. At about eighteen years of age, Wade left the farm to work at Bryan's Apple Orchard in Northeastern Maryland, where he met my grandmother, Helen Kathryn Hoffmaster.

Helen was born in Chambersburg, Pennsylvania, in 1922. Her father was Gabriel Hoffmaster, and her mother was Maizie Metzler. Maizie died of pneumonia at the age of thirty-five, leaving behind six young children. My grandmother was ten years old at the time. My mom said that Gabriel took all the children to a Mennonite orphanage rather than try to care for them himself, but my uncle Dan thought he only took some of the children or maybe only my grandmother. Either way, my grandmother's five siblings—Clair, Suz, Dot, Velma, and Grace—were each adopted out to good families, but my grandmother was not, for unknown reasons. At the orphanage, she was raised in the strict Mennonite religion and taught to be pious, work hard, and not complain. My mom only knew of one story from the orphanage, when there was a lice epidemic, and all the children had their heads shaved and doused in a purple liquid and then covered with bandages fashioned into a turban.

In stark contrast to Helen's upbringing in the orphanage, her sixth great-grandfather was actually a well-known and much-researched historical figure. He was Hans Herr, a Mennonite bishop originally from Switzerland, and was the first Mennonite bishop to emigrate to America, landing in Philadelphia, Pennsylvania, in 1910. There is a granite monument for him in the Willow Street Mennonite Cemetery in Lancaster, Pennsylvania, where all the family stayed until my grandmother left the area for Maryland. She was educated up to a point of probably eighth grade by the orphanage, but if she wanted to further her education, someone would have to pay for it. The only opportunity my grandmother had to earn that money was to work for a local family during the summer, with the promise that they would pay for her education for the following school year. She found a family who promised to do so and worked hard at their apple orchard all summer. When the school year started, however, she was told that there weren't enough funds for them to pay as promised. She returned to the family the following summer, doubtful that they would fulfill their promise this time but having no other options to possibly further her education.

That summer, she met my grandfather, Wade, who was also working at the orchard, and she was probably attracted to Wade's charm and humor. Helen was a stout, big-boned Swiss/German lady with large, masculine hands, but she was feminine, graceful, and had a plain beauty. At the time they met, she had long hair past her waist but kept it braided and wound around her head under a Mennonite cap. When the picking season ended and Helen was told again that there weren't enough funds for her education, my grandfather persuaded her to marry him instead, which she did. Wade was nineteen, and Helen was seventeen. At some point, Wade found work at the Aberdeen Proving Ground as a civil servant. He tested vehicles and heavy equipment for the military and was also a sometime chauffeur in Washington, DC, for government staff.

They settled in Stepney, an unincorporated area just outside of Aberdeen, Maryland, where Wade built them a cinder-block home. Between the time they married in 1939 and when they left this house in Stepney, they had seven children. The oldest was Donald Wade, born in 1942 in Pennsylvania, and then came Dean Laverne in 1944, also born in Pennsylvania. My mom, Sherrill Jean, came next in 1945 and was born in Bel Air, about eleven miles northwest of Stepney. Then there was Gerald Stanley, John Carroll, Daniel Joseph, and Samuel David. Around 1956, Wade had a stroke and was left with a limp and a slight speech impediment. He never held down steady work again and was able to draw Social Security Disability.

My grandparents were very religious, and my grandmother continued to be extremely pious. My grandfather, however, was a hypocrite in the cruelest way. My mom said that he donated so much money to their church that his name could be found on many items in the building, embossed on little metal plaques indicating his donation. My uncle Dan said he knew there was at least a pew with the family's name on it. At home, however, he provided the barest necessities to his family. They had little food and sometimes none at all. My mother told of the family eating potatoes one day and potato peelings the next. At times when they had nothing to eat, my grandmother and the children would sit at the table and read passages from the Bible to fill them in lieu of food. My grandfather, however, would take his meals in a restaurant in town, his favorite being a nice, juicy steak.

Food wasn't the only thing Wade deprived from his family. He had built them a simple home of mostly cinder blocks but never bothered to connect the home to indoor plumbing, although all the components were sitting on the land, ready to be hooked up to a water source and utilized. Thus, the family used an outhouse in the backyard. Dan remembered sitting on the seat in the outhouse once when a deer came up to the back door of the building, which was always open. He just sat and watched the deer for a while until it wandered away. Mom had a much worse memory of being bitten on her behind by a dog once when she was running from the house to the outhouse. Wade also deprived his children of heat. In the cold

Maryland winter months, he would place a sheet of plyboard over the entrance to the older children's room so that the available heat would be concentrated on the room where he slept with my grandmother and the youngest children. My mother shared a bed with her two older brothers, and they had no blankets or pillows or any bedding whatsoever. They slept in between a mattress and box spring, huddled together for warmth. My grandmother loved her children and did her best to care for them, but she demanded nothing of my grandfather. Having been raised with nothing in the orphanage and being a Mennonite, who believed that everything should be plain, she didn't yearn for nice things or even comforts for her or her children.

If only that were the worst my grandfather had done to his family. He was also mentally, emotionally, and physically abusive, horribly so. He beat my grandmother on a regular basis. My mother said that once, he even chained her to a tree in the yard for days and went out to beat her several times before finally freeing her. This behavior was tolerated because they lived out in the country with few neighbors and only one law enforcement officer in the rural county. This officer was very afraid of my grandfather and considered him violent and mentally unstable, which he was. My grandmother, who was also deathly afraid of my grandfather, for obvious reasons, would never complain to anyone about his behavior or seek help. The only people in her life were those at the church, which they attended Sunday morning, Sunday evening, and Wednesday evening, and the members of the church considered my grandfather a hero who lived for the Lord. That was all they knew of him. The monster was abusive to his children as well. One time, my grandfather drove a dump truck home, opened the tailgate, told my mother to scrape out the dried dirt with a stick, and went into the house. After some time, he flew out of the house in a rage; from what my mother didn't know. He yelled at her to get away from the truck. At this point, she was standing on the ground behind the truck, having scraped off all the dirt except what was on the back edge of the bed. He told her to get the hell away from the truck, and when she tried to protest that she was almost finished with the job and kept scraping, he slammed the gate shut on her arm, breaking it in the process.

He didn't just abuse his family during fits of rage. Sometimes, he was very calm and calculating during the process. When my mother's younger brother Dan was a baby crawling around the floor, my grandfather liked to call him over to him, then kick him back across the floor. He would then laugh at how stupid the baby was because he would come again when called. Dan was also told that Wade kicked him down the stairs once when Dan crawled up to his leg and was trying to hold onto it.

My grandfather really showed his cruelty when my mother had a terrible accident at about the age of three. My grandmother had an iron skillet full of hot grease on the stove, and while she wasn't looking, my mother put her finger inside the little loop at the end of the pan handle, and when she tried to pull her finger back, it caught in the loop, tipped the pan, and some of the hot grease poured down onto my mother's head and shoulder. The second-degree burns were treated at home, with her mother immediately coating them in butter, an old remedy that we now know only served to insulate the heat and make the burn worse. The evening of the accident, my mother sat at the dinner table with the family, bandaged and in terrible pain. Her father suddenly jumped up and smacked her so hard that she and her chair fell over onto the floor as he was screaming that the smell of her was making him sick while he was trying to eat his dinner. Remarkably, my mother was able to regrow some of the hair she had lost to the burn, although it was terribly thin. She was left with a gruesome scar that spread across her shoulder and upper arm. She was very self-conscious of both her hair and her scar for her entire life.

When the children grew older, they tried to intervene in their father's beatings of their mother. One time, the three oldest siblings—Don, Dean, and Sherrill—had a plan to kill Wade while he was beating their mother. The plan was to have Sherrill hit their dad from behind, which she did, and have him chase her to underneath the stairs, which he did. In the meantime, the two boys were waiting upstairs to pick up a heavy mirror to drop down on my grandfather, but they dropped it too soon when they couldn't hold it any longer, and it missed him. Their dad picked up a piece of glass from the mirror and cut Don with it, then beat him. I believe the three kids were very lucky that they didn't get worse. Another time, my grandfather was beating my grandmother very badly, and my mother's two older brothers were able to run to a public pay phone about a mile away to try and call for help. My grandfather was quick on their heels and caught them inside the phone booth before they were able to make a call. He beat them so badly that when my mother passed by the booth on the way to school the next day, it was coated in blood, and places in the glass had been broken by the boys' heads. They never made that mistake again.

Somehow, the family managed to survive these brutal beatings, all except for one: my mother's younger brother, Gerry, who happened to be her favorite at the time. When he was seven years old, my grandfather beat him very badly, with the worst part being when he stomped his foot into Gerry's abdomen several times. Gerry was bedridden and barely conscious for several days after the beating, then began to run a high fever, and my grandmother feared that he would die. When she begged my grandfather to get him help, he refused to take Gerry to the hospital, saying that the Lord would heal the boy. Finally, the family pastor came to the house to find out why the family had not been attending church services. He took one look at Gerry, picked him up, and carried him to his car to go to the hospital. My grandmother held her son on the way to the hospital with the pastor. The story told to the pastor was that Gerry had an accident on his bicycle, and his stomach was caught by the handlebars when he flew over the front of the bike.

My grandfather, in the meantime, quickly gathered his belongings and fled the home, knowing that his disgusting secret would be found out once his son had been examined. Gerry died in the hospital the next day of gangrene in his stomach. The doctors said that they probably could have saved him if he had been brought in sooner. Charges were never pressed against my grandfather for his murder due to my grandmother insisting that his bicycle accident story was true, but my grandfather's reputation had been ruined in the church—the only people whose opinion he cared about. Helen's sister, Grace, had moved herself down the street from Helen just before the incident with Gerry took place, and she tried to help her sister, urging her to get away from her evil husband, but my grandmother refused to leave Wade no matter how badly he treated her and her children. My grandfather did not appreciate Grace's interference, and he tortured her while she was living nearby, once trying to hit her with his car, and she was pregnant at the time. He would also make noises outside her windows to scare her, and he treated her with great disrespect whenever he was in her company. Grace was an attractive, worldly, and classy lady, but was also a tough gal who wouldn't take crap from anyone. My grandfather, however, terrified her.

As for Gerry, Dan believed the story that he was riding a bike too big for him, and then he hit a telephone pole, and the impact of the handle bars on his stomach caused internal bleeding, although Dan was only two or three years old when Gerry died. He said he did remember sitting on the couch with his mom who had a worried white face, and Gerry was throwing up in a basin, not long before he died. Dan agreed, however, that Wade wouldn't take Gerry to the hospital for days until the family pastor finally insisted and that Gerry did die of gangrene. If not from abuse, Gerry at least died from neglect.

Gerry had died in December, 1956. My mom was eleven years old at the time. Previously that year, on February 19, the last son in the family, Samuel David, had been born. When my grandfather left home the day after Gerry's funeral, he left the family with no money, and there were six kids to feed. Luckily, there was more food than normal for a short time because of Gerry's funeral and neighbors bringing food, so they didn't starve. My grandmother got a job at Bata Shoe Company right away, working third shift so that my mom could be with the little kids overnight and still go to school during the day. The little kids were newborn, two and four at the time. The two older boys slept in my grandmother's room and shared her bed, and baby Sam slept right beside the bed in his crib. It was Mom's job to keep the boys in the bed during the night and take care of the baby if he woke up. Luckily, Mom said Sam was a good baby, and she didn't remember him being any trouble. Dan was tougher to deal with before he started school, but when that time came, he calmed down and did well in school, getting good marks and being very polite. In the morning, Mom would feed everyone and get herself and John ready for school. They would leave when my grandmother got home from work. I'm assuming that my grandmother slept when the boys would nap during the day or maybe after my mom got home from school.

That situation must have been so tough for my grandmother but also a relief to not be beaten or see her children beaten any longer. It was also a lot of responsibility for an eleven-year-old girl, but my mom appeared to have taken good care of her siblings. She was used to babysitting already, from the time her brother Gerry was born. She told me a story about having to get baby Gerry to sleep every evening before she could go play. Being only four or five years old, she was anxious to get going, so she would gently trace her fingers down Gerry's face from his forehead, moving downward to close his eyes and on down to his chin. She would do this over and over to make him sleepy, and it usually worked to get him to nod off. Sometimes, however, it didn't work, and she would become frustrated. When his eyes would pop back open after she gently shut them, she would poke at them, stopping just short of touching them, to persuade him to keep them closed!

Although it might have saved Mom's family's lives for my grandfather to leave, the family still struggled with poverty. Then my grandfather added great insult to horrible injury by arranging to sell the family home from California, where he had fled to when he left Maryland, leaving the family suddenly homeless on top of being poor. He had chosen California because his sister, Aunt Jeannie, was located in Eureka, but then he moved on to San Francisco, although nobody seemed to know why. My grandmother kept her job at Bata, but she had to find a home she could afford for her and her children, and it wasn't easy. They ended up in a tiny one-bedroom travel trailer. Dan had a lot of memories from when they lived here. He remembered that my grandmother had the bedroom at the end of the trailer, with a crib for baby Sam. All the kids slept in bunk beds in the hallway. Don, Dean, and Mom each had a bunk, and John and Dan shared one. He also remembered a booth and table where they had their meals, and it was there that his brother Don called him a prick for the first time after saving him from choking on a nickel he had swallowed. He had a few other memories from this time, such as when a truck carrying watermelons wrecked nearby, and his oldest brothers Don and Dean gathered them up and put them under the front porch. Then my grandmother gave John and Dan a slice of the watermelon to eat outside in their underwear, and they were all sticky. Dan also remembered that Don and Dean had a friend named Charles Wilson, who drove a Jaguar with a sunroof in it. His dad sold fireworks, and they had an attic full of them. The teens would drive around and shoot roman candles at people's houses, and once, there were some people standing outside who jumped in their car and started chasing the guys. The Jaguar couldn't outrun the other car, so Dean stood up through the sunroof and started shooting roman candles at the car until they finally gave up.

Dan said that Charles had a developmentally disabled little brother or what was called retarded in those days. The older boys were mean to the young man. They would catch him smoking cigarettes, and make him eat them. Once, the young man took Dan off to the woods and gave him some big bear hugs but did nothing else that might harm him. When Dan told Don what had happened, he whooped his friend's younger brother's ass, and the young man didn't come around Dan any longer. Another memory that Dan had at this time was when he was hit by a boy on a bike, somehow ended up with the chain on his neck, and was run over by the tires. He thought that's where he got a little knot on his neck that is still there today. This was just the first of many incidents and accidents that Dan had with moving vehicles in his life.

Shortly after moving in the trailer, my grandmother got put on second shift instead of third, which meant a lot more work for my mom. She had to come home from school and get the dinner dished up for the kids that her mother had prepared earlier. Then she washed the dishes and bathed all the brothers, then swept the kitchen and did other household chores, along with completing any homework that she had from school. Mom got the boys to bed each night, and my grandmother would be there in the morning when they woke. It must have been better for my grandmother to at least get a few hours' sleep after work each night. The family was making their difficult life work, but Dan also remembered my grandfather coming around the trailer to torment my grandmother. He would force himself on her sexually, and once, he took her lipstick and used it to write "Bitch" and "Whore" all over the outside of the trailer. In the midst of this disgusting behavior, Dan also remembered his dad sleeping in his bunk with him one time and putting his foot on Dan's leg in a rare show of affection. Dan seemed to remember every show of affection that he was given as a child. When he was four years old, Mom was attending Havre de Grace High School, and she got to take him to school for the day. He told me that he really liked being able to do that.

The last time Wade came back to the trailer, he had hopped freight trains from California and got off at the tracks just behind the family's little camper. It was during the day, and the older kids were in school, so Helen was alone with baby Sam. Wade easily broke into the trailer and beat and raped my grandmother, getting her pregnant with another child. He then knocked Sam's crib over, stole some food, hopped back on the train again, and left. When the kids got home from school, they found Sam struggling to breathe under his crib mattress. My grandmother was lying on the floor, unconscious and with blood all around her.

Helen recovered and continued to struggle on her own. Sometimes, things would get so tight with money that they didn't have electricity because they couldn't pay the bill and also couldn't always pay the rent. Dan remembered bill collectors coming to the door. Their life was always a struggle. Once, Helen sent the kids to stay with her brother, Clair, in Pennsylvania to give herself some respite. Clair was married to a woman who later spent some time in a mental hospital and would get out for family visits. On one of these visits, her family was waiting in the car for her to go into the house and retrieve her purse. She then jumped out of the attic window of their house onto the sidewalk below, right in front of the family, and she didn't survive. She had allegedly found out that Clair was having an affair with one of their daughters and committed suicide.

When Dan was about five, the family moved to the Tranquility Place Townhomes, known as the Projects, in Havre de Grace. It was a neighborhood of townhomes connected to one another, with a lot of green space for children to play. They had been built in the 1940s as temporary housing for soldiers stationed at the Aberdeen Proving Ground nearby and wartime workers. They have since been demolished. Dan remembered someone had a car to help them move their belongings and that Dean rode on the same bicycle that Gerry was supposedly killed on during the last trip to the house, trying to beat the car. Dan remembered when my grandfather came to visit there once, and he gave Dan a bite of his banana. My aunt Patricia Gale (Patty) was born while they lived there. She was the child whom Helen had conceived during Wade's last visit to the trailer.

When Patty was about two or three years old, she and Sam were sent to stay with a Mennonite extended family member for maybe as much as a year for another respite for my grandmother, and they apparently loved it. Yet another time, John and Dan went to work on a farm in Pennsylvania for about two weeks. They liked it okay, except for the boredom of no friends to play with. The kids were always treated well and enjoyed themselves during these respites. Helen was close to her family, and Wade had taken her away from them in Pennsylvania to Maryland when they married. She didn't have much contact with them when she was with Wade but had much more after he left. I wonder why she didn't move to Pennsylvania to be closer to them. Dan didn't know why either. Maybe it was because she didn't want to give up her job, which she valued greatly.

Dan said they enjoyed living in Tranquility Place, and the boys would go out and play all day. They weren't there long, however, before they moved to the bottom floor of a house called Seven Brothers in Havre de Grace, maybe named for the trailer park right next to it. There was a diner next to the house, and my mom would take the kids over there whenever she got a nickel for the jukebox and dance her heart out. She didn't have money to buy food, just a nickel for the jukebox, and apparently, the owners were okay with that.

The family then moved to Bel Air for a short time. Dan remembered getting kicked out of that house and having all their belongings set out on the street by law enforcement. Friends of the family helped them move everything to a house in the Edgewood Heights. Mom said that the neighborhood was segregated at that time, with whites living on one side of Trimble Road in one-story row houses and blacks living on the other side, on Battle Street, in two-story row houses. Neither color was welcomed by the others in the Projects. Mom said it didn't feel like hate or even dislike for one another; it was just a lifestyle. She never gave black people any thought at all, except she had a real curiosity about their hair. The Edgewood Projects are still standing. I personally haven't been there since about 1975, but based on Google research, there's a large housing area there now called the Harford Commons. The one-story row houses are still there, and they and the neighborhood look very nice on Google Maps. I think that the two-story row houses have been demolished, and Battle Street doesn't exist anymore.

Back in my mom's day, there was no town of Edgewood per se, just a post office, sub shop, and a few mom-and-pop shops, but little else. There was a trailer park just below the Projects, and the kids from the trailer park used to fight with the kids from the Projects. Mom said you always had a lot of friends in the Projects because there were so many kids there, and you were all on the same level in your neighborhood. No one was any better than the other, or they wouldn't have been living there. You always got gossiped about when you first moved in and often accused of one hell of a history, but little by little, people would come around, and then you'd join the gossiping about the next new family. There was always some husband beating his wife or some wife running around on her husband and lots of abused or neglected kids; but you mostly just turned your back on it and went on with your own troubles.

By this time, Don and Dean had both gone out on their own and didn't move with the family to Edgewood. Dean went to prison for theft in Lancaster, Pennsylvania, during this time. He got out on parole and wasn't supposed to leave the state of Pennsylvania. However, he would hitchhike to Edgewood on Friday after work to see his mom and hitchhike back after the weekend so his parole officer wouldn't know he had left the state.

Life continued on with Helen's work and my mom helping to care for the children, although Helen became more relaxed about her religion. My mother didn't have to wear the very drab Mennonite dresses that covered everything but her hands and feet any longer, which had been a source of teasing in school and made her an outcast. My mother was thrilled by this rule change, but my grandmother was still pretty strict. My mother longed to be what she thought of as a normal girl—one who was pretty, short, could participate in what was popular at the time, and didn't have to care for children. She was very tall at five feet, eleven inches, as were her father and most of her brothers, but that wasn't a good quality for a pretty girl to have at that time. She was also attractive with pretty brown eyes that could sparkle, but she could never be convinced of that fact. Between the teasing she received at school, the beatings from her father, and the merciless bullying she received from her older brothers, she was convinced that she was ugly and stupid and worthless.

Things really changed for my mom when she was about fifteen years old when she met and became best friends with a girl from school named Carol. Carol was a beautiful, sweet, petite gal, who showed my mom how to dress, fix her hair and makeup, and dance. Mom had a hard time believing that Carol could adore her as much as she adored Carol, but she did. Music was the highlight of Mom's life. When she was finally able to get a job other than babysitting her siblings, she went to work at the Bata Shoe Company and bought herself a record player and one 45 record with her first paycheck. She bought "This Time" by Troy Shondell and played just that one record the whole week over and over again and never got tired of it, although I imagine everyone else in the vicinity did! From that point on, she spent $10 a week on 45 records, which got her ten records. She bought everything that was on the charts and had the music playing constantly. Some of the big hits at the time were "The Lion Sleeps Tonight," "Stranger on the Shore," "Wonderland by Night," "Dream Lover," "Hey Baby," and "Dear One." Mom also loved anything by Rick Nelson, Buddy Holly, The Shirelles, and her all-time favorite, Elvis Presley.

Mom had a beautiful voice herself, and she loved to sing. She even sang on a radio program once a week for a while, but the biggest thing she loved about music was that it allowed her to dance! She and Carol would practice all the popular dances at the time: the cha-cha, jitterbug, stroll, the monkey, the locomotion, and more. Dan remembered Mom always playing her records and dancing and making the kids dance with her. Years later, she did the same thing with me, my brother and sister, and even later her grandchildren and great-grandchildren. Mom said that young people back then danced all the time, and they even danced in the streets. If they were riding down the road and a good song came on, they would stop the car, jump out, and start dancing! Even the older people would often stop and watch and clap their hands, or they would just drive around them. Mom said she thought that life was easy then, no gangs or drugs or really anything to be afraid of. It was safe to be out late at night, and everyone knew everyone in their neighborhood. The hardest part was always being dirt poor, but she learned to adapt to having nothing since she had never had anything else.

After some time, Mom started to become a wild one, rebelling against her religious upbringing and unwanted responsibility of caring for her younger siblings. When she was sixteen years old, she ran away from home with a girlfriend. The two of them hitchhiked to Florida, where Mom was sexually assaulted, then arrested and sent back home. Around this same time, she got a tattoo on her upper right arm, which was not something that was done at the time, especially not for a woman. She hated that tattoo later and always concealed it with a Band-Aid. She was already ashamed of the horrible scar she had at the top of the opposite arm, so she never wore clothing that revealed either side. She started smoking cigarettes around this time, but she didn't care to drink at all and didn't for many years.

Around this time, my grandmother began dating a nice man named Bill Maines. He and Helen were on a double date with my mom and one of her beaus at the time. They got into a car accident, and my mom was injured, although the other three were relatively unscathed. Mom broke her collarbone and got her front teeth knocked out. Dan said she had also told a story that Dean was chasing her, and she ran into a clothesline pole, and that's how she lost her front teeth, but Mom always maintained it was the car accident. Dan remembered the kids having to stay with a neighbor while Helen and Mom spent the night at the hospital and that my mom came home wearing a cumbersome brace for her broken collarbone. He didn't remember her recovery or whether or not she had broken front teeth, but Mom said it took a long time to recover, and she had a great deal of difficulty wearing the brace along with a new dental bridge to replace her teeth. She said that's why she ended up quitting high school, but I get the feeling that graduating wasn't a big priority for her. This was what Mom was all about when she first saw that handsome Elvis look-alike in the Edgewood Project and fell madly in love.

CHAPTER 4

"Don't Be Cruel"

(Elvis Presley)

Dad said he couldn't help but notice my mom around the neighborhood. She was attractive, had a nice figure, and a lot of confidence. She hated being so tall, but Dad loved her gorgeous long legs. She was a little wild and rebellious and gained her share of attention from the guys, but Dad didn't even consider dating her because she was too young for him. He was twenty-six, and she was only seventeen.

Mom said that she loved Dad from the first time she saw him and thought he was the most gorgeous guy she had ever seen. He had really sexy eyes, but she thought she saw sadness in them too. She would find out later that they were hiding a lot of pain and bitterness. He was a large, muscular man, over six feet tall, and everyone thought that he looked just like Elvis Presley, who was my mom's favorite singer. Mom couldn't have been more enamored of Dad if he were the King himself, and she said she literally swooned any time she saw him. Dad was also a nice dresser and had a nice car. She did her best to catch his eye, and though he looked a few times, he never showed any interest other than a smile for the "kid" next door. She did everything she could think of to get him to see her as grown-up and somebody that he could date, but nothing worked.

Mom and Dad officially met for the first time in the summer of 1962 when she went over to Bell's house one day, and he was there. Bell had a short fence around the yard to keep the kids in, and Mom was wearing a dress so tight that she had trouble getting over the fence. Dad looked out and saw her and asked her if she needed help, but when she said yes, he just went back into the house. Mom managed to make it over the fence and into the house on her own and talked to Dad for a while. Dad didn't remember much about what they spoke about during that first conversation, but he did remember thinking that Mom was funny and warm and talkative, and he really liked that about her. He thought Mom was smart too even though she thought she was really dumb. Dad said it took him a lot of years to convince her that she was smart and could learn anything she wanted.

Although Mom said she was crazy about Dad right from the start, she apparently didn't let on because Dad had no idea. He didn't find out how she really felt about him until a little over a year later when they finally started dating. Mom said she couldn't believe that Dad didn't know how she felt about him because she thought she threw herself at him. She dated every friend that she saw Dad with just to get his attention. She hoped that the friend would tell Dad what a wonderful girl she was, and he would want to date her too, but nothing happened. By the next time they spoke again, about nine months later, they had each gotten married to other people!

I never asked my dad why he married his first wife, Margie, but Mom said that his family coerced him into it, hoping she could change his wild and crazy ways. She acted very sophisticated and sweet and had two young sons. Dad was always good with kids and would make a perfect stepfather to the boys. They had a short courtship and quick wedding and moved into a nice house in Bel Air, Maryland, about ten miles northwest of Edgewood. He was hauling furniture for a living, which would end up being his primary career throughout his life. He didn't run long distance then but did some overnight trips. Dad and Margie's life together looked good on paper, but it didn't take long for things to go really wrong.

When Mom heard that Dad had gotten married, she said a part of her died inside. She knew that all hope was lost for her, the kid next door with the big dreams, to marry her dream man, so she might as well marry somebody else! She chose to marry a gentleman named Jim because he was the first guy that she dated of whom my grandmother approved. My grandmother was always horrified for what would become of my mom, her wild daughter. She always called my mom a rebel, or Grace, who was Helen's sister and a real nonconformist, which was very frowned upon at the time. My grandmother said Mom should have been Grace's daughter because she acted just like her. Mom always knew that she was a huge disappointment to my grandmother, and she resented it, but she also adored her mother and would love to be able to please her. Mom said that marrying Jim was the first thing she ever did to meet her mother's approval, so it was no small thing.

Mom had met Jim when she was working at a diner in Havre De Grace, Maryland, which was about fifteen miles northeast of Edgewood. While she worked there, she stayed most of the time at her Aunt Grace's house in the Swan Meadows neighborhood of Aberdeen, Maryland, which was about five miles southwest of Havre de Grace. It was much closer than home in Edgewood. Grace's boyfriend, Ray, took her to work and picked her up most of the time, so transportation was no problem. Jim was a sailor stationed at the Bainbridge Naval Training Center in nearby Port Deposit, Maryland. He came in one night with a briefcase full of homework and was sitting in Mom's section. She waited on him, and he kept trying to chitchat, but she was not interested. She said she heard so much BS as a waitress that she had really gotten immune to it.

Jim was trying the old song-and-dance routine about Mom being the most gorgeous girl he'd ever seen and stopped just short of drooling on her. She just thought he was so dumb, as she did most guys who tried to get her attention. He asked her right away to go out with him, and she turned him down. He was very persistent and seemed nice enough, in fact, real square if anything. He didn't cuss or drink, but he did smoke. He told her about himself, as if she cared. He was raised Baptist and was from Danville, Virginia. He was a Radioman Third Class in the Navy and planned to make a career out of it. He stayed there in the diner all night, staring at her, trying to talk to her, and drinking buckets of coffee, but she really liked nothing about him.

Then one night, Ray called the diner and said he had to take Aunt Grace to the hospital, and he wouldn't be able to pick Mom up from work. She had off the next day, and she wanted to go to Edgewood to her mom's house anyway, so she got an idea. She told Jim, "I won't go out with you, but I do need a ride home if you're interested, and it's all the way down in Edgewood." He jumped at the chance even though it was the opposite direction of Port Deposit, where he had to go to get back to Bainbridge, making him drive about thirty miles out of his way. Rather than being grateful to him for saying yes, Mom couldn't believe that he agreed to her request. Jim took Mom home to Edgewood and talked her ears off the whole time, singing her praises with compliments the whole way. Mom thought he was so goofy and totally full of crap, but she needed a ride. When they arrived at my grandmother's house, Mom tried to just say thanks and jump out of the car, but Jim came right out behind her. He had to be at work the next day, and Mom didn't get off until midnight. It was about fifteen miles just for him to get back to the diner in Havre de Grace and then another ten miles to Bainbridge, so Mom couldn't understand why he wouldn't just leave!

My grandmother was awake and having coffee when they got there. Because of her working night shift during the week, she never went to bed early on weekends. Jim opened the front door for my mom, then walked right up to my grandmother, held out his hand, and said, "Hi, I'm Jim, and you must be Sherrill's lovely mother." Mom said it was easy to see my grandmother's shock and pleasure at Jim's beautiful manners. She shook his hand back, smiled really big, and offered him coffee, much to my mom's chagrin. He started calling my grandmother Mom that same night, and before he left, he told her that he didn't know how exactly, but he was going to find a way to marry her daughter. Mom laughed in his face and told him he was crazy, but my grandmother said something like she should be so blessed to have Sherrill marry a man like him. Jim's persistence, along with my grandmother's, finally paid off in getting Mom to say "I do," but she did so with the notion that Jim would be sorry for pushing her into marriage. My grandmother, Aunt Grace, and Jim handled all the wedding arrangements, and Mom didn't care what they decided. They chose the wedding chapel, flowers, and even the wedding dress. Mom was sullen and depressed and only thought about the man she wished she were marrying, Tom.

Somehow, Dad was by himself at Bell's the night before Mom was supposed to marry Jim, and in a last-ditch attempt at capturing Dad's heart, Mom made some goofy excuse to go over there. She was hoping that he would tell her not to marry Jim, that he would divorce his wife and marry her instead. She admitted to him that she didn't love Jim and that she was marrying him to make her mother happy, but all he said was that she should do whatever she thought was best. She was devastated and still didn't tell him that she was crazy about him, but it might not have mattered at that time anyway.

Mom and Jim were married on March 9, 1963, at the courthouse in Elkton, Maryland, located about twenty miles northeast of Havre de Grace. I don't know why they got married at that location, but at any rate, they went afterward to my grandmother's house for a very modest reception, during which Mom's older brothers, Don and Dean, stole her away in a car, drove her to a nearby town, and partied with her at a bar all night. Mom didn't put up much of a fight. She and her brother Dean returned early the next day to the home that Jim had rented for them. He was asleep on the couch, and Mom and Dean stretched out across the newlyweds' bed and passed out. Mom didn't even change out of her wedding gown until she awoke later that day. The newlyweds' house was located on Wilson Street in the Tranquility Place Townhomes in Havre de Grace, also known as the Havre de Grace Projects. Jim wanted them to move to Port Deposit to be closer to Bainbridge, but Mom refused. She had lived in the Havre de Grace Projects before and felt comfortable there. She and Jim later consummated their marriage in one brief act, and Mom said that Jim had stars in his eyes about being a newly married couple, but she despised him because no matter how badly she treated him, he would never confront her about her behavior. He never once even raised his voice to her.

Mom continued to be mean to Jim and spent most of her days playing her beloved records and getting lost in her music. Jim did the cooking and cleaning when he wasn't working because she refused to and just sat on her butt and watched him work. He also spent time studying for a higher rank in the military, and Mom would turn her music all the way up just to distract him, but he didn't complain. She didn't want to talk to him and only wanted to punish him for being foolish enough to marry her. Shortly after the wedding, Jim told his mother that he was bringing Mom down to her house over the Easter holiday so the family could meet her for the first time. Mom told Jim that she didn't want to meet anyone in his family, and when it was time to go, she refused and went off to her Aunt Grace's house instead.

In the meantime, Mom's oldest brother, Don, had turned eighteen and, like a lot of young people on the East Coast at the time, was itching to go to California. My grandfather was there in Eureka at the home of his sister Jean after having fled there after the death of my young uncle Gerry. Don went out there, and he met and married his wife, Rosie, who was originally from Porterville, roughly the geographic center of California. The couple came back to Edgewood and stayed briefly with my grandmother, but she really didn't have room for them, so my grandmother asked Mom if they could stay in her and Jim's spare room until they got on their feet. Mom said yes to please her mother without even asking Jim. Mom didn't like Rosie and had never gotten along with Don, but they mostly avoided each other. Shortly after Don and Rosie's arrival, Mom asked Jim the night before he was getting paid on the first of April if she and Don could come to Bainbridge and pick up his paycheck the next day. Jim agreed and asked Mom to make the payment owed on the loan that he had taken out for their wedding while she was on the base. Mom, Don, and Rosie took off for Bainbridge not too far behind Jim after he left for work the next morning, and they found the building where Mom was to pick up Jim's paycheck. They stayed on base just long enough for Mom to cash the check and then took off back to Havre De Grace, not bothering to stop at the bank and make the payment on the loan as Jim had requested.

Jim had also suggested that Mom go grocery shopping, which she had never really done before, and she agreed. She, Don, and Rosie went to the Acme store, and each of them got a cart, and Mom said that they started putting the dumbest things and quantities in the carts and ended up having so many groceries that they had to hire a taxi to take some of them home for them! They laughed all the way home at how hilarious it was to buy all that food when my mom didn't even know how to cook! They unloaded all the groceries from the car and cab and piled them in the kitchen, on the table, counter, chairs, and floor. Mom said she just couldn't bear the thought of staying home and being a good little wife to Jim, and she still had some money left over, so she took the register receipt for the groceries and stretched it across the floor, from the kitchen through the living room and to the back door. She taped it all the way, left all the groceries sitting where they were, and she, Don, and Rosie took off for Lancaster, Pennsylvania, to visit with their brother, Dean, who was living there at the time.

They picked Dean up and went out to a restaurant to eat. Of course, Mom used Jim's money to pay for all of them to eat. Afterward, Mom paid for a new set of tires for Don's car since he didn't have a job, not that he was really looking. She paid for the gas to Lancaster and back and bought each one of them a carton of cigarettes. She topped it all off with a bottle of wine that she and Don drank on the trip back home, and they laughed and talked crap about Jim the whole time. When they were almost home, the realization of what she had done hit Mom like a ton of bricks, and she really expected Jim to be at least livid with her and maybe even hit her from being so angry. She was actually worried about Jim's reaction to her behavior for the first time.

She walked in the door of the house and saw steam coming from the kitchen, where Jim was cooking dinner. All the groceries were put away, and the mess they had left was all cleaned up. Jim came out of the kitchen and said, "Hi! I see you made it back." He asked Mom if she had paid the finance company, and feeling emboldened again, she answered, "Hell no!" He asked if she had any money left, and she answered, "About $6.00." He just said, "Well, I guess the important thing is that you had fun!" Mom just shook her head at what an idiot he was. He had to borrow money from someone on base just to get through the month and pay the rent, etc. Mom realized years later that Jim was a good person, who never did anything wrong to her and didn't deserve her criticism or the mean things she did to him. She just didn't love him and hated herself and him for making her try. She loved Tom, but she couldn't have him. When Jim left for his Navy duty station in Newfoundland, Canada, in April, Mom was supposed to get his allotment checks from the Navy and stick to the budget that Jim carefully laid out for her, explaining to her which bills to pay and how. When she got her first allotment check in May, she, Don, and Rosie took off to Lancaster, Pennsylvania, to see Dean again. Don and Rosie had been talking about going back to California, and they talked Mom into going with them on the way to Dean's house. They then talked Dean into going along, and so after stopping back in Havre de Grace for their belongings, they headed West to California!

Dean had just gotten paid, and he and Mom were the only ones with money, but Don had the car, so he made Mom and Dean give him all their money for the trip. Mom said Don damn near starved them on the way out there, and she was sick almost the whole trip. When they reached San Francisco, they took Mom to a clinic, where she was diagnosed with pneumonia, and she also found out that she was pregnant! Mom was shocked and devastated. She had only had one quick sexual encounter with Jim, and she ended up pregnant. After the clinic, they went to see Wade, my grandfather, who was living in a hotel on Turk Street in the Tenderloin district. My mother had only seen him very briefly a few times since he had abandoned the family years earlier after he killed my uncle Gerry, so she was very anxious about seeing him as she never knew how he would behave. He was living with a woman named Vivian, whom Mom said was a doper, who popped prescription pills. After greeting each other and visiting for a bit, they were all supposed to take a nap in my grandfather's hotel room and then head on to Eureka, California, about 270 miles up the California coast, to Aunt Jeannie's house. Mom fell into a heavy sleep, and when she woke a few hours later, everyone else was gone. They left her a note that said they were headed to Eureka, the room was paid up for a week, and they would be back in a few days. They didn't, however, leave her any money, and there was very little food in the room. She was horrified that they would leave her all alone in the city. She had no way to call anyone, no one to run to, and she cried like a baby for the first two days! To say that her stint in San Francisco was hell is an understatement. Mom said she thought it was God paying her back for the way she had treated Jim.

Someone at the hotel finally told Mom about traveler's aid. Since Jim was in the military, they might help her to get back home. She walked to their office and told them that she was sick, pregnant, penniless, starving, and abandoned. All she wanted was to get to her mother's house in Edgewood, Maryland. They gave her a bus ticket and $25.00 in cash. She felt like God was back on her side. The trip took six days on the bus. They lost half of her luggage, and her feet swelled so badly that she could barely walk, but she finally made it back to Edgewood. She called Bell's house from the bus station and left a message for her new stepfather, Bob, to pick her up. Helen had met Bob while living in Edgewood, and they got married right after my mom married Jim. He came to get her and took her back to her mother's house. After crying in her mother's arms, Mom took a shower, then went to bed. When she woke up hours later, Jim was sitting on the side of the bed, beaming at how happy he was to see her and telling her that he had come home from Newfoundland to take her back with him. Mom expressed her opinion about that idea by jumping up and running to the bathroom to vomit. She then told Jim that she wasn't going anywhere with him ever again and that they were through. He pleaded with her until Bob finally convinced him to go back to Newfoundland and let Mom think about it for a while. Mom then begged my grandmother to let her stay with her in Edgewood, and Helen relented. Mom didn't tell anyone, not even her mother, that she was pregnant.

CHAPTER 5

"Can't Help Falling in Love" (Elvis Presley)

While my mom was ripping her first marriage to pieces, Dad's marriage was falling apart as well. He was doing a furniture moving job one day, and they sent him to New Jersey on another job. He had to get each shipment of furniture weighed before he could load another, and he didn't have any cash for more weights. He asked a coworker/friend to borrow the cash, and Dad wrote him a check for it. He made the trip, and when he got back home, Margie said he had a message to call the guy to whom he had written the check. Dad called him, and the guy said that the check had bounced. Dad said that was impossible as he had hundreds of dollars in the bank. To make a long story short, Margie had been taking all the money out of their bank account without Dad knowing it. She forged the bank book, which Dad always kept with him, and he had no idea what she was doing with all his hard-earned money. Dad had already been unhappy in his brief marriage due to Margie's controlling ways, and he disagreed with how she wanted to raise her children. Stealing from Dad was one of his cardinal sins, and he was livid. He told Margie that he was leaving to stay with his sister, Bell, for a while.

By the time Dad moved back in with Aunt Bell in August, 1963, Mom was happy to be free from Jim, was living back with her mother, and had started dating again. She saw Dad outside one day, and they started talking again. One night, Mom was waiting at her mother's house for her date to show up when my dad came over for a visit. They were enjoying their conversation when Mom's date showed up. When Dad asked the date what he was doing there, he said he was there to take Mom to the movie theater. Then Dad stated that *he* was taking my mom to the movies and that her date could go ahead and leave. The date asked Mom if that was okay with her, and she said, "Yes!"

After that date, Dad left Aunt Bell's house and tried to make another effort at his marriage. Mom was devastated that just when she finally caught his attention and had hope for their future together, he went back to his wife. She consoled herself by continuing to date other guys and, as she had done in the past, chose one of Dad's buddies to go after to see if Dad became jealous. Mom went out with the guy, and when he brought her back home, they found the street blocked by several large metal dumpsters and Dad waiting at Aunt Bell's to talk to my mom. They argued predictably about him having no right to be angry about her dating when he had gone back to his wife, etc. He said he was done with Margie for good this time, and he wanted to date my mom, and he didn't want her dating anyone else. Mom said she was okay with that. They became a couple at that point and started seeing each other on a regular basis. They had a lot of fun together, but Dad told Mom that he wasn't the type to say he loved someone unless he really meant it, so he hadn't said it to her yet. After a couple months of dating, however, he knew he was in love with her, and Mom had known that she was in love with Dad for a long time now. Of course, Mom's pregnancy with Jim's child was a huge secret that she was keeping from Dad as she was scared to death that he would end the relationship as soon as he found out. Finally, she knew she had to tell him and get it over with. Rather than Dad wanting to end the relationship, however, he didn't have a problem with it at all as long as she would let him raise the child as his own. Dad said he was just as happy and excited about the baby as if it *did* belong to him. Looking back, he said he felt like he really needed a family to give his life meaning and stability. He had been wary of what Mom's intentions were because she had dated a lot of guys and had broken a few hearts, including her husband's, and he didn't know if she was ready to be committed to him. Now, however, he knew that he loved her, and she loved him, and that they were going to be together.

CHAPTER 6

"It's Now or Never"

(Elvis Presley)

My folks had no doubt that they wanted to be together now, in spite of each of them being married to other people, and my mom being pregnant with her husband's child, but it wasn't going to be easy for them.

Dad was on the run from Margie, having left their home to be with my mom. He was couch surfing with family and friends because every time she would find out where he was, she would call the police and tell them that my father had been abusive to her. The police would find him and lock him up for a few days, so he would lose jobs over and over again. Not having work meant he couldn't afford to get a place with my mom. Margie told him that if she couldn't have him, Sherrill couldn't either. She told my mom that her reason for continuously having him arrested was because if he had enough thinking time, he'd realize he didn't love Sherrill but rather Margie. Mom told her that for every day Dad spent in jail on her account, he'd hate her more, and Mom was right.

Margie was clearly desperate to keep my dad. She even told him that she was pregnant with his child even though she'd had a complete hysterectomy after the birth of her second son, and it was impossible for her to conceive! Mom got so angry with Margie and her ridiculous behavior that she went after her to kick her ass even though she was pregnant at the time. She found Margie at the Edgewood Legion, but the bouncers were all over my mom, and she didn't even get to hit Margie before they threw her out. The next day, Mom went to see Dad in jail and take him cigarettes, and the jailer told her that he had a warrant for her arrest for assault and battery! She spent the night in the Bel Air jail, and the next day, when Margie visited my dad in jail, he was furious with her and ordered her to drop the charges on both my parents, then told her take the two of them to my grandmother's house in Swan Meadows in Aberdeen, where the family had moved to from Edgewood. She drove them, as ordered, while my folks sat in the back seat with their arms around each other. They might have won that round, but the war over my dad raged on.

While Dad was trying to hide from Margie, Mom moved back in with my grandmother in the Tranquility Place Townhomes in Havre de Grace, where the family was now living after leaving Swan Meadows in Aberdeen. In the meantime, Dad's sister Ruth and her baby daughter, Vickie, had moved in with my aunt Bell in the Edgewood project. Ruth had been going with a guy named Billy and gotten pregnant. Billy said he would marry her but went out right away and married some other girl. He wanted no part of Ruth or the baby. Ruth went after him and stalked him and cried and cussed and threatened, then slashed his car seats with a knife, but it did no good. He wouldn't have her or the baby. She even got my dad to go after him, and Dad beat his ass, but that only made Billy hate Ruth more.

In the end, Ruth had Vickie and took Billy to court to get $10.00 a week for child support, but he wanted nothing to do with his daughter. Dad was always his family's protector and especially Ruth. Mom said she could push all his buttons and make him feel so sorry for poor Ruthie, getting screwed over time and again. In fact, they weren't dating any time at all when Dad let Mom know that Ruth was number one with him, and if she was going to be with him, she better love Ruth too! Mom didn't love her, didn't even like her, but had to hide that from Dad because she sure loved him!

Ruth had some trouble with Aunt Bell's husband, Herb, so arrangements were made for her and Vickie to stay with my mom at my grandmother's house in Havre de Grace. At this time, my mom and my grandmother were both pregnant, with mom being two months ahead. My grandmother was very clean, and she just hit the roof over some of the things that Ruth did, like leave Vickie's dirty diapers lay on the floor, wherever she took them off, and the fact that Vickie was always dirty and had the worst case of diaper rash they had ever seen. Ruth would sleep and just let Vickie run wild, so my mom and grandmother had to watch her. She was unruly and wild, and Mom disliked her immensely. She was only eighteen months old, but she terrorized my mom.

Finally, Mom got sick of fighting with my grandmother over Ruth and Vickie's behavior, so she took the allotment check she received for Jim and rented a place in the Baldwin Manor, a complex of long rows of efficiency apartments in Aberdeen. Mom believed that the apartments were built initially as part of the housing for the Aberdeen Proving Ground, which was within walking distance. She didn't know when they were built but remembered that she went there when she was a little girl with people from her church. They had a section that had bedrooms and another with duplexes; but Mom's apartment was in the worst section. When you entered the door to the building, there were four apartments, two upstairs and two down. I never got to see the apartments as they were torn down before I ever lived in Aberdeen myself.

There were clotheslines strung between the buildings, and women were always fighting over someone else taking their clothes. There were mostly losers, derelicts, and transients there, along with some GIs. It was within walking distance of town, so conveniently located. The apartments were all furnished alike, with a hide-a-bed sofa and a small end table in the living area. The kitchen was tiny, with a table and four chairs, and none of the chairs matched. There was a hallway that had a closet and a chest of drawers and the tiny bathroom, and that was it! Mom didn't have anything pretty to brighten up the place, but she was sure thankful for it.

Aberdeen was bigger than Edgewood and was more like an actual town. Driving through the town on Route 40, you saw mostly clean and neat little stores and some houses and other buildings. Because of the Aberdeen Proving Ground, you could always see soldiers hanging around on the corner waiting for the bus. From this perspective, the town looked much more civilized than it actually was. You didn't have to get far off the beaten path to find trouble, like GIs walking in a bar and the local rednecks not liking their looks, and then all hell would break loose. The barroom clientele were mostly neighborhood guys, and you had to fight your way into acceptance from them. People were clannish, and like tended to stay with like.

Mom had hoped that when she moved out of her mother's home, Ruth would go back with Bell, and just she and my dad could live in the apartment, but that didn't happen. Ruth and Vickie moved in right along with Mom. They had to rent a rollaway bed from the landlord for Ruth and Vickie to sleep on in the kitchen. My dad was in West Virginia at the time, where he'd gone to help his dad get coal in for the winter. It was during this time that John F. Kennedy was assassinated. It was very telling that my mom, dad, and Uncle Dan each told me where they were when Kennedy was killed. Dan remembered that he was in school at Halls Crossroads Elementary in Aberdeen, and he didn't understand why everyone was so upset about the death of someone they didn't even know. When Dad got back to town, he came to the apartment, and Mom begged him not to leave. Mom said that people didn't live together back then, and she knew they would be talked about and looked down upon by people, but she didn't care. She just wanted them to be together. Dad agreed, and he moved in. It was October 1963, and they began their life together. What a life it would be!

CHAPTER 7

"I Got You Babe"

(Sonny and Cher)

My favorite story about my parents happened shortly after they started living together. Life was bleak for them during this time, but they were determined to stay together no matter what. My dad's wife continued to have him arrested, and he kept losing jobs as a result, so he earned very little money. It made matters worse that they didn't have a car. My dad had given it to Margie when he left her so she wouldn't be without transportation as a single mother. This made it even more difficult for Dad to work. He was one of the hardest-working men I've ever known, so it must have been agony for him to be in this situation and not be able to provide for the family. My mother was pregnant, so my dad didn't want her to work. They had very little food to eat and often went hungry. My mom said there were times when they just drank water. Things would have been easier for them if they had assistance from their families, but that wasn't going to happen because neither family approved of the relationship.

My dad's family thought my mom was too young, a one-night stand, and a home-wrecker, among other things, and they told my dad not to bring her around. Even my aunt Bell, who adored my grandmother, wouldn't allow Mom into her home. My mom's family didn't approve of my dad for many of the same reasons. My grandmother thought he was using my mom, breaking up her marriage, and was too old and too troubled for her. She decided too that he was unwelcome in her home. As a result, they were alienated from any help from their families because they refused to go anywhere that the other one wasn't welcome. When they didn't have food to eat, my dad would insist that my mother go to my grandmother's house to eat because he was concerned about the baby. Mom hated to go, but she relented in the best interest of the baby. My dad, however, wouldn't go to his family for any help at all.

On Thanksgiving, my uncle Dean visited my mom and told her that my grandmother wanted Mom to come to dinner, but Dad was not invited. At the same time, my aunt Bell had invited Dad to dinner but not my mom. Mom and Dad discussed it, and both decided they would rather be together than eat, so they didn't go to either place. Ruth tried to persuade Dad to come with her and Vickie to dinner, but he wouldn't budge, so they left without him. Mom and Dad sat on the couch all day with their arms around each other and talked about how pretty the snow was that was falling. They also talked about their hopes for the future, convinced that things would get better for them. Mom was very immature, and she believed that as long as she was with Dad, everything would be okay. Dad had strong beliefs about how he wanted to live his life, what kind of man he wanted to be, and how he wanted to raise his children. His thoughtfulness would become very evident in our household in spite of all the craziness that ensued.

At about nine that night, Ruth and Vickie arrived home, and Ruth had a turkey drumstick that Bell had sent for Dad. It looked like heaven to my folks, and they couldn't have been more excited and grateful. They sat at the table together and fed the turkey to each other. In between bites, they laughed, giggled actually. They thought they had everything they needed in that moment, to have each other and food to eat. All too soon, the turkey was gone, and they had made sure to clean every single bit off the bone. Sadly, Mom took the bone to the trash to throw it away. Before she could toss it, Dad said, "No. Let me have it." He took it and scraped off the inedible bits that were left on it with his pocket knife until it was perfectly clean. Then he washed it and dried it and put it up on an empty built-in shelf that they had nothing to put on. Mom laughed at Dad and asked him what in the world that represented. He said, "We aren't going to be broke and hungry all our lives, and I want to always keep this bone to remind us of today and of when we had nothing but each other." There happened to be a can of wood varnish under the kitchen sink, so Dad put some on the bone and made it shiny. When anyone came to the house and saw the bone, they'd always laugh and ask, "What is that?" Mom or Dad would answer, "That's Tom's bone." That's all the explanation they got.

CHAPTER 8

"Hey Paula"

(Paul and Paula)

When it came time for Mom to give birth to her first child on January 5, 1964, she was all alone. Dad, my grandmother, and her husband, Bob, were all at the hospital with Mom for hours when she first went into labor, but the doctor said it would be hours until time for delivery and suggested they should all go home and wait. Having little children at home, Grandma and Bob decided to go, and Dad reluctantly went with them because they were his only ride home. Dan remembered that they were all home watching *Bonanza* when the hospital called my grandmother the next day to say that Mom had given birth. Mom said they had drugged her with something that knocked her out for two days. The family came to see her and the baby that day, but Mom didn't remember. The nurses had to keep waking her up to feed the baby, and she would fall asleep holding her. When the baby bottle hit the floor, it woke her up and horrified her that she could have dropped the baby. It didn't happen again. She was more coherent the next day when the family came. Dad fell in love with the baby immediately. He wanted to name her after an old love of his, Carolyn, I think, but Mom adamantly refused. Instead, they called her Paula for the song that was popular at the time and gave her the same middle name, Kathryn, as my grandmother Helen.

When my folks took their precious bundle home to Baldwin Manor, Dad said they were happier than ever together, but times were still terrible. Dad's ex, Margie, was still having him arrested, so he continued to lose jobs, and money continued to be scarce. It was even tighter now because they had to pay $5 a month extra to the landlord to rent a crib for Paula. Mom loved being a mommy and adored Paula, but Dad was crazy about being a daddy and took the utmost care of my sister. He insisted on washing her clothes by hand, hanging them to dry, then ironing them himself. He had worked in the laundry for a time while stationed in Korea in the Marines and was an expert launderer. He later taught me to be the same.

It wasn't long before they were out of food again, and they needed money for baby formula. Dad was going to find someone to loan them the money, but Mom had another plan. Back when they had first moved into the apartment, Mom bought a can of Johnson's paste wax, thinking that with a lot of scrubbing, she might get those ugly floors to shine. She just never seemed to get the elbow grease necessary to do all that on her hands and knees, so the can sat in a kitchen cupboard, forgotten. Now she remembered the paste wax and the fact that it had been pretty expensive. She told Dad that she and Ruth could return it to the grocery store where they'd gotten it, and they could get Paula's formula.

They went to the store, and Ruth haggled with the manager for the return since they no longer had a receipt. In the meantime, Mom had a big purse that hung almost to her knees, which happened to be in style then. She walked through the store, putting three cans of baby formula and a bag of pinto beans in her purse. Then she was horrified that someone had seen her, so she walked around looking at people and trying to figure out if they looked at her suspiciously. When no one seemed to be paying attention to her, she walked over to the candy aisle and put one of the giant Hershey bars in her purse too. My mom loved chocolate probably more than anyone I've ever known. Then she found Ruth, who had gotten the refund, so they picked up more baby formula, went through the line and paid for it, and left the store. They couldn't afford to buy anything else. After they got outside, Mom confessed to Ruth what she had done, and they laughed all the way home. Mom was feeling pretty proud of herself. She had taken care of the baby, gotten beans for dinner, and even some dessert—for *free*! When they got back home and told my dad the story, however, he was livid. It was the maddest he'd ever gotten at Mom to this point, and he said not to ever do anything so stupid again. He felt strongly that it was wrong to steal under any circumstances and was horrified that she could have been arrested and gone to jail with a newborn baby at home. So much for Mom being a hero. Needless to say, she never did that again, but she maintained that was the best piece of chocolate she ever had in her mouth.

My grandmother gave birth to Virginia Ann on March 9. Mom said that she and her mother loved being mommies to their baby girls together. In addition, as families are often brought together by a new baby, Helen was spending time with my dad now, and she had gained respect for him when she saw how he cared for Paula. It was a blissful time for everyone, but it only lasted about one month. Dad's ex, Margie, continued to be obsessed with my parents, and they felt that the only way to escape her troublemaking was to leave the area. They decided to move to Alexandria, Virginia, and rented a room in a boarding house. They thought it best not to tell anyone where they were going so they wouldn't feel any pressure to reveal information to Margie or law enforcement. That ended up being a huge mistake.

CHAPTER 9

"Tragedy"
(Thomas Wayne)

On May 13, 1964, my grandmother was home preparing herself and her baby, Ginny, for her six-week checkup with the doctor. They were upstairs at the house in the Havre de Grace Projects, which was split down the center by a staircase that ran from the front door of the house upstairs to a bathroom. There were two bedrooms, one on each side of the staircase. My grandmother was in one room getting ready, and her daughter was in the other bedroom, sleeping in her crib. Dan said that on that morning when the three boys were leaving for school, Helen gave them a hug goodbye, which was unusual. Dan knew his mom loved him, but she was always busy, and he didn't think she had time to be really affectionate.

Meanwhile, my uncle Dean was outside siphoning gas from the dump truck he drove for work to put in his personal car. He took the first can of gas into the house to store it there by the front door until he could retrieve it after work that night. There was an open flame on the water heater right inside the front door. Dean set the messy gas can down and went back to get another one. When he opened the door with the second gas can, it combusted and created an explosion, which blew Dean back out the open front door and sent flames directly up the stairs. The flames immediately blocked Helen's passage across the hall to her daughter. The fire department was called by a neighbor, and they responded quickly. When they arrived, Helen was at her bedroom window screaming for someone to rescue her infant daughter. Maybe they didn't realize that the daughter was on the other side of the house, and they began to set up a ladder to the window that Helen kept appearing at, growing more and more frantic. She kept running back to the hall to try and see a way to get to her daughter, and she refused to leave the house without her, in spite of the firefighter on the ladder at the window encouraging her to come.

My Aunt Patty, who was five years old at the time, had been at the playground across the street when the fire occurred, and when she saw the smoke coming from the house, she ran to her home. She saw her mother the last time she appeared at the window. Mom said that my grandmother was on fire. Patty tried to run in the front door and then tried to run in the back door while the firefighter was trying to get Helen to come down the ladder. The firefighters asked a neighbor, Mrs. Mason, to take Patty. Mrs. Mason held and comforted Patty while the fire was being fought.

When the fire was finally out, the house and all its contents were completely destroyed. Sadly, my mom had stored Dad's one prized possession at my grandmother's house, the shellacked turkey bone, so it was destroyed as well. One of the firefighters approached Mrs. Mason and told her that my grandmother had died of smoke inhalation. My uncle Dean and baby Ginny had both been taken to the hospital. They also told Mrs. Mason that my grandmother had three boys in school at the moment, so she and Patty went there to retrieve them. Dan said he had heard the fire truck sirens when he was sitting in class and joked that they were coming to get him. They did get him, along with his brothers, and took them to the office. Apparently, nobody knew who to call to take the children, so Mrs. Mason said she would keep them for a while. The boys insisted on seeing the house, so she drove them past it. Then she took them all to her house and got them settled in with her husband. She went to the store and bought them pajamas, toothbrushes, and one outfit apiece.

My uncle Dean suffered burns, but he left the hospital and stayed at my grandfather's cousin Arnie's house in Darlington, Maryland, about ten miles northwest of Havre de Grace. He recovered from his injuries, although not from the terrible guilt he carried with him from then on. Ginny only survived for a few hours in the hospital. My mom said she had been horribly burned.

The kids ended up staying with Mrs. Mason and her husband for two weeks and were out of school during that time. Dean visited them at her house and was invited to stay, but he refused and stayed with distant relatives instead. Mrs. Mason bought each of the kids' clothes for the funeral, and she accompanied them. I'm assuming that my grandmother's husband, Bob, was devastated by the deaths and really wasn't capable of caring for four young children at the time. After the funeral, Mrs. Mason said that the four kids walked away together with John holding on to all three. The four kids weren't all close to one another, but everyone was close to John. My dad said that from the minute Helen died, John took on the role of caretaker to his younger siblings. He had always been a good brother, but now felt that he had to be the one responsible for them. He was a mild-mannered kid that never got into trouble and tried to keep Dan out of it. It's my opinion that if he couldn't keep Dan out of trouble, he would join in with him to stay close and try to protect him.

My folks didn't attend the funeral because, since they hadn't told anyone where they were, there was no way to contact them. When they finally called someone back home and got the news, my mother completely fell apart. She frightened my father so badly with her reaction that he told her he thought it best to have her committed to a mental hospital. This apparently caused her to control her behavior and push it inward to avoid that fate, but Mom was mentally and emotionally scarred by her mother and baby sister's deaths for many years. She had an irrational fear of fire, and she told the gruesome story several times throughout my childhood about Ginny's tiny hand being melted to her cheek by the fire. She frightened me when she talked about the fire and railed against a God that could allow it to happen.

Mom said she could talk all day about Mrs. Mason and what a godsend she was, but she could never sing her praises enough. In fact, the entire town of Havre De Grace did everything they could to help Bob and the children after this horrible tragedy. The man that owned the house where my grandmother died offered Bob and the children a house rent-free for a year. The neighborhood and local stores furnished it, and it was beautiful. They even stocked it with tons of food, linens, dishes, and everything and they could possibly need. They donated clothes for the family and toys for the children. They gave gift certificates from every store in town, and they gave a lot of money. The plan was for Mrs. Mason to keep the children until the house got all done, and then Bob was going to move them in there. The kids were clearly on their way to a new life if they had been allowed to stay there.

CHAPTER 10

"Five Hundred Miles"

(Peter, Paul, and Mary)

When the fire occurred, my uncle Don, his wife, Rosie, and three-month-old daughter, were living in their car in Porterville, California. Neither Don nor Rosie worked, and they were receiving food stamps, which they had sent to Rosie's mom's house. My grandfather also lived in Porterville at a hotel. When they got the news about Helen's death, they decided to take my grandfather's Social Security check and drive back to Maryland. When they arrived in town, Don took my grandfather to his cousin Arnie's house in Darlington, Maryland, because my grandfather didn't know if he was wanted by the law for any previous crimes.

Don and Rosie found the Masons, and they went there and asked Mrs. Mason if they could take the kids for the day and take them on a picnic. It was a Friday afternoon, and they said they would have the kids back home by 7:00 p.m. Mrs. Mason had no problem allowing the children to visit their oldest brother and his wife. Instead of going on a picnic, they took the kids to Darlington to pick up my grandfather and Uncle Dean and headed out for California. Don said his mom told him once that if anything happened to her, she wanted all the kids to stay together, so he thought she would have wanted him to take the kids.

When the kids weren't back at the Masons by 8:00 p.m., Mrs. Mason called their stepfather, Bob, and he went to their house. He called the police from the Masons and tried to file kidnapping charges against Don. The police put out a ten-state alarm for the bunch but told Bob that if they did find Don, all they could do was ask him to bring the kids back. They told Bob that a stepfather had no more chance of getting those kids than a stranger did if any of their blood relatives wanted them. Bob hired a lawyer, and the lawyer told him that my mom would have the best chance of getting custody of the kids since she was their oldest sister. My mom arrived in town the evening of Bob's appointment with the lawyer. Mom told Bob she would do anything she could to help him get the kids. She wanted to see them settled in their new home with a good, dependable person and have all the things they'd been given. Mrs. Mason told Dan later that Bob had also hired a private investigator to find the kids, but he couldn't find them and eventually gave up.

When they arrived in California, Don took the kids to Porterville, where he couldn't find work, and they didn't have enough to eat. Rosie's parents bought each of the kids another outfit because they only had the clothes on their backs. Wade went back to Eureka to join Vivian, whom he had since married. Don, Dean, Rosie, and the kids followed them to Eureka after about one month. My grandfather's sister Jean (Aunt Jeannie) and her husband, Lawrence (Uncle Larry), had been living in Eureka for some time. Uncle Larry loaned Dean the money to get them a house in town. Apparently, work was scarce or couldn't be had, so again, there was never enough food to eat. The kids would steal fruits and vegetables out of neighbors' garages. They got kicked out of the house after one month when they couldn't pay the rent, and they moved to the town of Samoa on a peninsula about three miles west of Eureka, where they stayed for maybe two months. There was nothing out there, so food was even more scarce, with no garages for the kids to steal from.

At some point, Don and Dean got into a fight over Dan. Rosie had overheard Dan say, "Mrs. Moore is a whore," talking about

Rosie's mother. Dan actually liked and respected Mrs. Moore. He only said that because he had recently learned the word *whore*, and it rhymed with Moore. He didn't even know what the word meant. Rosie was obviously upset, and when she told Don about it, he wanted to spank Dan. Dean defended Dan and his innocence and told Don he couldn't spank him. They ended up getting into a fist-fight, and Don and Rosie left. After that happened, Wade bought Dean a car and told him he had enough money to take the kids back to Virginia because my parents wanted to take care of them. Before heading back east, they stopped in Porterville to see Don and found Don and Rosie living in their car and eating canned dog food. Dean told Don he should leave Rosie there and come back east with them, so he said he would, and Wade gave Don money to make the trip in his own car. They headed out of town, and that evening, Don said he needed to go back to the last town to get toothache medicine but never came back, so Dean and Wade took the kids to my parents without him.

CHAPTER 11

"Together Again"

(Buck Owens)

While the Smith kids were going through their California chaos, my folks were on the move, and I'm not certain of everything they were doing and where they were doing it. I know that my mom had shown up back in Havre de Grace after the kids were taken. Meanwhile, Dad ended up in Hampton, Virginia, staying with an old friend from West Virginia and looking for work. Hampton is located on the southern end of the Chesapeake Bay, close to where it meets the Atlantic Ocean in Southeastern Virginia. Dad found a job in a retread shop in nearby Newport News and then went back up to Maryland to pick up Mom and Paula and take them back with him to Newport News. They lived in an apartment there for a month and then moved to a tiny little house on Fifth Street in Hampton. Mom thought they were set up pretty good, and their home was the perfect size for their family of three.

Dad had no experience in the retread business, but they hired him anyway, and he ended up earning a master retreader certificate from Firestone. He enjoyed the work, but he wasn't making enough money at $64 a week, so he went back to the local furniture moving business. He was now making just under $100 a week, which was just enough for the three of them. They didn't have the money for a car, so they took the city bus to the grocery store, then caught a cab back home with the groceries. They were very happy together then. Dad remembered fondly when he would come home each day, and Paula would run in her walker to greet him. Dad loved children, and they loved him. I asked him why he liked kids so much, and he said he didn't know but that he thought everyone should like kids. He always wanted to help children and did so with a lot of them throughout his life. I asked him what was his philosophy on raising children. He said if you love them and talk to them, you won't have any problems. He said he thought a lot of people have kids when they shouldn't have, and then they don't know what to do with them.

One morning, Dad told Mom that he had listened to her cry in her sleep for the last two nights, and he knew she was grieving for her family. Dad said he wanted to take care of the Smith kids because he felt sorry for them, and they had nobody else that was going to take good care of them. Mom had mixed feelings about the idea. She was enjoying her new little family, recovering from losing her mom, and happy to have only her own child to take care of. She did love her siblings and wanted them to be well cared for, just like Dad did. They made up their minds, and Dad said he would try to find them and see if they could get the little ones back with them. Before they could even start the process of finding the kids, they got their wish.

One day, Mom saw a car pull up out front, and out came her younger brothers and sister! She said that seeing their condition was beyond a huge shock. They looked worse than any orphans she'd ever seen. John didn't even have a matching pair of shoes; he had on two different kinds. All the boys were wearing literally rags, and Patty was beyond pathetic. She was wearing a pink sateen dress that was ripped on the waistline all the way from the side to the back and had safety pins in it, trying to hold it together. Her hair looked like it hadn't been brushed since my grandmother died. It had leaves, briars, lint, and fuzz all knotted up in it so badly that after days of trying to get all the mess out of it, they finally had to cut it, just to get it combable. John was aged twelve when they got there. Dan was eleven. Sam was nine, and Patty was six.

Mom had another shock that came out of that car too when her father got out, saying that he just came along to help Dean drive. Mom had only seen Wade very briefly since she was eleven years old when he abandoned the family. The last time was for just minutes at his motel room in San Francisco years earlier. What's worse was that he and Dean said they needed to stay there at my folks' house until my grandfather got his Social Security Disability check to have the money to travel back to California. Wade was just pretending that he didn't have any money because he didn't want to spend it, but my folks never questioned it. They thought that surely, a father of these poor destitute kids would help his children somehow if he even had one penny. They forgot with whom they were dealing.

Dan said the kids were so excited to get out of the terrible situation they had been in even though they were now living in a tiny one-bedroom house with eight people. Dean and Wade slept on the fold-out couch; Mom and Dad slept in the bedroom with a crib for Paula, which was now shared by Patty. The boys slept on the kitchen floor on a blanket. To get my dad off to work in the mornings, my folks would have to climb over the couch, which took up the entire living room when it was opened. They would then wake the boys up in the kitchen and have them climb over the couch to go and get in my folks' bed. This arrangement lasted for about a month until Wade and Dean went back to California. The kids had arrived in August, and school started in September. My folks had no idea where the money for clothes would come from on Dad's salary of less than $100 a week. Their immediate thought was food now that they had four more mouths to feed, not to mention having to feed Dean and Wade for a month. My folks didn't know anything about the Social Security benefits that the kids were eligible for, and Dean and Wade contributed nothing, so they knew that the only hope they had was coming from my dad.

The family got so broke so fast that they borrowed $20 from a church so they could buy pinto beans, potatoes, and flour and salt for fried bread, just basics that they hoped to stretch out and feed all of them. It absolutely killed my dad to have to borrow that money because his work ethic was his greatest and strongest asset, and he prided himself on being able to work for anything he needed. Mom remembered one time she asked John to run down to a friend's house and borrow one egg because she needed it for something she was preparing to eat. Dad said, "Absolutely not!" He told Mom that if they couldn't afford to buy it, then they couldn't have it! In the meantime, Wade never offered a dime, and yet Mom began to notice that when they had their dinners of pinto beans, fried potatoes, and fried bread, Wade rarely ate with them. Mom hoped that he was just being fatherly and letting his poor kids eat his share. She should have known better.

Right after the kids arrived, John got a job at the local barbershop shining shoes. He would also run errands or do odd jobs for the owner, a nice man named Jerry. One day, Jerry asked John to go to the restaurant next door and bring him a cup of coffee. When John walked in, there sat Wade eating his favorite T-bone steak dinner, complete with baked potato, salad, and green beans. John just died. He was so upset that he asked Jerry if he could take off for a few minutes after he returned with the coffee. Jerry told him that was fine, and John went home and told Mom what he had seen. Of course, Mom was livid. She told Dad about it that evening, and Dad talked to Wade about it. He asked Wade something like, "How can you have money in your pocket and eat expensive food in a restaurant but allow your kids to suffer like this with barely enough to eat?" Wade just laughed and said something about those "little bastards" of his. Dad told him that he would work his ass off, if need be, to take care of Wade's children, but he'd be damned if Wade was going to spend another night in his house. Wade and Dean left that evening, with Wade having enough money to get them back to California and then some.

After Wade and Dean left for California, the family started to settle into their new lives with one another, and they had some problems. Dad said it was hell taking on the kids, especially Dan. The other kids weren't too bad, but Dan would start trouble, and the other kids would go along with him. It wasn't long before Dad had to give Dan a spanking for the first time, and afterward, Dad went into the bedroom and cried because he hated doing it so much. Dan required a lot of discipline, and Dad found himself spanking him nearly every day. He finally decided that he couldn't do it any longer. He said he was afraid that Dan would end up in reform school or worse, but after the beatings Dad suffered in his childhood and the promise he made to himself not to beat his own children, he couldn't stomach it any longer. He said Dan seemed to get a little better after that, but he still got into trouble for many years. Dad said that Dan probably had ADHD, and today, they would have likely given him medication to slow him down.

Another problem they had was that the kids generally didn't do well in school, and Dad would not allow it. I had grown up hearing the story that if the kids came home with a failing grade, then they were made to sit at the dining room table from the time they got home from school until bedtime, having dinner with the family when it was time. Dad said that he couldn't force them to study, but they had to sit there with their books open until they brought their grade up, so he hoped they would take advantage of the time they spent. Dan said that if that were the rule, it wasn't strictly enforced, and instead, he remembered getting rewarded by Dad for good behavior and good grades. He said one time, Dad bought rotisserie chickens home for dinner, and he gave Dan his own half a chicken for getting good grades on his report card.

John, who was a really good kid, surprisingly ended up being another problem. He didn't like that my mom was going to be their mother figure, and they didn't know Dad very well at all. Dad sat all the kids down and told them that they would have to respect both my folks if they were going to live there. John said, "Sherrill is just our sister," to which Dad replied, "No, Sherrill is my wife." Mom had been a babysitter of the kids but was never a role model or mother figure to them. She had no maternal instincts toward them, and they only developed to some degree after she had Paula. Mom hated having to care for her young siblings again, and Dad assumed that the kids knew it. At first, Mom didn't try to discipline them and would only report their behavior to Dad when he got home from work.

Dad quickly realized that he was in the same position his father had been in when he was growing up. He didn't want the kids waiting in fear for him to return home from work to get their punishment, so he told Mom that she had to start disciplining the kids on her own. Dan remembered that Dad gave him a dollar once and not the other kids because he hadn't had to spank him for one whole week.

John soon fell in love with Dad and became his right-hand man. He seemed happy to turn over the role of caretaker for his younger siblings and trusted Dad to do the job. Whatever Dad was doing, John wanted to be right there with him. John had been best friends with Rocky, my aunt Bell's oldest son, so he was at Bell's house quite a bit when Dad was staying there, but Dad didn't really have a relationship with any of the Smith kids before their mother died. Mom always loved John but said she was jealous of John and Dad's relationship at times. John had a good relationship with everyone in the family, and he kept the family in harmony. He couldn't stand for anyone not getting along. Dad never had to spank John. He only spanked Patty once when my folks found out that she and Dan and Sam were terrorizing the neighborhood, tearing clothes off the lines and dumping over trash cans. Apparently, this behavior had been going on for some time, but the neighbors knew that the kids were orphans and that the folks were struggling to care for them, so they didn't say anything. Finally, when they couldn't take it any longer, they got together and came over to tell the folks what the kids had been doing. Dad said he thought that was the only time Sam got a spanking as well.

Dan said that everything happened so fast after their mother passed, and they were going through so much that the kids didn't have time to grieve, and they just worried what tomorrow would bring. Mrs. Mason had said that they were very well-behaved children, but not long after their mother died, they got defensive, especially Dan. He didn't want to take crap off people. John never really got crap from anyone, and Patty and Sam just took whatever they got. Dan didn't like anyone abusing his family, and all the kids were very protective of one another. He said that it was pretty good living with my folks; they got plenty to eat, but Dan got a lot of whippings.

He said that my mom liked to show off in front of her friends and would call the kids heathens and dog them in front of her friends, but Mom denied that this happened. Dan also said that one time, Mom made John smoke and inhale cigarettes so much that he threw up to make him give them up, as he had recently started smoking. Dan understood that she didn't want John to smoke but thought that was a very cruel way to try and stop him.

It wasn't long before the landlady found out that there were four extra kids living with my folks when the people upstairs told her that the family reminded them of the old woman in the shoe and swore that there were kids climbing out the windows. That last part wasn't true, but they got kicked out anyway. They found a furnished three-bedroom house down by the beach on the corner of Buckroe Avenue and Third Street. The place was a real dump but was at least bigger. The house was across the street from Mr. Hobgood's grocery store, and the folks were able to establish credit in the store, which was a huge help. They had to lie about the number of kids they had and prayed that this new landlady wouldn't find out the truth. The landlady, however, was a nosy old biddy, and she snooped around the house all the time. Mom would have to keep the kids in the house during the day so she wouldn't see them. Then one hot afternoon, Mom finally relented and let them go play in the side yard. They didn't have any toys, so the boys balled up a couple pairs of Dad's socks and made a football out of them. They started out just passing the makeshift ball around, but soon Dan tackled John, and they ended up in the landlady's prized lilac bush. She called the cops and, when they arrived, brought the kids and the landlady to Mom's door. The landlady screamed and yelled and gave the family three days to move out. Mom was scared to death about what would happen to them, but Mr. Hobgood came to the family's rescue and offered to rent them the apartment above his store.

CHAPTER 12

"Sherry"

(The Four Seasons)

Mr. Hobgood's store was located at 112 Buckroe Avenue just a few blocks from the beach. He had rented the apartment above the store to my folks by the week, and he even knew the truth about how many kids they had. They continued to have credit at the store, and that's the only way they had food to eat sometimes. Dad's whole paycheck would often go to Mr. Hobgood, but at least they were surviving, with a roof over their heads and just enough food to eat. John had gotten the job shining shoes in the barbershop and brought all his money home, which sure came in handy. The owners at the barbershop, brothers named Jerry and Ralph, liked John really well. They gave him a matching pair of shoes when he went to work for them since all he had were two different ones. When John had no customers, they would make sure there was some kind of work for him to do, and they always paid him fairly. Mr. Hobgood also gave the boys little jobs to do for a dime sometimes. The Smith kids never had a problem working their entire lives.

One day, a nice man came in the barbershop where John worked and had John shine his shoes. While he was shining them, the man started questioning John as to why he wasn't in school, and John made up some unknown story. Unbeknownst to John, the man was a truant officer, and the next day, he showed up at the family's home with two women from the school board. They gave Mom the third degree about who all these kids were and wanted to know why they weren't in school. Mom hemmed and hawed around and said they were just visiting, and she didn't remember what all she said, but seeing that they weren't buying her story and they wouldn't be put off, she broke down crying and told them the truth. She showed them the way the kids were dressed and said that was all the clothes they had and asked if they expected her to send them to school dressed like that.

The three visitors then softened up a bit, and they told Mom that they had a room at the school that had donated clothes in it and said that Mom could come and pick out a few outfits for each boy, enough to get them started. Mom told them that she had no transportation, so the next day, they sent a lady to pick up my mom and the kids and take them to the school. Mom had arranged for a neighbor lady to stay with my sister Paula while she was gone, but she took Patty with her even though she wasn't old enough to start school yet. Thankfully, they let her pick out two outfits as well. She got two nondescript dresses, and she found the ugliest pair of high-top shoes that had once been white, but someone had tried to paint them red! They were horrible, but Patty cried to have them. Unfortunately, the lady gave them to her. Patty continued to have a unique fashion sense throughout her life. The lady also told Mom about Social Security for the kids and told her how to file for it, which was a big blessing.

Mom enrolled the kids in school the next day, Dan and Sam in Phoebus Elementary and John in Buckroe Junior High School. School lunches would have been very expensive for the family to afford, so Mom packed lunches for the two youngest boys, who rode the bus to school and back. John came home for lunch every day instead of buying it at school since we only lived a few blocks away, although he wasn't supposed to leave campus. He even walked home one day during a hurricane to have his lunch, and of course, Mom kept him home instead of letting him walk back in that kind of weather. When he went to school the next day, the principal called him to the office and told him that he knew he had left school grounds at lunch and then didn't return. He told John that if he left school grounds again at lunchtime, he was going to get a paddling. John went ahead and walked home at lunchtime that day too and told Mom that he was going to get paddled when he got back to school. Mom went right away to the pay phone downstairs and called Dad and told him what the principal had said to John. Dad said to keep John home, that he would be right there. He got home right away, and he, Mom, Paula, and John all went back to the school. Dad had a company truck that they rode in. When they arrived, they all walked uninvited into the principal's office, and Dad confronted the principal. Dad said to him, "After you spank me, then you can spank John." The principal threatened to call the police, and Dad said, "Go ahead, but I'll be whipping on your head until they get here!" After that, the principal became very nice, and he even told John that he could have free lunches. Dad told the principal that John didn't need free lunches, but he needed to be allowed to come home for lunch. He did so from then on.

This was just the first time that my folks stood up for us kids if we were being treated badly at school. We were expected to follow the rules, mind our manners, and always respect our elders, but we weren't allowed to be mistreated. Dan remembered another example of my folks coming to the kids' defense when he was in the fourth grade at Phoebus Elementary. One day at school, he was playing keep-away with a beanbag at recess. He and a boy both went for the bag on the ground at the same time, and Dan ended up pushing the boy over. The boy told the teacher that Dan had pushed him, so the teacher grabbed Dan by his T-shirt and poked him over and over with her knuckle in the chest. When Dan got home and showed Mom his chest, she called the teacher on the pay phone at Hobgood's and told her not to ever put her hands on Dan again. After that, he was teacher's pet. Years later, in 1984, Dan ran into the teacher, Ms. Ric, in Louisa, Virginia, when he was living in nearby Mineral. What a small world!

Christmas was coming, and my folks were stressing terribly about having no money for a tree, much less presents, for their five kids who believed in Santa Claus. Three days before Christmas, Mom and Dad took Paula in a cab to the store, and they bought gloves for each of the kids, plus some groceries, and took the cab back home. They were so sad that they couldn't buy anything else that resembled presents for those poor kids but were happy that they could buy two chickens for Christmas dinner. When the cab pulled up at the house, the driver had to double-park because there were so many vehicles on the street. They noticed commotion in front of their house, and when they opened the door, they were shocked! There were boxes and boxes of food, presents, Christmas decorations, clothes, and even a beautiful Christmas tree had been put up. The food was piled all over the kitchen and dining room, and there were fruit baskets in the living room.

It turned out, the owners of the barbershop where John worked, Jerry and Ralph, were in the Lions Club or Moose Club or some such group, and they had told John's story to the club, who decided to give Christmas to these poor little orphan Smith children. Wow, did they ever! Mom just started crying, and she didn't know how many people she hugged and thanked, and she still never felt like she had thanked them enough. Their generosity was so overwhelming to my folks. Mom was pregnant with me at the time, and they had even gotten newborn clothes for the baby who wasn't due until the summer. The family had a ball! They had food like they had never seen before. They giggled and oohed and aahed for hours. The kids were in seventh heaven and had so much of everything that it was a long time until they needed anything else in the way of clothes or toys. In addition to these gifts, some members of a church also came and got the kids one at a time to shop for a Christmas gift. Dan remembered that he got a rifle, and Sam got some Army men. He also remembered that Jerry and Ralph bought the boys race cars.

The family got another godsend between Christmas and New Year's. Their first Social Security check finally got there, and it was very large due to all the back pay that it included. Mom and Dad called a family meeting to decide where it would be best served for the family, and they all decided that the best thing they could do was buy a car. So they bought a 1959 Ford, and man, were they proud! They were able to pay cash for it because Dad never liked having bills to pay. They even had enough left over to go to Maryland for the New Year weekend, and the kids hadn't been back there since my grandmother died, so they were looking forward to it. They had a good time, but it was really sad when they all went to my grandmother's grave. After that trip, things were pretty uneventful until just about the time that school was out for the summer.

I was born in Dixie Hospital in Hampton, Virginia, on June 6, 1965. My folks had been making monthly payments to the hospital for my impending birth, but I arrived two months early, so I wasn't paid for yet. I was healthy in spite of being premature, and when Mom and I were well enough to go home, Dad came to pick us up but was told by a gentleman in the accounts payable department that Dad would not be taking us anywhere until our bill was paid in full. Dad explained to the man that they had been making regular payments all along, but that I had arrived early, so surely, they would allow him to continue to make payments until the debt was settled. The man said that a payment plan was no longer possible now that I had arrived. Having really no other choice, Dad told the gentleman that he saw that his wife and new baby seemed to be well taken care of by the hospital, so he was fine with leaving us there until the bill was paid. He said he had five more mouths to feed at home already, and the hospital would take good care of these two. When he kissed us goodbye and began to walk down the hall, he was chased down by the gentlemen. A payment plan was arranged, and Mom and I got to go home. Dad paid the bill off within the next two months.

My hometown of Hampton has a rich history but not all of which I am proud. Captain John Smith and the Virginia Company built Fort Algernon on what is now Fort Monroe in 1609. Fort Monroe had its share of significance during the Civil War. Off its shores, the battle of the first ironclad ships, the *Merrimac* and the *Monitor*, was held, and the Union gained control of the bay. Fort Monroe was also the location of the prison cell where Jefferson Davis, the president of the Confederacy, was imprisoned for several months after his capture at the end of the Civil War. Sadly, Hampton or specifically Point Comfort was the location where the first African American slaves arrived in Virginia in 1619. However, Fort Monroe was also the site of the contraband decision in 1861. After the Civil War began, three local enslaved men fled to the Union Army that was in control of the fort. Because the men were being used as forced labor by the Confederates, the Union's commanding officer, Major General Benjamin Butler, claimed the men as contraband of war and refused to return them to the Confederates. Within weeks, thousands of slaves had converged onto Fort Monroe, seeking refuge. This was one of the first steps toward the eventual collapse of slavery in the United States.

During World War I, Hampton became the site of the United States' first aeronautical laboratory, NASA Langley Research Center, where many scientific and engineering breakthroughs have been made. Human computers, such as those featured in the book and movie *Hidden Figures*, were located there. During World War I, on April 14, 1942, the first German U-boat was sunk off the American East Coast, east of the Outer Banks of North Carolina. What is significant about Hampton in this incident is that the following day, twenty-nine bodies of German seamen were recovered from the ocean and were secretly buried in a full ceremony that night at the Hampton National Cemetery in graves dug by German prisoners of war, who were imprisoned at Fort Monroe.

So back to my less-than-historical story. Not long after I was born, my mom's Aunt Grace from Baltimore asked if she and her husband, Brownie, could have the Smith kids for the summer so that Mom could have some time with the new baby, especially since I was a seven-month baby, and the family had not been prepared for me to be there that soon. The family had a meeting to discuss the idea, and the kids said they would like to spend the summer in Baltimore, so Mom told Aunt Grace to come and get them. Mom and Dad thought it would be a real vacation to not have six kids, but just their own two now, but they were lonely and found themselves worrying about the Smith kids all the time. Being the transients that they were, they decided the solution was to move to Baltimore so they could be close to the kids, and they moved one street away from Aunt Grace. Mom said that we were able to move at a moment's notice because we owned almost nothing. Everything we had could fit in the car for years. Mom said that if a place had a lease, they wouldn't stay there because of the restrictions a lease would often impose, i.e., the number of people in the house or the time they must stay at the property. Every place we moved to was furnished; sometimes we got good furniture, and sometimes we got junk, but not having our own furniture made it possible to move easily. The fact that Dad was a professional mover had its perks too because he could pack everything really tight. Later on, when the folks began to acquire more belongings, Dad could use a company truck to move us.

Mom and Dad were able to see the kids every day in Baltimore, and that eased their minds. The kids liked living with Aunt Grace, and she took really good care of them. They were still living with her and her family when school started, so she enrolled them in school. Unfortunately, Dad hadn't been able to find good work in Baltimore, so my folks decided to move us back to Havre de Grace, Maryland, where Dad found a furniture moving job. Not too many guys had any interest in working that hard, but my dad loved it. The Smith kids stayed with Aunt Grace in Baltimore. We were living in a little two-bedroom apartment on Union Avenue in Havre de Grace when my mom's brother Don, his wife, Rosie, and their two children showed up at our door, from California, to stay.

This was the first time Dad and Don had met. The two were discussing Don's slim chances of getting a job in Maryland when Dad told him that he knew a place in Virginia that if they walked in the door, they would be hired as furniture movers on the spot, even though Don had never moved furniture before. Don refused to believe it was possible for Dad to get them work so easily, so Dad and Don took off that same night and drove to Hampton, Virginia. They got there the next morning and walked into Brooks Transfer, a moving company where Dad had worked previously. His old boss, Mr. Francis, loved him and was like a father to my dad, and they would have many years together in the moving business. When my dad walked in with Don and asked Mr. Francis if he had any work available, he looked up from his desk and said, "Punch in, Tom, and get your buddy a time card too!" Don was shocked that my dad was right, and they could really walk in and get a job on the spot. He really wasn't happy about moving furniture for a living because it was very hard work, but he had no choice at the moment. They worked there for a week and went back to Havre de Grace on the weekend to get Don's family along with Mom, Paula, and myself, and we moved back to Virginia. We moved into a house trailer in Newport News, and Don got a house in Hampton. A couple days later, my mom's brother Dean, his wife, Reba, and her son, Steve, also showed up at our house from California. Apparently, they were there to stay as well as Don.

Meanwhile, back in Baltimore, things got a little crazy. Dan remembered that while they were at school one day, Grace and her husband got into a fight, and Grace stabbed Brownie when he was on top of her, and she couldn't breathe. She used the pocketknife that she got out of his pocket. The kids came home to an empty house with blood everywhere. They had never seen Grace and Brownie fight before, so it was a real surprise. He remembered them going to court, but apparently, it all got settled. After this happened, my folks, Don, and Dean all decided to get the kids from Baltimore and take them back to Virginia. Not only were they concerned about the situation with Aunt Grace, but they had also heard that my mom's Aunt Velma was talking about putting Dan and Sam in the Hershey School for Boys in Pennsylvania. Everyone thought that was a bad idea until years later when they realized it might have been a great opportunity for the boys. Dan said that the kids didn't really want to leave Aunt Grace, and they had to pull Patty, crying, out of Grace's arms. At any rate, they were now headed back to Virginia.

Mom and her two brothers made a deal that they would split the Smith kids up so that each couple had three children because none of them had the money to take care of all four kids by themselves. Mom and Dad got John since they had my sister Paula and myself. Don took Dan since he, too, had two children of his own, and Dean took Sam and Patty since he only had one child, Stevie, who actually belonged to Reba from her first marriage. Mom and

Dad moved into a big furnished house on Fourth Street back in the Buckroe neighborhood by the beach in Hampton. Dean and Reba moved into a little house behind our big one, and Don moved one street away. That way the kids could still be close together and go to the same schools, etc. It sounded like a great plan to me. Mom said the kids were happy with these living arrangements, but Dan said he was really bored living with Don and was there alone with Rosie most of the time. All he could do for fun was climb trees in the yard. He did remember having fun trick-or-treating with his siblings there on Halloween even though a lot of the houses by the beach were just summer homes and nobody lived there that time of year. Mom said that's another reason why they liked living in Hampton besides all the military installations in the area that gave furniture movers lots of business: because you could get a place for cheap when it wasn't summer. The downside was that they often had to sign an agreement to be out before the tourists came or pay triple the rent.

The whole family gathered at Mom and Dad's for dinner almost every evening, and Mom was delegated family cook but not because she wanted to be. Rosie portrayed herself as a vegetarian who would neither eat nor cook meat, and since meat was the main staple in the family dinners, she couldn't be the one to cook it. Dean thought that Reba was much too good to slave over a hot stove, so that left Mom. She said she didn't mind cooking so much when there was plenty of food to cook for everyone; she just hated it when there wasn't enough to feed all of them. Fifteen people was a hell of a lot to try to fill up.

Dad had been made supervisor at the moving company now, and Don was one of his employees. Don still hated the furniture business but had no choice unless he wanted to find another job. One Sunday, Don broke into the moving company warehouse, broke open the soda machine, and took all the money. The next morning, when Dad opened the warehouse and saw the mess, he knew immediately who had done it. Don wore a size 15 shoe, and he had left the imprint of his shoe on the insulation that he tore out of the soda machine. When Dad confronted Don, he denied it, but Dad knew it was him and was prepared to fire him over it. Dad went to the boss,

Mr. Francis, and told him what happened, but he said, since Don was Dad's brother-in-law, he would just let it go this time.

At about the same time, Don and Rosie got kicked out of their house for not paying the rent and moved back in with us again along with their two kids and Dan. Apparently, Don had only paid the rent one time. A few days after the soda machine incident, Dad sent Don and three other employees out on a job to deliver an Army colonel's household goods. The colonel came up with missing jewelry and called in to speak to Dad the next day. Meanwhile, Don had come home and given Mom a watch and Rosie a watch and three rings. He said a shipper had given them to him. Of course, when Dad got the call about the jewelry, he knew it was Don, whom he was happy to fire. He wasn't as happy to fire the other three employees as well since Don wouldn't admit his guilt, so he had to let all of them go. Dad also collected Mom and Rosie's ill-gotten jewelry and gave it back to the colonel. Don just laughed about it and said he was relieved that he didn't have to hump furniture anymore. To top it off, Don was now out of work, so Dad was supporting him and his family.

The last straw finally came when Don stole $40 out of Dad's wallet, and Dad was going to beat his ass. Don knew Dad could hurt him pretty bad, so he asked Dad to please just let him take his family and go back to California instead. Don talked Dean into going too since he wanted Dean to pay for the trip. Dean almost always went along with whatever Don said anyway. Dad said it was fine with him if they all wanted to leave, and in one afternoon, they had both vehicles loaded up for California. Before they left, they said they were taking the Smith kids with them, except for John because he was old enough to refuse to go. Mom and Dad pleaded with them to leave Dan, Sam, and Patty with them as well, but they refused, saying that the kids were their family too, and they had as much right to them as Mom and Dad did. So they left John and took the younger three kids with them. The next time the folks heard anything about them, they had taken all three kids to Aunt Jeannie and Uncle Larry in Eureka, California, and left them there!

CHAPTER 13

"California Shoeshine Boys"

(Laura Nyro)

Dan said that when he, Sam, and Patty left the house in Hampton, he hated to leave without John. He remembered Mom, Dad, and John standing on the front porch, waving goodbye when they left. When the group made it to just outside Needles, California, Don's car died. Dean and Don got into an argument about Dean towing Don's car into town because Dean was afraid his car would break down if he did. Dean ended up pushing Don's car into town with his car. They all stayed the night there, and the next morning, the kids were running around playing when Dean just got into his car with Reba, Stevie, Sam, and Patty and left Don, Rosie, their daughter, and Dan stranded there in Needles with no money. There was nothing he could do for them anyway. Dean was headed to Reba's father's house in Porterville, where he dropped off Reba and Stevie. Then he drove to Sacramento with Sam and Patty, where he dropped them off with Wade, who was living there at the time. Apparently, he wanted to get everyone situated before he turned himself in to the police in Eureka. He was wanted there for stealing from a farm he had worked at before leaving California and going to Mom and Dad's in Hampton. He turned himself in, and he got locked up, as expected.

Meanwhile, back in Needles, Dan took Don's toolbox to a gas station and sold it to someone for money so the group could eat that day and use a pay phone to call Rosie's folks in Porterville for help. Her folks came and got them that evening and took them all back to their home in Porterville. Don then called the Porterville police and told them where he was at because apparently, he had a warrant out for his arrest as well. We don't know what crime he had committed, but Dan remembered that the police came to Rosie's parents' house, picked Don up, and put him in jail. A few hours later, Wade showed up on a bus from Sacramento to get Dan, while Sam and Patty stayed with his wife, Vivian, back in Sacramento. The kids were with Wade for about a month, waiting for him to get his Social Security check so he could buy all of them bus tickets to Eureka to his sister Jeanie's house, where he planned to leave the kids.

When I asked Dan what he thought about his dad, he said he was cool, and he enjoyed being with him. He was nice to the kids and was always laughing and cutting up. He took the kids to a thrift store, and he bought Dan an erector set and Sam some tinker toys, probably for Christmas. Dan didn't remember what he got for Patty. On Dan's birthday on January 5, he bought Dan a shoeshine box. Dan took it with him when they left but didn't remember the toys going to Eureka with them. Wade's wife, Vivian, was also nice to the kids but was still a doper strung out on some kind of pills. She ran around in her underwear and couldn't walk without holding on to the wall. She would sit on the bed for hours at a time in nothing but her panties, while Dan and Sam would shoot rubber bands at her bared breasts. One morning, Wade woke the kids and told them they were leaving. He said to get their stuff together very quietly so they didn't wake Vivian. They were downstairs getting in a taxi to leave when Vivian came out on the second-floor walkway of the apartments. She asked Wade if he was going somewhere and told him to wait while she got her coat. Wade told the taxi driver to get the hell out of there and take them to the bus station!

When they arrived in Eureka, Aunt Jeannie picked the kids up at the bus station, but Wade left on another bus, probably to Porterville. She took the kids back to her house, where apparently she was supposed to keep them for about two weeks until there was a place for them at a foster home. She took the kids to visit the foster home that they were supposed to live in, but the kids really didn't want to go there; they liked being at Aunt Jeannie's. She was very sweet and gentle but insisted on good manners and behavior. She and Larry decided to keep the kids after all, maybe so the boys could work for Larry. They were there for about eighteen months and became different kids because they were expected to be what Dan called squared away. Dan loved his shoeshine box, and he washed and shined the family's shoes every day, only for them to get dirty again the next day in the Eureka mud. Soon Jeannie would let Dan ask people who came to the house if they wanted their shoes shined, and he would earn a quarter for each pair. Then Jeannie started dropping Dan off downtown for about six hours a day, from about 10:00 a.m. to 4:00 p.m., where he would walk around all day, shine shoes, and hang out. He would make about $5 a day at the most. He would go to Woolworth's lunch counter and get a hamburger lunch for about seventy-five cents and also buy candy, never coming home with any money. Once, he bought Aunt Jeannie a bottle of perfume and was very proud of that. He said that John would always split his money with the other kids but not Dan, unless they were with him at the time. Speaking of John, the three kids got to Eureka in early 1966, and they didn't see John again until the summer of 1967 when Aunt Jeannie took them to Orting, Washington, to visit with their brother, where he had relocated to with Mom, Dad, Paula, and myself.

CHAPTER 14

"Little Star"

(Dion)

Before we got together with Dan, Sam, and Patty again in Washington, we had done a great deal of our typical moving around. We moved from the house on Fourth Street not long after everyone had left for California due to lack of money. We had to move to a dumpy apartment on Layton Avenue in Buckroe, but we only lived there for a couple weeks and then found a little house on Pembroke Avenue, still in Hampton but away from the beach. It was small but adequate, and Mom said it seemed like we lived there for quite a while. She discovered that she was pregnant again while we were there. A funny story happened at this house that illustrated how much my mom loved to rearrange furniture; sometimes she would even rearrange the whole house once a week. She just got so bored with looking at everything in the house situated in the same way over time. This time, she was rearranging her and Dad's bedroom and was trying to move a tall chest of drawers. It was heavy, but she managed to get it out far enough from the wall so that she could push her behind against the wall for leverage to move it. Instead of the chest of drawers moving, Mom's back side went into the wall, leaving a very large hole! She ended up scooting the piece back to the spot it had been to cover up the hole. Dad didn't know about it until we were moving out of the house, and he had to repair the damage in a real hurry.

Dad's sister Ruth was spending a great deal of time with us when we lived there. We had found her and Vickie living in the Edgewood Projects with a friend of hers during a visit to Maryland back when we were still living over Hobgood's store. We brought them back to stay with us for a little while. I have no idea how we fit two more people into the two-bedroom apartment, where there was already eight of us living. She very quickly met some married guy from Newport News, where they moved in together. We saw them periodically after that but not often. After we moved to Pembroke, however, they would come over a lot. When Mom started hemorrhaging due to her pregnancy, Ruth convinced my folks that she, Vickie, and her married boyfriend needed to move in to take care of my sister and me since Mom was confined to bed for nearly a month prior to her delivery. Mom said that Ruth neither cooked nor cleaned and mostly just played solitaire or watched soap operas on TV. She didn't even watch Vickie, so Mom ended up having to protect us smaller girls from the aggressive Vickie.

When we started seeing rats the size of small cats in that house, Mom and Dad knew it was time to move. Dad walked into the kitchen one morning to find a full loaf of bread standing on end on the kitchen table. When he inspected it, he found a large hole eaten through the entire loaf from the top to the bottom. He soon found us a beautiful house on Patrician Drive in a real fancy neighborhood in Hampton. Mom said it had the nicest furniture she had ever seen. We even had a pool table in the garage, and John was in his heaven out there! Ruth, Vickie, and the boyfriend moved with us, but things were not going well. It all came to a head one morning when Mom got up and discovered that Vickie had shit in the dining room and was now smearing it all over the place, including on the lace tablecloth that covered the dining room table. Mom knocked on Ruth's door and told her to get up and get this kid before she choked her! Ruth said something along the lines of "Go to hell!" so Mom went in the dining room and picked up Vickie, shit and all. She took her into Ruth's room and put her in the bed with her mom. Ruth jumped up, ran out of the room, and she and Mom had a screaming match until Mom told her to get out of her house. Ruth said, "We'll just see what my brother has to say about that. You'll be the one he makes leave!" She then went back in her room and stayed there until Dad came home. Mom said she spent that whole day wondering if Dad would defend Ruth or her; she really didn't know. When he arrived home and was told the whole story, he upheld Mom's decision, much to her relief, and he told Ruth that she, Vickie, and her boyfriend needed to move.

Shortly thereafter, Mom went into labor with her baby, and even though she was only six months pregnant, she delivered seven minutes after they got to the hospital. The baby girl, whom they named Tammy, weighed one pound and ten ounces, and she lived for twenty hours. Her lungs were too underdeveloped to save her. Afterward, Mom was still recovering in the hospital when Dad came back for visiting hours. She told Dad that she was going home with him! There was nothing she could do there but grieve and hear babies cry, but none were hers. She would see the new moms scurrying down the hall to the nursery to get their babies to feed them, but they had her in a room all by herself, and the loneliness was killing her. She had two little girls at home who needed her and could comfort her. When Mom was preparing to leave, the hospital staff argued with her that she shouldn't leave the hospital, but Mom refused to stay. Then a nurse said something to Dad about making arrangements to "dispose of it" for us, talking about the deceased baby, Tammy. Mom thought Dad would get arrested because he raised so much hell. He loudly announced that Tammy wasn't an it. She was their baby and that you dispose of garbage, not babies. They wanted a funeral for their little girl. The staff quickly began to apologize, and my folks said they would call with funeral home arrangements within the hour. They did.

Another tragedy occurred in Hampton at around this time on a much larger scale. On June 20, 1966, at about 8:50 p.m., two Marine jets were flying low on a training mission when they collided over Buckroe Beach. One of the planes crashed in flames in a residential neighborhood at Old Buckroe Road and Marion Road, killing two people, a mother and infant. There were varying accounts of the story, with the *New York Times* reporting as many as eight people dead. There were approximately forty-five people injured, ten homes destroyed, and seventeen others damaged, but again, there were varying reports of these numbers. The four Marines aboard the planes were much more fortunate. They ejected from the planes, landed in the Chesapeake Bay along with the other plane, and were rescued.

CHAPTER 15

"Daddy's Home"

(Shep & the Limelites)

It was now 1966, and the moves were coming faster than ever. We actually moved from the house in Hampton to an upstairs apartment in Newport News while Mom was in the hospital. Dad brought her home, got on the phone to make funeral arrangements for the baby, and then called his boss. He was still working for Mr. Francis at Brooks Transfer but decided that he had to make more money, so he had begun to work driving long distance instead of local. Dad said he hated driving long distance at first, mostly because he was away from his family, but he grew to love it. He was very good at his job, and the long-distance money was terrific. He started to have a hard time when he was sitting at home, drawing a somewhat decent salary, knowing that he could be on the road making double or triple the money.

At any rate, he was supposed to deliver a furniture shipment to Alabama but asked Mr. Francis if it could wait until after Tammy's funeral. Mr. Francis agreed and couldn't have been nicer, even though it was an industry with strict deadlines. He even loaned Dad a car to use at the moment since ours was broken down. When my folks went to pay the bill for the funeral afterward, they found out that Mr. Francis had paid for the whole thing and refused to take any money from them.

Dad had started the long-distance trucking little by little. It began as a few in-and-out trips occasionally, and then more and more, he went farther and longer. He explained to Mom that it was the only way he could afford to buy a house and give us the life he wanted for us. It was also their goal at the time to get the other kids back, and that would take all the money they could get. Mom was devastated at first when she no longer had Dad home. She had no idea how to do anything on her own and felt that all she was good at was playing with and caring for us kids. She said you would have to search long and hard to find a wife and mother more naive, irresponsible, and immature than herself. She didn't know anything about fiscal responsibility. Dad always handled the money and paid the bills. He set it up with his company, which was now Bekins, to send Mom a paycheck weekly and keep his settlement money for him to collect each time he came home. Mom's money was adequate to pay the bills and have a little left over. Dad would call her and tell her what to pay, and if he left one off the list, Mom didn't pay it; she didn't even think about it, just paid what Dad said to pay.

As usual, I don't know why we needed to move again, but it was time. Dad's old friend from West Virginia, who had brought him to Hampton for the first time, told Dad about a house on Seaboard Avenue back near Buckroe Beach in Hampton that he and his brother-in-law had bought together. It had a smaller house in the back of the big house, and he said my folks could rent the small one from them until the larger one was empty, then they could move in there. This happened at the same time as Tammy's funeral, so when Dad left for Alabama right afterward, Mom and Dad's friend's wife moved them into the little house on Seaboard. It wasn't uncommon for people in that area to have a smaller house behind their big one because they had a gold mine to rent out to the tourists in the summer. Dad had thought about doing the same thing, with us buying the big house to live in and renting the small one for extra income. He'd talked to his friend about it before he left town, and they were going to work out the details when Dad came in from his long-distance trip. I'm not sure what happened with that deal, and I didn't get the chance to ask my folks, but I can't say that I'm surprised that they didn't end up buying the house. They never bought a home until 1986.

Not long after this move, Mom's brother Dean came back from California again for a visit along with his wife, Reba, stepson, Stevie, and my grandfather. They stayed a while and, as usual, never offered a dime to help pay for food or anything else. Mom said our family wasn't as needy then, with Dad working long-distance, so it didn't matter as much. She said the five of us were living just fine at the time. Dean hadn't seen the rest of the Smith kids since Wade dropped them off in Eureka with Aunt Jeannie, but he had talked to them on the phone and assured Mom that they were all doing better than we were, living there on Humboldt Hill with the rich people.

When Dad called from the road and heard about Dean's impromptu visit, he asked Mom if they would watch me, Paula, and John long enough for Mom to make a trip on the road with Dad for her twenty-first birthday. They agreed to keep us kids, but Mom was too afraid to agree to fly to New Mexico to meet Dad, so instead, she took a bus to Hammond, Indiana, and met Dad there. She had never been around his job before and had no idea what it was like. She said that moving furniture was the hardest work she had ever seen any man do, and Dad loved it. He was also an excellent truck driver, and he loved that too. She spent about a week with him, and she wanted it to be fun, but she mostly felt like a fifth wheel in Dad's way while he was loading and unloading people's furniture. She was horrified to have to meet the shippers. She had no social graces and said she was pretty much ass backward, really. She felt like a hick and a fish out of water and realized that she was most comfortable around her kids. We didn't require much more than a song or a nursery rhyme, and she didn't have to discuss current events or other things about which she had no clue. She was actually an excellent mommy at that time. She made sure we were fed, washed, clothed neatly, safe, and entertained. She could be so good with kids when she wanted to be, singing, dancing, playing games, and being very silly to make them laugh. She said she missed us kids the whole time she was gone and really didn't have much fun on the whole trip.

When Mom got back home, she discovered that my grandfather was terrorizing Reba's son, Stevie. He would shake his fists at him and make faces at him and call him a sneaky little bastard. Stevie was terrified of my grandfather, and he was scared to death when Reba would make him go outside where Wade was always sitting on the porch swing. Wade had only come along to help Dean drive because he loved traveling, and he certainly wasn't coming to see my mom or John or us girls but rather to see Hampton, specifically Buckroe. Finally, as a result of his fear and hatred of my grandfather, Stevie crawled under our house one day to the room below where Wade was taking a nap, and he set fire to some cardboard he'd gathered under there. Mom said he must have panicked and came in the house and asked John to come out back. John came running back in and told us all to get out; the house was on fire! He grabbed me and Paula and took us outside, while Mom called the fire department and yelled for Wade to get out. Luckily, the cardboard was damp and caused more smoke than fire, but the investigator showed the adults where Stevie had really worked hard to get the fire going because of all the match head marks on the damp paper. Reba called Dean home from his temporary job, and to say that Dean beat Stevie is putting it mildly. Mom had never witnessed such a horrible beating, and that's saying a whole lot, considering her own father's behavior. Dean kept screaming at him about his mother's house burning down and her getting killed, and it was as if Stevie had set *that* fire. Of course, the whole family was traumatized by my grandmother and aunt's deaths and especially Dean, being the one to accidentally start the fire. Reba and Mom finally got him to stop but only after he had inflicted what must have been a great deal of pain on a little ten-year-old boy. Then two days later, Stevie set the hedges on fire outside of Wade's bedroom window. That sent Dean over the edge again, but he didn't just beat Stevie this time. Instead, he crawled all over Wade for being the real responsible party. He unleashed hell on Wade and threatened to kill him if he ever looked in Stevie's direction again. He chewed long and hard enough on Wade that he left the house and caught a Greyhound bus back to California. Dean and his family left soon after.

While we were still living on Seaboard, the transmission went out of the folks' car. Dad put it in the shop during his time at home, intending to pick it up and pay for it with his settlement check after he got back from the road on his next trip. Then Mom got a thirty-day notice to vacate the house, although I don't know why, especially since they were renting from Dad's friend and his brother-in-law. Anyway, as luck would have it, Bekins accidentally sent Dad's settlement check to Mom along with her weekly allotment. She had so much money that she could have paid all their bills, including the last month's rent that was due, and gotten the car out of the shop and still had a lot of money left over, but she said that never occurred to her. The only thought she had about paying the rent was that she deliberately didn't pay it because they were getting kicked out. Before she discussed any of this with Dad, she decided to load John, Paula, me, and herself into a cab and go to the bank to cash the check. It was the most money she had ever seen! She got us back into the cab, and we went to downtown Phoebus, a neighborhood in Hampton. We got out in the heart of town and just walked in each store on the street and bought whatever we wanted. She got us all got new wardrobes and we kids got new toys. We ate lunch in a drugstore and caught a cab to take our new purchases home. Then we went to Buckroe Beach Amusement Park, which was a couple blocks from the house. We rode all the rides until we were tired of them. We laughed and had so much fun. Mom said she was a bigger kid than we were. Then we went back home to our treasures. Mom had bought Paula a huge doll that was bigger than she was, and she was so big that Paula could only drag her around by her hair! The best thing Paula liked about that doll was her red plastic shoes, and she took them off the doll and wore them herself! Mom also bought both of us girls tricycles and a new bike for John.

When Dad got home a few days later, he was less than pleased with Mom but only raised minimal hell. At that point, he sat her down and explained how she was to act with money from then on. He said that after all the bills were paid, she could have play money if there was any left over, but the bills must come first. Mom did a pretty good job with that plan after that. Since we had to move again, the folks found a lovely upstairs apartment in Phoebus while Dad was home. It was located on Court Street, because the courthouse was our neighbor. Dad also got the car out of the shop and paid all the bills, and then he told Bekins not to ever send Mom his settlement money again! He went back out on the road again, and he always called while he was away, usually after we kids were in bed and he was done driving for the day. When the phone started suddenly being busy all the time, he was getting worried. When Mom finally answered the phone, she told Dad that she was always talking to her girlfriend Tish because our television was broken, and she had nothing else to do. Dad called Mr. Francis the next day and asked him to come to the house and take Mom to Western Auto to buy a new TV. He picked Mom up that same day, and she picked out the biggest and best Curtis Mathes color TV in the store. Mr. Francis insisted on paying for it, brought it and Mom home, and hooked it up for us. The man was obviously the best you could ever find. You would think that my dad would never leave him.

After we had been in Phoebus for a few months, however, an opportunity arose, or should I say that it was created. Dad got his settlement check, and it was more than he had expected. The folks were debating whether to buy a new Plymouth Sundance car or go to California to see Mom's long-lost family with the money. Mom's brother, Don, had been writing and telling Tom how crazy he was to work so hard. Don said that he was a foreman in an orange packing shed in Porterville and that he would guarantee Dad a job hauling oranges if we would move out there. Don had always been a con man, and it was blatantly obvious to all who knew him, but he had the magic Smith charm. He was so lovable, and he had a fantastic sense of humor, doing anything to get you to laugh. Dad never fell for any of Don's cons, but we were missing all the family, especially the kids. Plus, we had never lived in California, and it was considered the promised land of America, so we decided, "Why not?" School was out, so we had John's summer vacation to make the move. Thanks to the new TV Mom had gotten, we had to rent a small U-Haul trailer to fit all our belongings, and Mom said that made her feel that we were rich!

CHAPTER 16

"California Dreamin'"

(The Mamas & the Papas)

We loaded up and moved to California, not knowing what to expect, but Mom and Dad felt that we had enough money to face whatever came next. We pulled up to Don and Rosie's house in Strathmore, California, about six miles north of Porterville. It was early afternoon, so we expected Don to be at work, but as soon as we got out of the car, we heard him playing guitar in the house. At first, my folks were happy that he was home until it occurred to them that it wasn't a good sign for him to be home at that hour. Turned out, he and Rosie were both unemployed, and they were living on welfare. Don assured Dad that he could get jobs for both of them, but Dad wondered why Don didn't already have one like he said he did.

We went to Porterville and rented a very nice apartment on Sunnyside Street. Dad paid the deposit and first month's rent, and my folks just knew that in no time, Dad would have a job. Don and Dad partied through the weekend, and come Monday morning, they headed to the employment office. Dad was convinced that even though there were no moving companies in town, he was a truck driver, and they can get a job anywhere. Not Porterville, California! The only job they found was picking oranges in the orange groves, and Dad spent half a day doing that, then said, "No way!" The work was demeaning, and the pay was pathetic compared to what he was used to.

Little by little, my folks' money dwindled down to nothing. They were feeding Don and his family nearly every day because they didn't have enough food. They even bought Don's cigarettes and the gas for his car. Dad continued job hunting, and Don kept assuring him that he just picked the wrong time of year to come out there. In no time at all, Dad couldn't pay our rent, so Don insisted that we move in with them and pay his rent instead since it was cheaper. We moved into Don's place, almost totally broke, and my folks were getting really scared about the job situation. The day after we moved in, Don left to go to Stockton, California, where Wade was living at the time. Rosie and their kids left the same day and moved in with her parents in Porterville. So there we were stuck in their house with no food or money. Dad called his sister, Helen, who lived in Sumner, Washington, about twelve miles east of Tacoma on the way to Mount Rainier, and he asked her for help. She said that she had no money to send him, but if we could get up there, we could stay with them until Dad got a job.

John's Social Security check was due in about another week, and Dad decided that if we stretched it tightly, we would have just enough money to make the trip up there. He pawned the Curtis Mathes TV and got enough food to last until we left. Then they turned the gas and electric off in Don's house because he hadn't paid the bills, so Mom had no way to cook anything. The family ate oranges for three days. They bought milk for my baby bottle, six cans of potted meat, and a box of crackers, and that's what we ate on the trip to Washington. Of course, they had no money for a U-Haul trailer this time, so a few things had to get left behind. That was only the first time of many.

CHAPTER 17

"Busted"

(Ray Charles)

With the car loaded to the max, we took off and headed north to God only knew what. Mom had never met or talked to my aunt Helen, and Dad hadn't seen her for years. My folks were desperate and figured that we couldn't be any worse off in Washington than we were in California. We made it to Sumner, pulled into Helen and her husband Larry's driveway with thirty-eight cents to my folks' name, and there was nobody home. Mom and Dad weren't sure what to do, but I needed milk, so we went to a store to spend the last of the money on a pint of milk for me. It turned out that Larry's mother lived up the hill from them, saw our car lights at the house when we got back from the store, and came down to see who it was. She let us in the house and then went home and got two jars of canned pears for the family to eat. Mom said they tried not to act ravenous, but she didn't think they fooled Larry's mother. Helen and Larry came home soon after to us five weary travelers. Mom liked Helen right away, but she didn't like Larry. They had a son named Timmy, and he was a good kid. They showed us to our bedrooms, and we hit the beds like rocks.

The next day, Dad went to work with Larry, doing roofing. The fly wheel went out of our car right after we got there, and Dad's first check had to go to get that fixed and to pay Aunt Helen for our board and groceries. Mom got a job at Nalley's Fine Foods, and she used the car, while Dad rode with Larry. Mom didn't even last a week at her job, which was inspecting beef stew. She was on the conveyor line at five thirty in the morning, and she started getting dizzy. The hot steam coming off the food felt stifling, and she passed out. They took her to the nurse's station and lay her down and then called Dad to come and pick her up. The nurse told Mom that she suspected she was pregnant. Sure enough, she was. Since Mom was having a hard time working, she made a deal with Helen to clean their house to earn her stay, and Helen was happy with that. We were supposed to stay there until we saved the money to move out, but my folks were having a hard time saving because they were giving Helen and Larry more than half of everything Dad earned. They had just enough money to buy cigarettes and gas and go to the Laundromat, and that was it.

I got my first of several scars while we were living there. My cousin Timmy and John were playing with my sister and me on Timmy's bed, letting us jump and bouncing us around. Sure enough, someone was going to get hurt. I jumped on the bed, bounced off, and hit my face on the corner of his night stand. I cut my eye just below my eyebrow and had to get three stitches. Of course, it could have been so much worse. I had a scar for many years, but it wasn't too bad because it followed the bottom line of my eyebrow and faded with time. It would be the first of many accidents that I had, probably because I was fearless as a child.

Fate intervened with us leaving Aunt Helen's one day when John was riding bikes with a boy who lived up the hill. They had a path that went in and out of the woods that they rode on. They were riding in and out, and Penny, Helen's dachshund, was following them. On one of the times that they came out of the woods, a car was there, and it hit and killed Penny. John picked her up and carried her home, crying and very upset. He and the other boy explained to everyone what happened over and over, but Helen and Larry were hysterical and started blaming John for killing Penny. It ended up getting really ugly with Mom, Dad, Helen, and Larry all arguing with one another, and my folks knew it was time to leave. By the grace of God, Dad had gotten paid that day and hadn't yet given his sister any money. My folks found a dumpy trailer to rent in Orting, Washington, that weekend. The rent was very affordable, and we were able to move in immediately. Orting was about eight miles south of Sumner and even closer to Mount Rainier.

CHAPTER 18

"Going Up the Country"

(Canned Heat)

Orting was a real experience, a culture shock. It's a picturesque little town that sits at the foot of Mount Rainier and at the time, consisted of one main street. Unfortunately, if Mount Rainier ever erupts, it also sits directly in the path of danger. Maybe that's one reason why Mom said that Washington State was scary to her. In spite of all her moving, she didn't consider herself well traveled, and Washington seemed to represent beauty in the most rugged way that she had ever seen. The women she saw out there looked masculine to her, hunting, fishing, fighting, like real pioneers. She usually stayed to herself anywhere that we moved but became even more withdrawn after moving out there.

Our home in Orting was way out in the woods, which Mom said terrified her. The place wasn't much better than a shack. It was a little trailer house, with two bedrooms, and there was a built-on part that consisted of a big living room with a woodstove, a small bedroom, and a utility room. It was livable, but there was nothing pretty about it. However, like many places that we lived while I was growing up, with much scrubbing and TLC, Mom and Dad made a cozy home out of it. Dad worked for Atlas Van Lines in Tacoma then, so he had a pretty substantial drive each day. Dan said that he thought John got a job at a concrete place in the town of Auburn and that my dad would take him to work every day on the way to his own job, but that would have been about ten miles out of Dad's way. At any rate, we didn't do much during the week because of how far away everything was, but we would all go to Tacoma to shop on the weekends. We had iron water in Orting, which we couldn't stand to drink, so Dad carried water from Tacoma for us to drink. The owner of our trailer house offered to sell it to Dad, but Mom said that iron water was three strikes against buying it for sure. It turned everything yellow and rusty and was a real mess. All the scrubbing in the world wouldn't get that rust off, and that was just one more thing to make that place a little dumpier.

We moved into the trailer house in early January, and it was mid-March before Mom let us kids play outside. It rained incessantly, and where Mom came from, you didn't let kids play out in the rain; you waited until it stopped. John finally convinced Mom that if she waited until the rain stopped, we kids would all go stir-crazy. My sister Paula and I were three and two respectively. Mom said we were chomping at the bit to get out of that bleak house and do some exploring. She finally relented, and we waited until the rain became more of a mist than a downpour, then ventured outside of the house. Mom didn't like that we had deep woods on three sides of us, and what was supposed to be the front yard was so grown up it seemed like more of a field than a yard. The grass and weeds were almost too high to see over the top. Deer would come out of the woods almost daily, and they were so tame and totally unafraid of humans that Mom would have a hard time shooing them out of the way to drive off in the car. It frightened her how they would easily approach her and us little girls. She could also work herself into a sheer panic thinking of what other kinds of creatures lurked out there in those woods. Us girls seemed to take to the great outdoors immediately, and Mom said that trying to reign us back in became an impossible chore. John took us out on short walks occasionally, and we found all kinds of berries just growing wild there. Mom gave us empty egg cartons to gather our berries in. We were delighted to be able to play outdoors and not have the restrictions of a yard. There was a little stream over across the road where John would take us, and we would pretend to go fishing or wade in the very shallow water when it got hot. The only downside for us kids to being outside were the stinging nettles growing everywhere, and Paula and I learned early on to watch out for them. Mom said that we called them "those old dummy medals!"

Dad and John enjoyed the great outdoors there as well. They went fishing at Lake Kapowsin about ten miles south of Orting. At home, they shot a bow and arrows out in the yard and chopped and stacked wood for the woodstove. It just seemed like life was so much more on the outside than in and that was new to all of us except Dad, from his young days in the mountains of West Virginia. Mom had never been an outside person, and she had to get used to us girls getting dirtier there than we ever had, yet we were always giggling, holding hands, skipping, and just exploring and enjoying the great outdoors. We were inseparable, so you never saw one girl without the other. Mom dressed us alike because that was always the way we wanted it. If one of us picked out what we wanted, the other insisted on having the same. People often thought we were twins, especially since we were only seventeen months apart, so were almost the same size. We both had long, beautiful hair, and Mom would usually fix it in braids or ponytails, and there again, we had to be the same. Paula gave me my nickname, Sis, from the time I was born because I was her new baby sister. It was really Sissy when I was little, and Dad would call me Sissy Lynne or my least favorite, Sissy Lynder Hicks. Luckily, after I became an adult, it was mostly Sis.

One weekend, we were all walking down the sidewalk shopping in Tacoma, as was our habit. Paula and I were holding hands, as usual, and I must have become distracted or slowed down for some reason. Mom and Dad were walking behind us, and they heard Paula suddenly say, "C'mon, Sis!" Then she pulled my hand so hard and fast to catch up to her that I went flying face-first into a parking meter! I started to cry, of course, and she cried too because she had hurt me. She was loving on me and telling me she was sorry, while

Mom and Dad were loving on both of us and trying to inspect my injuries, which were not anything serious.

One evening after dinner, we all went to Lake Kapowsin, and Dad caught a little sun perch. We girls both squealed with delight and wanted to play with it because it seemed to be changing colors right before our eyes. Dad took it off the hook and laid it at our feet. We jumped away with fright but soon returned with curiosity. Mom said we were hunkered over the fish, gently touching it, saying "Tickle, tickle," and squealing each time it jumped. We were convinced it was our tickling that made it flip and flop. We were sad when Dad had to put it back in the water before it died, but we were very entertained for a while.

My dad was my hero, and I was always eager to spend time with him, so I tried to insert myself into as many of his projects throughout my childhood as I could. He usually liked my company and sometimes had difficulty reaching into small spaces with his giant hands, so my small hands could be very useful. That was a huge source of pride to me that I could actually be helpful to my hero, who could do anything. One day, the oil heater that we had in the house trailer stopped working, so after dinner, Dad tore into it to try to get it fixed. We girls wanted to stay near and watch, but the job was turning into a black, sooty mess, so Mom made us go to the living room at the other end of the house. Mom said I kept trying to come back in with my dad, and Mom kept chasing me away. When Dad determined that he had to buy a part for the heater and couldn't get it before the next day, everybody decided to go in the living room, watch television, and forget about the heater for the night.

Apparently, I had snuck out and gone back to the heater, but Mom didn't realize it until she went to the kitchen to get a drink of water. When she reached the hallway, she had a straight view of the heater, and there she saw me. I was holding a stick, stirring it all around in the black soot in the heater, working hard, and was completely black with the soot. Mom quietly back-tracked to the living room and motioned for Dad to come see. When he saw me, he asked, "Sis, what do you think you're doing?" I looked up at my folks and smiled, showing my teeth to be the only white spot left on me.

Then I said, "Daddy, I dus tyin to wix it!" and kept stirring (meaning, "I'm just trying to fix it"). That expression became one of tons of mispronunciations used by my family. We were so fond of them, and they were our personal shared idiosyncrasies. Mom and Dad had to laugh, but it wasn't so funny to Mom when she had to work hard to get me clean again.

In the summer of 1967, just before Mom was due to give birth, Aunt Jeannie contacted her and said she would like us to keep the Smith kids over their summer vacation, and she would bring them up to us from Eureka, California. We were all delighted, and John was especially happy to be reunited with his younger siblings again. Mom and Dad went out and bought a bigger kitchen table with more chairs, another set of bunk beds, and a chest of drawers so we could accommodate everyone. Aunt Jeannie brought them up to our house when they got out of school, and she spent one night. She asked Mom if she could keep getting the kids' Social Security checks even while we had them because she didn't want the Social Security office to get confused. Mom said yes; Dad had a good job moving furniture in Tacoma, so they didn't have to have the money. Mom and Dad were never greedy for money. It was happy times having all of us together again, and Mom said all of us kids just seemed to be in a party mode. Paula and I loved our aunt and uncles, who were much more like an older sister and brothers, and we were always happy to have them around, I'm sure in part because we got so much extra attention from all of them. Dan, Sam, and Patty fell in love with our place, just as John, Paula, and I had, and we had a great time showing them around the woods and stream.

On July 31, Mom gave birth to my brother, Tom Jr. The closest hospital was Good Samaritan in nearby Puyallup about ten miles northwest of Orting. This meant that my brother was saddled with a birthplace that people outside of Western Washington would always struggle to pronounce. The birth of my parents' first son was a joyous occasion indeed, but fourteen years later, that hospital would play a large part in a terrible tragedy for our family.

Mom had to be in the hospital for three days with Tommy, and she was really worried about how we would get along without her.

Dad was plenty capable of caring for us, but he worked during the day. John, however, was old enough and responsible enough to watch us kids during the day, and we managed to survive. When Mom came home, she asked John what he wanted for supper that night. He said, "Fried chicken, mashed potatoes, and corn." Mom said that was okay with her, and she got some chicken out of the freezer. Then she asked John what Dad had made us for dinner while she was in the hospital. He said, "Fried chicken, mashed potatoes, and corn." She laughed and asked what else Dad had made for dinner, and John said, "Fried chicken, mashed potatoes, and corn." Then Mom asked, "What did you have the other night?" You guessed it, John said, "Fried chicken, mashed potatoes, and corn." Mom laughed and told John she couldn't believe they were eating the same thing for dinner four nights in a row, to which he replied, "It's our favorite dinner!"

Mom said that looking back, life was really good then. It was simple, but everyone was happy, and we had great times just being outside, running through the woods, and seemingly doing nothing. My sister and I, however, were not happy about having a baby brother. It was a wonderful novelty in the beginning, having a live baby doll to play with, but as he grew to become more and more like a boy, and a headstrong one at that, we were not interested.

CHAPTER 19

"California Sun"

(The Rivieras)

When summer vacation was over, Mom and Dad took Dan, Patty, and Sam back to Aunt Jeannie's in Eureka, but when they arrived, Aunt Jeannie said that she didn't want all the kids back. Mom and Dad said that they wouldn't take Dan back because he was a little hellion and wouldn't do what Mom told him to do, so Jeannie relented and kept Dan with her. Patty and Sam came back to Orting with John, Mom, and Dad. Not long after they returned, Don went to prison for stealing some jewelry from a lady, but he hadn't actually stolen the jewelry. He did, however, take the woman's car and trade it in for another car, which he kept. Dan thought that Uncle Larry was the one who turned Don in to the cops when he left their house one day. Dean ended up coming to Orting with his family the following summer after Sam and Patty moved there, but he didn't like it there, and when he left, he took John, Sam, and Patty with him back to Eureka. John and Sam joined Dan at Jeannie's house, and Patty stayed with Dean and Reba. Dan said that the previous year he had spent alone at Aunt Jeannie's had been good for him and that Jeannie had taught him to speak properly. He could really tell how far he had come when he was reunited with his brothers again after that year, and they spoke like they were from the ghetto. After Dan left Aunt Jeannie's, though, he said he went back to his old ways. John had gotten a guitar and learned to play while he was in Orting, and now he taught Dan to play as well. He taught him to play "Tom Dooley" and "Little Black Egg." Don also played guitar, but he didn't teach the boys much, and they had trouble keeping up with him.

Jeannie and her husband were very active in the Pentecostal church, but when Jeannie was kicked out of their church along with two other influential women for having women's prayer meetings, they started their own church meetings in nearby McKinleyville. Eventually, this group decided that the Lord told them all to move in together, about twenty-seven people, in one house. Jeannie and Larry moved in with the group along with the Smith boys, but they still kept their home in Eureka, and Larry was there a lot for business. When the group was kicked out of the rental house in McKinleyville by their landlord, Larry moved everyone into his and Jeannie's house in Eureka. They believed they were all chosen by God and were very special, but when the rest of the group tried to bring in even more people, Larry and Jeannie kicked everyone out, on the advice of prominent Pentecostal Evangelist A. A. Allen, their spiritual mentor.

Then one day in the spring of 1968, Jeannie told the boys that instead of going to school, they needed to pack their bags. She took the boys down to Don's house in Porterville and dropped them off. Patty stayed in Eureka with Dean. Don had just gotten out of the penitentiary after serving nine months. Don was stabbed by a Mexican in prison, and he ended up beating the guy up so badly that he was in a coma. It happened right before Don was supposed to get out, and Don could have had time added to his sentence, but the warden liked him, so the incident was kept quiet, and Don was released. The boys started school there at Don's in Porterville, and Dan met a boy named Bob in school who was from Arkansas. In the winter of 1969, Dan went with Bob and his family back to Denning, near Ozark, in Northwestern Arkansas. The nearby town of Altus is where Paris Hilton and Nicole Richie filmed their television show

The Simple Life many years later. Dan stayed with Bob's family there until the spring when they gave him $10 and put him on a bus back to California because he said they were tired of him.

Dan had recently received a letter from someone in California saying that John and Sam were in a foster home there, but he didn't know where to find them. He only hoped that Wade was still staying in the Porterville Hotel, which he was. Dan got off the bus and walked to the hotel, then he and Wade surprised John at his car after school that day. John told them that he and Sam were being fostered by the Jones family. Dan went out to the farm where Don was living and moved in with him, but he visited John and Sam on the weekends. After about a month, however, the Joneses took over care of Dan as well, and he moved into their home full-time with John and Sam. He said they had the first air conditioning he had ever seen. He had quit the eighth grade after leaving Arkansas, and he didn't want to go back. Since Mr. Jones taught school in the small town of Poplar, which was about nine miles west of Porterville, the school district let Dan finish the eighth grade there with his foster father.

Right away, Mrs. Jones, the boys' foster mother, began molesting Dan with kisses and petting. She told him that she loved him before she even met him, based on what she had heard from John and Sam. Mrs. Jones ended up taking Dan's virginity when she was thirty-two and he was sixteen, and they had an affair. This living arrangement lasted for a year. Dan said the kids loved that they could eat all the food they wanted there, and he ate like a horse. During summer vacation, they took all the kids on a road trip in the car around the country and into Canada for about six weeks, and they loved it. They even took the kids to where their mother, Helen, was buried at the Baker Cemetery in Aberdeen, Maryland, and they bought a little glass box with pink artificial roses inside of it to place on her grave. It was a lovely box that I saw when I visited there after we moved to Maryland when I was around eight years old. Helen was actually buried with baby Virginia Anne in her arms in one of the five plots she had bought there when Gerry died. Gerry is buried in another plot, and neither of them is marked. Dan has talked about placing markers on the graves and maybe buying the remaining three plots for other family members, but neither he nor any of the other family members has ever done so.

Even though they were treated very well, Dan was defensive and would get an attitude with all his foster parents, including the Joneses. After about six months, Dan got pissed off at Mrs. Jones and ran away from the house in Porterville and set out to hitchhike to Eureka to see Dean about 550 miles north. His ride took him all the way to Redding, 140 miles short of Eureka. He started walking west from there to hitchhike the rest of the way to Eureka, but after walking about forty-four miles with no ride, he arrived in the town of Weaverville, and he was done. He still had about another one hundred miles to get to Eureka, but he was exhausted. Dean had told him a story about how one time he had nowhere to sleep, so he went to the police station in whatever town he was in and asked if they would let him sleep there. It had worked for Dean, so Dan found the police station in Weaverville and asked them if he could spend the night. They did let him stay the night, then found out he was a runaway, so he stayed there five days in jail until the Joneses picked him up and took him back to their home in Porterville. Shortly after Dan's return, John got upset with the Joneses when they threatened to take his car as punishment because he had been working on the car and revving it up outside the church and disturbed the service. He refused to give up his car and left the Joneses to go and stay with Wade in his motel room. He graduated from high school shortly after and then started at Porterville Community College.

CHAPTER 20

"The Unicorn"

(The Irish Rovers)

After Dean and all the Smith kids left Orting, Mom and Dad decided to move to Tacoma, Washington, because it was closer to Dad's work. Within the next three years, we lived on Fife Street and Ainsworth Avenue in South Central Tacoma and McKinley Avenue on the east side before we left the state for Porterville, California. Mom and Dad were convinced by my uncle Don to go back there again, and this time, we lived on Orange Street in an apartment, then moved to a house on Springville Drive. When we got to California, Dan and Sam were living with the Joneses, their foster family. Patty was still with Dean and Reba, who were living in Porterville at the moment, and John was with Wade. This meant that all seven of the Smith siblings along with their children and their father Wade were all together in one place at one time. That would never happen again. Mom got a job at the Paul Bunyon restaurant as a waitress, then John got a job as a busboy and Dan as a dishwasher. When a lady named Kathy was hired as a waitress, she kind of liked John until she met my uncle Don. Don had left his wife, Rosie, while she was pregnant with their fifth child. Dan said that she didn't allow

Don to see his children after they separated. Dan also said that Mom told everyone Don left Rosie for Kathy, but Dan said that Don didn't meet Kathy until after he had already left Rosie. Either way, Don and Kathy became a couple.

I don't have much to share about this time in Porterville for our family of five, and two of my three memories are not good. I loved the fact that we had a lemon tree in the front yard, an almond tree in the back, and best of all, a small pomegranate tree on the side of the house. That started my life-long love of that fruit. After we moved back east, most people had no idea what the exotic fruit was or what to do with it, but my mom would find them for us kids, and it was such a treat to eat them! She would open them for us and put us outside or on the floor in play clothes that could get dirty because she was so afraid that we would do permanent damage with the red juice of the fruit staining something. We would pick out the berries one by one, savoring each bite. This is still one of my favorite things to eat in this same way to this day.

The first bad memory involved the lemon tree in the front yard. We had a neighbor nicknamed Tanky, who was developmentally disabled. Of course, at the time, we called him retarded. He was very sweet and would come over and try to play with us kids. Sam would come over to our house with his BB gun and tell Tanky to stand under the lemon tree while he shot the lemons, making the juice drip down all over Tanky's head, face, and clothing. He would tell him not to move, and Tanky wouldn't. I can remember him standing there, squeezing his eyes shut and shaking his head from the burning juice, while everyone around would laugh. Sam, who was always quiet and compliant, could be cruel in the tricks he played on people.

The other memory is even worse. Paula and I had acquired a tiny kitten from somewhere, possibly not even weaned yet. We played with the kitten all day, pushing it around in a baby doll buggy, wrapping it in a blanket, trying to put doll clothes on it, etc. At some point, we began to argue over whose turn it was to hold the kitten, and I'm assuming that our argument was very annoying because my dad picked up the kitten and threw it across the yard and into the street, killing it instantly, and told my sister and me that we wouldn't have the kitten to fight over any longer. It was the first time that I remember witnessing such cruelty that a living thing was killed, and I was absolutely devastated. To think that my father, who was my hero, could do something so heinous caused a real fear in me. It was certainly warranted because that would only be the first incident that I witnessed my father do something cruel, violent, or scary. It didn't change my hero worship of him, but it gave me a healthy fear of him that would last until my late thirties.

We moved back to Tacoma because apparently things weren't going well in Porterville, and Dad was encouraged by an old friend from back in West Virginia, Jim, who was now stationed at Fort Lewis in the US Army. Jim had met and married a lady from Tacoma named Dolly, whose wealthy family owned several successful businesses in town, including a car repair shop. Jim secured a position for Dad repairing tires in his in-law's shop because of Dad's experience with retreading. We stayed back in South Tacoma with Jim and Dolly at their house on Warner Street, then moved a few blocks away to our own place on Junett Street. I have good memories of our time in Tacoma, but I can't be certain if some of them are from when we lived there this time or the last time. Mom was really an excellent mother at this time in our lives, and she was particularly gifted at teaching preschool children. She saw to our every need—physical, mental, and emotional. We adored her and the attention that we got from our precious mommy who hadn't ever disappointed us or broken our hearts—not yet. She taught us nursery rhymes, read books to us, and colored with us. I thought that her coloring books pages were so beautiful! The way she shaded her colors, always stayed within the lines, and went over all the lines with a black crayon. I never did learn to color as well as she did. She played and danced with us and sang songs with us, especially in the car. One of our favorite songs at the time was "Who Put the Bomp" by Barry Mann; for me it was because I always had a fixation on background singers, and this song contained many of the silly sayings found in songs from the 1950s and 1960s, like "Bop shoo bop" and "Dip da dip." Another of our favorite songs was "The Unicorn" by The Irish Rovers, about leaving the unicorn off Noah's Ark. My favorite lyrics were "Humptyback camels and some chimpanzees" and "The loveliest of all was the unicorn."

In fact, most of my childhood memories involve music and songs. It seemed as if I were born into a movie with the soundtrack always running. Mom was definitely my biggest musical influence. She loved her 45 records and played her favorite songs over and over again. She particularly loved the classic fifties rock and roll music, and because of that, I am very knowledgeable on the genre. Really, I'm very knowledgeable about all popular music from the 1950s to the 1990s, as is my brother. He and I often joked as adults that we should have our own radio show and that nobody could stump us at music trivia.

My dad enjoyed the same music as Mom, but he also loved classic country music. Some of his favorite artists were Hank Williams, Johnny Cash, and Merle Haggard. Both my parents followed contemporary country music as well, and I remember the big hits by artists like Dolly Parton, Loretta Lynn, and Conway Twitty. Dad was particularly fond of Charlie Pride, which always confused me a little given the way Dad spoke about black people. I wasn't yet old enough to understand the racist theory that "you can enjoy their music; you just don't bring them home with you."

We had many idyllic moments during this time, and I am especially grateful for them, considering the life that was to come down the road. Idyllic, yes, but we kids did some especially crazy stuff during this time too. My folks were both working at the time. Dad worked nights at the repair shop, and Mom worked days as a waitress. The plan was for them to take turns watching us kids. My sister Paula was three to five years old when we were in Tacoma, and I was two to four years old. She was so smart and so good, and I worshipped her. She was also very curious and was really the one that was always getting us into trouble when we were together. I was sweet, gullible, and generally a people pleaser by nature, so I was the perfect sidekick who went along with whatever she wanted me to do. My brother Tommy was a baby or only up to two years old at this time, so he was truly an innocent victim in our shenanigans at the time. My sister's curiosity had already caused her to supposedly drink bleach by this time, although there were no ramifications for that action that was ever mentioned, so that is a puzzling story. Another thing that occurred here was my first choking. Paula and I were eating a roll of Life Savers, and apparently, I put three of them that were stuck together in my mouth and started choking on them. Mom and Dad were right there, and mercifully, Dad figured out what was wrong with me right away when I started turning blue and then went limp. He picked me up, held me upside down by my feet, and beat on my back. Mom was frantic and wondering what in the world Dad was doing until I coughed up the Life Savers. It just occurred to me that they were almost Life Takers. Ha!

So let's get to our first adventure here. My mom left for work one morning, and my dad had fallen asleep on the couch after a long night of work. My sister and I awoke, and apparently, she decided that we needed to go on an adventure. We changed out of our pajamas into wearing nothing but a pair of Mom's underwear each, the big brief kind, that we found in the dirty clothes hamper. I would give anything to know what prompted that decision. Then we managed to push the kitchen table over to the back door, and my sister unlocked the lock up at the top of the door, the one that was meant to keep the children from opening the door. I don't know how we did this without waking my dad, but then Paula and I left the house together and embarked on our adventure. Neither of us has memory of what we did during that time, and I don't know how long we were out before my father awoke and discovered what we had done. At any rate, he found us holding hands, walking down the sidewalk in our residential neighborhood, with my borrowed underwear falling off and me struggling to keep them on and my sister doing a much better job and holding hers up to her neck. I should mention that it was wintertime in Tacoma, Washington, so it was probably thirty to forty degrees that morning, and there was snow on the ground. After that, we had a babysitter whenever my parents were at work.

That babysitter really came in handy after our next stunt. It was a weekend, and our parents were still asleep in bed when we three kids awoke early in the morning and made our way downstairs to get some breakfast of Cheerios with honey. My mom had been discussing my dad trimming mine and my sister's hair, and he was supposed to do it that very day. At the time, my sister had hair that fell to the middle of her back, and mine was down to my waist. My father loved our long hair and brushed it for us quite often. He was also in charge of trimming the ends, including our bangs. Apparently, my sister had decided to take the job off my father's hands, and we all cut each other's hair—before, during, or after our breakfast we are not certain which.

So Mom and Dad woke up and realized that us kids were already awake and active when they heard us making noise downstairs. They came down, walked into the kitchen, and discovered a combination of Cheerios, honey, and lots and lots of hair spread all over the kitchen. Apparently, they both cried. My hair was now just above my shoulders, and Paula laid the scissors on the top front of my head and cut, leaving hair about one-eighth-inch long in that spot. She thought that was how you trimmed bangs. Paula's hair was cut above her neck with very short bangs, although not as short as mine. Tommy didn't have a surplus of hair to begin with, but he also got a trim. It was a disaster. Something had to be done with our motley-haired bunch, but my folks were too embarrassed to take us to a beauty parlor to get us repaired, so they paid the babysitter to do it. My brother ended up with a buzz cut, and my sister had a cute little pixie style. My hair remained just above my shoulders but had to be combed over to the side in the front and fastened with a barrette to hide my little crew cut on top. Nothing else could be done, but time would eventually solve the problem. I think that just about every kid cuts their own hair, but I've never heard of a more spectacular job than the one that we did.

I have mentioned how much I adored my sister and the fact that we were inseparable, so it completely devastated me when it was time for her to start kindergarten. I was absolutely lost without her, my best friend, mentor, and partner in crime. Our babysitter would walk Paula to school every morning, with Tommy and me in tow, and it never got easier for me to say goodbye to her. One day, I managed to sneak out of the house and make my way back to the school to be with her. I was quickly discovered wandering around the school, and my mom was called to come and fetch me from the premises. I must have finally gotten used to the idea of her being gone, but I never really recovered from the loss of our close relationship. It wasn't the same after she started school, and we no longer did everything together anymore. She started finding other friends of her own age, and I started getting left out for the first time. It was a dynamic that marked my childhood and my self-esteem.

CHAPTER 21

"Dizzy"

(Tommy Roe)

In 1970, we decided to leave Washington and move back to Maryland. I'm assuming that what prompted this move was a job for Dad moving furniture back in Aberdeen, Maryland. Our friend Dolly made the trip back east with us. Dolly was always happy and laughing, and I felt seen and loved in her company. She will always have a special place in my heart. As many times as we traveled across cities, states, or even cross-country to move to another home during my childhood, this road trip was one of the few of which I have any memories. We three kids rode in the back seat of our station wagon, with Mom and Dolly up front. The rest of the car was packed with our belongings, as was the U-Haul trailer that my mom pulled behind us. Mom was very thoughtful about our well-being on this trip and bought us new toys and snacks to open for each day of the four-day trip. I can remember the barrel of monkeys but nothing else specifically. We never got to stop anywhere or do anything fun on our road trips, so this one was different because we at least got something special each day of the trip.

We arrived at our temporary—even more temporary than usual—home in a boarding house outside of Aberdeen, Maryland. We found out about the boarding house from an old friend of my dad named Ersel, who had a room in the house with his wife, Shirley, their son, and Ersel's two stepsons. Dolly and her husband, Jim, who had traveled separately from us, had another room, and our family of five were in another. I loved living in this boarding house! I remember going from room to room, visiting with each of the occupants, collecting snacks and attention. Just as Dolly made me feel seen and loved, so did Ersel and Shirley, and they will always have a special place in my heart as well. I don't remember much about the oldest stepson, Eddie, at this time, but I always liked him and thought he was cool and handsome. Georgie, the second of Ersel's stepsons, slept in a screened-in porch on the second floor. He was a teenager and probably loved the privacy. We kids used to visit him there, and we wished we could sleep outside as well. Georgie was such a sweetheart and was always patient and loving with us kids.

Since I had already developed a love for architecture at a very young age, I loved the boarding house. It was a big, plantation-style white building, which I believe was three stories. It was classic Georgian colonial, which is one of my favorite styles. There was a common living room for guests, but we kids weren't allowed to be in there without our parents. In fact, if we went outside to play, the owner would often lock the door behind us so we couldn't get back in. It wasn't so bad being locked out, unless we had to use the restroom, because we had a great time playing on the grounds with all the kids from the boarding house. My mom told the story of something that happened there, but I don't remember it myself. While out playing on the grounds, we found a nest of newly hatched snakes, and we were picking them up with sticks. When my mother discovered what we were doing, she was horrified. She had a serious phobia of snakes, and I thought it was funny when people teased her with them until I was old enough to understand how terrible it was for her.

From there, we moved to Havre de Grace, Maryland, to live in the same Projects where my grandmother and aunt had died in the fire years earlier. I know that Patty was with us here because she took us kids to the movie theater to see a Charlie Brown flick. It's the first movie that I can remember seeing, but I couldn't enjoy it because Tommy, who was three at the time, kept running down the aisle, getting up on the stage, and touching the movie screen, trying to play with Charlie Brown and his friends. We were finally asked to leave the theater because poor Patty could not keep control of Tommy and make him stay in his seat. Patty was so good with us kids, and we adored her. She was kind and gentle and patient with us. When we were living here, she accidentally pulled Paula's arm out of socket while lifting her from the bathtub. Paula recovered just fine from the incident, but I'm sure Patty was devastated. She would never, ever inflict pain on anyone. My best guess for how she ended up with us in Maryland is that Dean and Reba brought her back, but nobody can remember exactly.

The Havre de Grace Projects were a fun neighborhood for us kids to live in, just as it had been for the Smith kids years earlier. We played a lot with our new friends that lived next door in our townhouse duplex. They had a girl that was mine and Paula's age and a boy who was Tommy's. Most of our playtime outside was on the swing set out in the common yard. One day, my sister and I were swinging on the set when one of our friends came out to join us. I very graciously surrendered my swing to the little girl. However, when I saw how much fun she and my sister were having on the swings while I had none, I decided to walk up behind my sister and push her off her swing and onto the ground. By the time she got herself up from the ground, I realized what a big mistake I had made and began to apologize profusely. Paula, however, was having none of it! She started to chase me through the yard, and we ran for what seemed like miles until she eventually caught up with me. I was running so fast that when she finally gained on me and just barely touched my back, I went falling to the ground. Just my luck, we were on the sidewalk, and my knee landed on a piece of a broken Coca-Cola bottle when I hit the ground. My sister ran for help when she saw that I was bleeding, and I remember Dolly picking me up off the ground and carrying me into the house. The next thing I remember was Dolly carrying me into the house again, but this time I had a Tootsie Pop in my hand, given to me at the hospital, where I had received a total of seven stitches in two places on my knee. Strangely, the scars that started out just under my knee are now located just above it. I suppose they got relocated with my growth.

Soon our whole family became friends with the neighbors next door, not just us kids. We would be close to the mom, her little sister, and especially her little brother, Henry, for many years. The father, however, was a very different story. One day, my sister and I were playing with the girl next door at her house. Mom allowed us to play at their house because our friend's father assured Mom that it was okay and he would keep an eye on us. He worked nights and was watching his daughter while his wife was out shopping with their little boy. Mom always told us that there was safety in numbers and felt okay about us three girls being together. But I was alone when I was sent downstairs by the older girls to fill our teapot with water from the kitchen sink for our tea party. My friend's father was lying on the couch and told me to come over to him. I did so without fear, but when he unzipped his pants and pulled out his penis, I knew something was very wrong. I started to run away from him, but he grabbed my hand and, despite my struggle, forced my hand to touch his penis. I don't remember anything else bad happening after that, so I'll assume and pray that nothing else did.

The next thing I remember, I was home, and my mom was telling me that a police officer was going to come and ask me about what happened and that I needed to tell him the same thing that I had told her. I vaguely remember talking to the officer. Whenever the story would come up later, over the years, my mom said that my friend's father had left his home and family immediately after the incident and fled from the wrath of my father for what he had done. My dad had a lot of connections in Havre de Grace and nearby Aberdeen, Maryland, but he was never able to locate the man after many years of searching. I am grateful that my dad couldn't find him because God only knows what he would have done to him, and I don't want to have to live with whatever it would have been. Certainly, my dad wouldn't have gone to the police because they were generally the enemy in our family of outlaws, and I'm surprised that my mom called them in the first place.

Another, much worse tragedy occurred here, but it was after we had already left. There had been a German Shepherd dog chained to a tree near our building in the project. My mom warned us to stay away from the dog, but my sister and I would disobey and pet the dog sometimes or share food with it if we had it. After we had moved away, someone told my mom that a little girl about my same age went up to pet the dog one day, and he mauled her to death. If the story is true, it's just one example of many times that my life could have been damaged even more than it was or possibly be gone altogether. I remember that we kids got lucky in another way while we lived here. Apparently, a lot of kids in the neighborhood had been found to have worms. When my folks found out, they inspected our bottoms to make sure there was no sign of the parasite, and there wasn't. We were told, however, that we couldn't go barefoot outside any longer so that we wouldn't be exposed to the worms. We were not happy about it, as we were usually barefoot anytime we were outside, but we didn't like the idea of having worms in our bodies either, so we complied. My only other memory of this place is that I started kindergarten, and I can remember sitting at a table in class, playing with clay, and I really liked it there. Very shortly after, however, it was time to move again.

CHAPTER 22

"Porterville"

(Creedence Clearwater Revival)

A few months after Dan got back to the Joneses from Eureka, in the summer of 1970, he got an attitude and ran away from their home again, this time to stay with my grandfather. He was put into a new foster home with a nice older couple on Springville Drive, the same road our family of five had lived on for a short time. The place was kind of a farm with cows and a walnut grove. Sam joined Dan shortly after, and they were given so much freedom that they would stay out all night hanging out with girls and sleep all day. Dan learned about huffing paint from his foster parents' daughter, who was in her early twenties. She showed him how to spray-paint into an empty bread bag, hold the bag so that there was only a small opening near the top, seal your mouth over the opening, and inhale. Apparently, it gives you a really euphoric buzz. Dan then showed John how to huff paint too. Dean had left Porterville and moved back to Eureka, taking Patty with him along with John, who was on summer break before starting community college. Since it was summer break for Sam and Dan also, they were able to get permission from their foster parents to take a bus to Eureka to see Dean and their siblings. John and Dean had little Honda motorcycles, and Dean never let Dan touch his bike while they were visiting, but he changed his mind and told him he could ride it one morning. He and John were out riding, and John picked up a hitchhiker on his bike who was on his way to Oregon. He didn't have anything to his name, so they went into a Sears store and stole a sleeping bag for him.

After they let the hitchhiker go, they were back on the road when a cop got behind Dan and in front of John. Dan said he was always in the lead. The cop turned his lights on, and rather than stopping, Dan got on a path beside the road, then entered into the Sequoia Park. The cop chased Dan all through the park, but he got away. Dan knew the park well because the boys used to get dropped off there when they lived with Aunt Jeannie, and they would play there all day. Dan headed toward Dean's house, and he found John waiting on the side of the road for him. Dean had told the boys that morning to come to the saw mill in Arcada for lunch, where he worked, so they headed there now.

They got behind a logging truck, and Dan was daydreaming, going about sixty miles per hour, as fast as the bike would go, and wasn't paying attention when the logging truck hit his brakes. Dan saw the brake lights and knew he wasn't going to be able to avoid hitting the truck, so he just closed his eyes and waited. His front tire hit the back tire of the truck, and then the bike flew forward and was run over by the truck, but when he opened his eyes, Dan was flying about fifteen feet in the air upside down, back away from the truck. He landed in a yard and was knocked out. His left leg had ended up around his neck, wrapped around his head. He woke up when a man came up with a medical kit and put his leg back down where it belonged. When the man started to cut Dan's jeans with a pair of scissors to see the damage to Dan's leg, Dan started cussing the guy, telling him not to cut his brand-new jeans. John ran over to Dan after lying his bike down in the road and followed the man with the medical kit as he carried Dan into a nearby house. There was a nice lady there, and the man laid Dan on her couch while John ran to the sawmill to get Dean. Dan heard Dean's heavy work boots clomp into the house and knew he was in trouble, but Dean wasn't mad at him; he was really concerned and kept saying, "You poor son of a bitch."

Dean then took Dan back to his house because he refused to go to the hospital. Dan had a huge, soft knot on the back of his head, about eight inches across, but it didn't hurt. His left leg, from his ankle to his knee, was skinned down to the bone on his shin, and it had black skid marks on each side from the truck tire. Dean finally made Dan go to the hospital, where he spent the night in terrible pain from his knee. The next day, the doctor drained three large syringes full of fluid from Dan's knee. His kneecap was cracked but not broken. They released him from the hospital with crutches but without a cast so that the wound on his leg could heal. He spent two weeks on Dean's couch. One time, Dan was drinking a pint of Southern Comfort that Dean had bought for him and was lying on the couch with a blanket over him but had his injured leg hanging out over the side of the couch. Dean was drinking too, and he was joking with Dan, kicking the couch like he was going to kick Dan's bad leg, until he actually did kick Dan's bad knee instead of the couch because he couldn't see it hanging down under the blanket. Dan said that, of course, it hurt like hell, and Dean felt really bad about it. After the wound healed, Dan got a cast on his leg from just under his butt down to around his foot—his entire leg. It wasn't a walking cast, but he refused to use crutches, and he walked on the cast, smashing the bottom of the foot portion and making it easier to walk on. He ended up having to cut his new jeans to get them on over his cast. He wore the cast for six weeks and was still wearing it when he and Sam got back to Porterville to their foster home. He went out to the lake in a boat with Don, and the boat had water in it, and his cast got wet, so he cut it off up to the ankle. He was so happy to be able to wear his favorite cowboy boots on both feet again. When they finally took the cast off, he had a huge scab on his leg, and the scab came off with the cast, which Dan thought was really neat. His leg was tender for about six months, and it took about a year for him to be able to run and jump like normal.

Things were going well for Dan after that until his foster parents said he was spending too much time with a Mexican family down the street and wouldn't let him go there any longer. Dan felt like the Mexican family was his own family, and he was really upset that he wasn't allowed to spend time with them anymore. Dean was now back in Porterville, and Dan convinced him to take him to stay with Don and Kathy, who were now living in Eureka. Don had taken a job driving a log truck after leaving Porterville and then spending a short time in Gold Beach, Oregon. Dean started on the way to Eureka with Dan, but then he decided to turn around and do things properly through the state so that Dan could stay with Don and Kathy legally. After getting permission from the authorities, Dean took Dan to Don's place. He was there for a few months when Dean decided to move to Eureka also and take a job as a log truck driver as well. Dean stayed in the little apartment with Don, Kathy, their baby son and Dan until he got his own place. At Christmas, they all went to Porterville to see family, then came back to Eureka. Shortly after they got back, Dan turned seventeen. It was January, 1971. It wasn't long before Dan told Don that he was homesick for Porterville, so Don took him to a truck stop in Eureka so he could hitch a ride to Porterville. My grandfather was renting a house for himself and John, and Dan stayed there for about a week before he wanted to hitchhike back to Eureka. John said he was going to quit community college and come with him. When they got there, Dean gave John a 1958 car. They stayed a few weeks, and then they wanted to go back to Porterville again. They stole some toolboxes out of trucks and sold them along the way to pay for gas.

When they got to Porterville, they went to see Sam at his foster family's house. They parked nearby to catch him on his way to school that morning. They visited for a minute, and Sam left for school. John walked to a county building nearby to pick up his Social Security check from his mother's death, about $335, while Dan waited in the car. Somebody who was visiting the foster parents saw Dan in the car and told the foster parents about it. They called his social worker because Dan was supposed to be living with Don in Eureka. Before John had returned, the social worker and a police officer got Dan out of the car and took him to juvenile hall for a few days until they found him another foster home. His social worker told him that if he ran away again, he would go to Sacramento to the Youth Authority, which was like a juvenile prison.

Dan's next foster home was in Poplar, California, where he said everyone was kin, hillbilly, and crazy. It was a rough place, and everyone knew not to mess with people from Poplar. Dan knew some people there already because that was where he finished the eighth grade when his foster father, Mr. Jones, taught school there. Don's ex-wife, Rosie, and their children lived a couple blocks away from Dan's foster home. He would visit them there and babysit so that Rosie could go out with her sister Sissy.

Meanwhile, Sam wanted to run away from his foster home in Porterville, so he and John devised a plan to have Sam pack up all his things in his bedroom, including all the posters he had on his walls, and put it all in his footlocker. John waited until late at night, then picked up Sam, who snuck out through the bedroom window along with his footlocker. They took off in John's car, but shortly after, the car broke down. They had no choice but to walk Sam and his footlocker back to the foster home, where Sam snuck back in the bedroom window. John fixed his car, and they tried a couple days later, but unbelievably, the same thing happened again. On the third try, John borrowed my grandfather's girlfriend Wilma's car and got Sam to the airport in Bakersfield, where he flew to Virginia to live with us in Richmond, where we had recently relocated. Apparently, his foster parents never went in his bedroom, so they didn't notice the few days when all his belongings were packed up. John and Dan would come to live with us in Virginia as well, but not for a few more months.

Don and Kathy had now left Eureka and were living in the town of Brawley, California, which was 370 miles south of Porterville, close to the Mexican border. John and Dan wanted to go see him, so John hitchhiked to Poplar, where Dan ran away from the foster home even though he would go to the juvenile prison if he got caught. He was seventeen at the time. He and John hitchhiked to Brawley together, and they got a ride from a trucker hauling sugar beets. They didn't know where Don lived in Brawley but hoped to walk around and recognize his car. When they got to town, they walked around the corner, and they saw Don getting out of his car! Don was supposed to be getting a birthday gift for Kathy, so he bought some ice cream and beer, took the boys home, and told Kathy that they were her birthday present. The boys stayed there with them for a couple months, and then they were all ready to leave town. Don got the idea to sneak out of their rental house, so they wouldn't have to pay rent. Dan said they snuck everything they had out the window so nobody would see.

Don took the boys back to Porterville, and he and Kathy went to Benton, California, just north of Death Valley. One day, John and Dan were at the police station in Porterville, where they had been questioned by the police for stealing a car, which they hadn't done. After they were released, they were walking down the street when Don and Kathy pulled up in their car. They had come to Porterville for a visit and were on their way back to Benton. The boys got in the car and went with them. They would hitchhike the three hundred miles back and forth from Benton to Porterville several times to see their friends and would crash wherever they could. Then Don decided he wanted to move to North Fork, California, to get a job. It wasn't far from Benton, as the crow flies, but you have to drive around the Sierra National Forest about four hundred miles to get from one town to the other. When Don and Kathy arrived in town, they lived in a tent with their new baby until they got a house.

John and Dan were now hitchhiking regularly from Porterville to North Fork to see Don. It was a little over one hundred miles. There were missions that people set up for kids who were hitchhiking and needed a place to sleep and food to eat, and they visited them sometimes. Dan said that they might have hitchhiked a lot, and they dressed like hippies, but they weren't real hippies because they didn't live in communes and really embrace the lifestyle. One time when they were visiting Don and Kathy in North Fork, they showed Kathy how to huff paint while Don was at work. When Don got home and saw what they were doing in the tent with the baby there, he was furious with the boys. It was a small space for all those fumes for a baby to breathe. Don took their paint away from them, and that made Dan mad enough that he took on the much bigger and stronger Don. He jumped up on his back, holding him by the neck, but Don easily slung him off and onto the ground. As usual with our family when we had a disagreement, all was quickly forgiven and forgotten. Because the boys were doing so much hitchhiking back and forth, Dean and my grandfather both told the boys that they should hop freight trains instead, so they started doing that too. My grandfather was living in Fresno at this time, which was on the route between North Fork and Porterville, so the boys would stop there sometimes too.

On one of their journeys from North Fork, they made it to Strathmore, which was about six miles north of Porterville, and they were so tired that they couldn't walk anymore even though it wasn't that far. They saw an eighteen-wheeler parked in a motel parking lot and got the idea to try and steal it to drive the rest of the way to Porterville. It was unlocked, and the keys were in it. They were going to pretend that they thought it was their brother Don's truck if they got caught, but they didn't, so it wasn't an issue. John had learned how to drive semis by then, so he took it to Porterville and left it in a big, open parking lot so the driver could easily find it. On another one of their journeys from Porterville to North Fork, they had been selling speed for someone and had used enough of it themselves that Dan had been awake for five days when they showed up at my grandfather's house. My grandfather and his girlfriend, Wilma, wanted them all to drive to North Fork to see Don. Dan had crashed really hard once he was in the car, but Wilma wanted to stop at a buffet restaurant to eat. He managed to get out of the car and go in the restaurant, but he wasn't really awake still. Sitting in the restaurant, he started hallucinating that he was on a boat and was freaking out, so John took him in the bathroom and told him to straighten up, that he was blowing it. They made it to Don's, where my grandfather and Wilma spent the day, and the boys stayed for about a week. They had decided to come back to Virginia to be with Sam, Patty, and the five of us, and they took off hitchhiking one morning, starting on their journey. Don had already gone to work, but Kathy said goodbye to them and watched them walk away while she stood in the yard, holding the baby in her arms. She told Dan later that she was thinking about how they were just a couple of kids going out into the world alone, trekking all the way across the United States with nothing but one bag apiece. Dan couldn't remember if they said goodbye to Don the night before they left, which ended up being very important in the near future.

CHAPTER 23

"Joy to the World" (Three Dog Night)

We five, along with Patty, had moved from Havre de Grace to an apartment in Richmond, Virginia, by Halloween 1970. I loved kindergarten in Richmond, and I loved my teacher. I can remember my classroom with all its play stations, and I learned to tie my shoes with an old tennis shoe attached to a board. I received the most adorable report card from this school. For each category of achievement, such as putting away belongings and being kind to others, there was a stick figure drawing depicting the activity. I've never seen another one like it. My favorite part of school was getting to be the nap fairy. Every day, a different child was picked to get up early from nap time and go around to each child on their mat. The job was to place a small treat next to each child's head and tap them gently with the wand that was provided to let them know it was time to get up.

We lived in a row house apartment, and Dad's baby sister, my aunt Judy, and her fiancé, Wayne, were our neighbors. Sam came in early 1971 after he had run away from his foster home on Springville Drive in Porterville, which I mentioned earlier. I can remember watching the Osmonds and the Jackson 5 on TV here, and they had recently built a new playground in the large courtyard that was surrounded by the apartments. It was a wonderful place to play, and my favorite activity was playing leap frog on the concrete poles they had placed in the ground that got taller and taller, so we competed to see who could go the highest. My sister probably taught me to do that, as she would many other gymnastic-related tricks.

Life either started to become pretty crazy here or I was just noticing it at five years old. On Halloween, we three kids dressed up, and Patty took us out trick-or-treating in the neighborhood. I don't recall anything being amiss when we left the house, but when we had finished our rounds, returned home, and tried to open the front door, it was locked. We could hear loud voices inside as mom came to the door and opened it just a crack. She told Patty to take us out a little longer before we returned home again. We were happy to get all the candy we could, so we didn't mind going back out, although all we could do was return to the limited number of homes in our vicinity. A few people asked us, "Haven't you been here before?" but we didn't mind. We finished the second round and returned home, only to find the door locked again and Mom cracking open the door and telling Patty to take us out again. Patty argued that we had already been to all the houses twice and that we wanted to come inside. We had been seriously warned not to eat even one piece of candy until my folks had checked it to be sure nothing looked as if it had been tampered with and that there weren't any razor blades in apples. We had been very good and not touched our candy but were becoming very anxious to do so. Mom, however, was adamant that we couldn't come in, and we needed to go back out one more time.

This time, many people were giving us dirty looks, commenting on how many times we had been there, and some even shut the door without giving us treats for the third time. We were also the only kids still out on the street. It was very dark and getting cold. We were tired, and the fun was over. Luckily, when we returned home, we were finally allowed to enter the house. I don't really remember if the house looked different or anything else that happened that night, but apparently, the adults had been eating dinner on TV trays in the living room and watching television when my dad got pissed off with someone. My best guess is Henry, our neighbor from Havre de Grace, who had come with us to Richmond. There was a big mess made with the food, and my mom was trying to clean it up and calm everyone down before letting us in. This was when she was still trying to hide the adult's bad behavior from us kids.

Dad was driving a semi-truck, hauling furniture, while we lived there. This would be his primary career for the remainder of his life. My daddy was a trucker and a good one too. He was an excellent driver and won many contents among his peers backing and maneuvering their semis. He also took a great deal of pride in his work, always meeting his delivery dates if at all possible and many times early. He was very careful with his customers' belongings and almost never had any claims of damage or loss. He really was the best furniture hauler and mover that I ever saw, and I saw a ton of them.

Dad was out on the road, and he was working out of an office in Aberdeen, Maryland, at the time. He ended up in a bar outside of Aberdeen very late one night, and he recognized some guys that he had known in the past, and they recognized him. Unfortunately, they were not old friends but enemies. I'm not sure why. They approached my dad in the bar and told him they would deal with him outside. Dad was never afraid of a fight, but this was five against one. He used the pay phone in the bar to call a friend to gather up some guys and come and help him out of this bad situation. His friends were in another town, and it was going to take a while to gather everyone and get to Dad, and it was almost closing time at the bar. Dad waited on edge for his friends to show up when finally, everyone but the five guys, the bartender, and my dad were gone. The bartender told all six of the men that they had to get out now in no uncertain terms. So the five went outside, and they were waiting for my dad to come out. My dad asked the bartender to please allow him to stay inside until his friends arrived or the men outside were going to beat him badly. The bartender said he absolutely had to get out now, that he didn't want to get involved with the matter, especially since the five were his regular customers.

My dad had no choice but to exit the building, where the five men all jumped him and beat the crap out of him in the parking lot, just as he had known they would. His friends got there in time to find Dad lying in a mud puddle with not another soul in sight, not even the bartender. They helped him up and said they were taking him to the hospital, but my dad insisted that he would not leave his truck at that bar. They could not stop him from climbing up in that truck, beaten, bleeding, and with his left arm hanging down by his side at an awkward angle; and driving it to a friend's house. At that point, he let his friends take him to the hospital, where his wounds were treated, his broken ribs were taped, and he had surgery to repair his left shoulder. After the surgery, he was left with a long scar and a pin through his shoulder sticking out of the top. They put a cork on the end to help people see it, so it wouldn't be disturbed.

Dad returned home with his shoulder injury, stitches, and the temporary pin in place, and he wasn't supposed to drive his truck or do much else for that matter, especially with his left arm. He insisted, however, on continuing to drive, although he couldn't do any other labor, so he had to hire helpers to do all the furniture moving. My dad was in this condition when the next incident occurred. He was getting drunk with his sister Ruth one night after we kids had gone to bed. She was living in Newport News at the time. They were having a great time together, listening to the oldies from their youth and dancing together. They both lost their footing at the same time and fell, all twisted up, to the ground. In the process, my dad broke his ankle. There was a picture taken of Dad's cast with what Ruth had written on it, "Ruth did it." That's Mom's version of the story. According to Dan, it was Thanksgiving, and everyone was waiting to eat dinner, but Dad was drunk and wasn't ready to eat. Ruth got pissed at him for his behavior, and they got into a tussle that ended with Ruth, who was a stout woman, coming down on Dad's ankle and breaking it. Maybe Mom was trying to protect us kids from the drunken, violent truth and told us they were dancing instead. Whatever the truth was, now Dad really couldn't drive his truck, and there was no trying. This was the only time in my life that Dad was unable to work. It didn't seem to upset the family, but I know that we were very poor while my dad was out of work and lived on pinto beans and fried potatoes. Eventually, he made a full recovery and went back to work. After the pin was removed from his shoulder, my parents kept it in a tall glass jar for many years.

This is the first time I've ever known my dad to be drunk and for there to be any kind of drinking, partying, or chaos in our house. This, however, would be the norm from now on. I don't know how or if my teacher at school knew anything about my crazy homelife, but at my parent-teacher conference that year, my teacher very cautiously and gracefully told my mother that she would be willing to adopt me if my parents would consent. I don't remember them being angry about it, so the teacher must have handled the situation very well, but my mother declined her offer. It's crazy for me to imagine what would have happened if they had let that teacher adopt me, or that she would even make such an offer. It wasn't mine, but there would be an adoption in the family in the near future.

I had my second experience with a developmentally disabled person when we lived here. We had a next-door neighbor named Gertie. She was the single mother of a daughter named Linda, who was what we called retarded back then. Linda was always sweet to our family, but apparently, she could become very violent with her mother, who had bite scars all over her arms from her angry daughter. Linda was fascinated with Patty as they were about the same age, and Patty was always very patient with her, as she was with everyone for that matter, except for her brothers. Linda had a big crush on Sam. He avoided Linda like the plague but was teased mercilessly by everyone in the family for being the object of her affection. We picked up some family mispronounced words from Linda. Her mother took her shopping one day, and she came over to tell us that she had bought an "undenbrell" and a "pregent" dress. From that day forward, we never used the words *umbrella* or *maternity clothes* in our family.

CHAPTER 24

"Everything Is Beautiful"
(Ray Stevens)

I finished kindergarten in Richmond, and we moved right after to a house in Hampton. It was the summer of 1971. We stayed with Dad's sister Ruth for a few days on Wickham Avenue in Newport News until our house was available to move into. We kids went to see *The Six Million Dollar Man* with my cousin Vickie at the nearby Newmarket shopping center, and we spent a lot of time climbing the big tree they had in the front yard until Vickie fell out of it and broke her arm.

Our new house was located on Mojer Drive in the Holly Homes subdivision of Hampton, Virginia. It was a post–World War II housing development, tract homes that were typical for that era. The neighborhood consisted of probably ten streets, and all the houses looked alike. Some people tried to customize their homes to make them more unique. The popular trend at the time was adding shutters to the windows, the kind with pictures on them, like eagles and horses with carts.

Our house was not customized. It was dark brown and very plain. There was no landscaping, save for a few bushes right next to the front of the house. It had the typical tract home floorplan—living room, dining area/kitchen, three bedrooms, and one bath. It did have sliding glass doors opening onto a patio out back. The front and back yards were plenty big enough to play in, but the inside didn't seem big enough for anything, even for a six-year-old. Maybe this was because there were always so many people in the house. What looked like an ordinary house in an ordinary neighborhood for an ordinary family turned out to be anything but that. So much happened at this house that the street name and the group of people on it earned the title of this book.

I turned six on June 6, right after we moved to Mojer Drive, and Patty planned a birthday party for me. We didn't have many birthday parties in our family, so it was special to have one at all. Patty got the idea to decorate my dad's empty semi-trailer with balloons and create places to play in it. In a furniture moving trailer, there are slots all along the walls, up and down in rows. The slots hold straps across walls of furniture to keep loads from toppling. With an empty trailer, you can use the straps to create swings across the trailer, and you can put flat empty boxes and furniture pads under them on the floor to keep you safe when you fall off because they are not very stable and you *will* fall off. Of course, you can get creative and put two right next to each other and wrap them in a furniture pad to make a more stable swing. Make this configuration a little wider and you have an awesome hammock to sleep in too. We invited all the neighborhood kids over, and we had a blast!

I'm sure it was one of the most unique and creative kid's birthday party ever. There were seats for the guests where the wheel boxes were located, complete with more furniture pads for comfort. The rest of the truck was decorated with festive balloons and streamers attached to the walls. Mom was baking me a birthday cake, and that was a real treat in our house too. Dessert, if there was any, was usually something like Mom's rice pudding, which we kids thought was wonderful. When I would remember the pudding fondly as an adult, my mother would inform me that it wasn't "real" rice pudding, just rice, a little sugar, and some raisins because that was all they could afford. I remembered it fondly just the same. Anyway, Mom tried to decorate my cake with frosting, but I can only remember now that it looked like a mostly green blob. To this day, I don't know what she was trying to create on that cake, but I loved it just the same. Mom was one hell of a cook and was truly the best meat chef I have ever known. However, she always said about herself, "I don't make nothin' pretty."

Patty and I were very close during this time. She was a sweet, forgiving, and helpful young lady to everyone in the family, except her brothers, sometimes. She was seven years older than me, and I adored her. I can remember being in the bed with her at that age and pretending that the key on the chain around her neck was a little person. I would walk him from his school on one shoulder, across the field on her neck, and over to his home on her other shoulder, adding dialog all the while. The key opened her jewelry box, which was a rare sacred item in the house. I was very curious about what all was in that box, but I wouldn't let my curiosity get the best of me yet. Patty attended the sixth grade at Captain John Smith and was never a good student. Sam was the only one of the Smith boys still in school as Dan had dropped out. John had graduated from high school back in Porterville, California, which was very unusual for our family. He even started classes at Porterville Community College, but dropped out soon after.

Life was nothing but good for me on Mojer Drive. I attended first grade at Captain John Smith Elementary. I had a wonderful teacher and classmates, one of whom was a boy in a wheelchair whose father was apparently a higher-up in the Hampton Police Department, so we got to go on a field trip to the jail one time, and us kids had the best time locking our teacher up in a cell, then being locked in one ourselves. I had so many wonderful school field trips in the state of Virginia, like to the Jamestown Settlement, Yorktown Battlefield, and Fort Monroe, and I'm certain that it shaped my lifelong love of history. I only had one bad experience that school year. I had to use the restroom one day when we were out at recess, and the grouchy teacher's aide on duty wouldn't let me in the building. I finally hid on the playground and peed on myself. Rather than waiting to line up with the other children when recess was over, I walked around to the front entrance of the school, went into the front office, and announced my predicament to the secretary. She let me wait in the nurse's office while she called my mother to bring me a change of underwear, socks, and shoes. I hadn't soiled my dress, so when I went back to class to join my classmates now lined up for lunch, they didn't notice that I had on different shoes and accepted my explanation for my absence that I had a sick stomach and went to the nurse's office. I sure dodged an embarrassing bullet that time.

My best friend, Elaine, was in my class, and she lived down the street from me. We were allowed to play freely at each other's homes, and we loved to be outside and climb the big mimosa tree in her backyard. We also had permission to play at a nearby ditch when we were in her mother's care, but not mine. My parents could be very protective with our safety at times and thoughtlessly neglectful at others. They had good, solid ideas about raising their children, especially my dad, but it all went out the window when they were in the midst of their own dramas and wrestling with their demons. Once when we lived here, I was left home without adult or elder supervision, which was very unusual, and I took advantage of it. I was playing at the home of a friend on the next street over, and she convinced me that I should take home one of her new kittens and ask my parents if I could keep it. I wasn't optimistic, but it was an opportunity to hold and spend more time with the kitten, if nothing else. When I got home, my folks were out shopping, and I'm assuming that some of the boys were in charge at the moment because Patty wasn't there either. I took the kitten in my room and decided to play with it on Patty's bed. She wouldn't have been happy with me for doing that, but I couldn't resist lying on the beautiful, silky teal bedspread that she had on it. I was always tempted by what I considered her very beautiful and interesting belongings. After a short time of playing with the kitten, we both fell asleep. When I woke up, Patty was yelling at me and crying to Mom and Dad that I had a kitten, and it had pooped all over her bed! I discovered that she was correct about both those things when I sat up and saw the dark, loose stool that the kitten had gotten on her beautiful bedspread and on me.

Needless to say, I didn't get to keep the kitten, and I didn't win any points with Patty.

I had other friends on our street as well. There was a little girl a few houses down that my sister and I played with sometimes. The best thing about her was that her mother had a box of lace curtains that we loved to dress up in and pretend we were brides. Being a bride was a big deal to me at that age. I had a little boyfriend at school named Danny, and when I realized that I wanted to grow up and marry him one day, it posed a huge problem for me. You see, I was planning to marry my dad when I grew up, and now I was forced to choose between the two. One day, when dad was in town, I asked if I could talk to him about something very important. We went in my folks' bedroom and sat on the bed face-to-face. I told him my dilemma, and he could see my distress over this life-altering decision. He was very respectful and thoughtful and told me that it was okay if I wanted to marry someone else besides him. He would be okay because he already had one wife, and I would be okay because as my father, he would always be in my life anyway. I was very satisfied with that answer and decided to plan on marrying Danny.

I couldn't have been more enamored of my dad at that time in my life, and he couldn't have done any wrong in my eyes. He was truly my hero, and I wanted to do everything he did. He used to whistle around the house, so I asked him to teach me, which he did. He also taught me to whistle two different songs, "The Happy Whistler" by Don Robertson and "Skoiaan," an old South African song about an illegal alcoholic drink that had been made popular by Louis Armstrong, whom Dad loved, as did I and still do. I was so proud of the fact that only he and I knew how to whistle those songs, although I don't believe anyone else in the family even cared to attempt it. I also decided that I was going to eat everything that Dad ate, and that was no easy feat. Although he could afford to eat most anything he wanted, he liked many of the same foods that he was forced to eat as a child because the family couldn't afford anything else. He taught Mom to cook him pig ears and feet and cow brains and eggs, and she would buy him chitterlings and head cheese. When he ate these foods, all seven of us kids would say how gross and disgusting they were, and Dad would get angry and tell us to shut up. He would say that we didn't like that food because we had never been hungry. To this day, I never say that I won't eat something but rather that I hope I never get hungry enough that I have to eat things I find disgusting. So I thought it would give Dad and me another special bond if only he and I ate certain foods. I gave it my best effort and tried everything that Mom made for Dad, but I soon gave up that particular challenge that I had made for myself. It was easier to whistle!

Dad had a way of loving people that made you feel so special. His love and belief in me had a huge effect on my life and helped me to make fewer bad decisions along the way. He loved very deeply, as do I, and affected many other people in his life with his love. Everyone who knew my dad respected and admired him, so to be loved so well by someone that you felt that way about meant that you must be pretty special too. There were always two sides to both my parents, however, and their negative sides sometimes did more damage to their relationships than their positive sides did good.

As I mentioned, I was already consumed with being a bride, and after my cousin Vickie got to be a flower girl in my aunt Judy's wedding, I became fixated on being a flower girl at someone's—anyone's—wedding. Vickie, who was three years older than me, handed her dress down to me, and I was obsessed with it. It had a beautiful white lace overlay with sheer lace long sleeves. The best part, though, was the little strand of faux pearls that was sewn onto the front of the dress like a necklace. I wore the dress around the house constantly and even convinced my mom to allow me to wear it for my school picture that year. Mom was very particular about how we dressed, so it was a big ask to wear something so unusual and eccentric to school and especially on picture day. She was so sweet in her indulgence that she curled my hair especially for the occasion, and when it was raining that morning before school, she paid for a taxi to take us kids to school instead of the usual walk that would have ruined my hair. That was one of the nicest things Mom ever did for me. It meant the world to be able to show off my beloved dress to everyone at school.

I had the opportunity to meet some other cousins for the first time on Mojer Drive. My dad's sister Bell lived in upstate New York with her husband and seven of her eight children. The eldest, Rocky, had already left home and was on his way to being a chemist for Eastman Kodak. Everyone in the family was impressed with Rocky and the fact that he attended college and ended up with a distinguished career. It was unheard of in our family. Anyway, the family traveled down from New York, and they spent a day with us. I can remember playing with all the cousins in the backyard and having a meal together. The kids ranged in age from a few years younger than me to a few years older than me, so every one of them was a good playmate, boys or girls. I don't have any other specific memories of the visit, but I know I was thrilled to spend time with them and felt blessed when I got to spend even more time with them in the future.

Probably the most unique circumstance that occurred at this location is that all four of the Smith kids lived with us again for the first time in quite a while. Not at first. We brought Sam and Patty from Richmond along with Henry, and then John and Dan would arrive from California in July. As I mentioned, this was a three-bedroom house, which made it cramped for two adults, five teenagers, and three small children, but gradually, there would be even more people living there. One bedroom was for the girls—Patty, Paula, and myself. The other bedroom was for all the boys. That was in theory. Realistically, there ended up being sleeping bodies lying all over the house wherever they could find a spot, except us girls' bedroom and Mom and Dad's bedroom. There were really only a few sacred places in the house. I mentioned Patty's jewelry box, and there was also Mom and Dad's bedroom, and mom's purse. Other than that, everything was fair game, including pillows, blankets, and any food in the house. Tommy slept with Mom when Dad was gone, but I don't remember where he slept when Dad was home.

It was around this time that Dan and I developed a real love-hate relationship. He was my favorite of the older kids but also the only one with whom I ever had any conflict. I adored him, but I was starting to be a hellion at times, and he already was one, so we would really clash. I guess we had the same type of dual personality, being the most charming and loving but also the most difficult of all the children. Everyone in the house was aware of my burning desire to be a flower girl, and once Dan arrived, he decided to use it to his benefit. He promised that I could have the job when he got married one day, and whenever I balked at making him a sandwich, bringing him a drink, or doing some other favor for him, he would tell me that I couldn't be his flower girl, and I would jump to it.

I have fond memories of our family of nine watching TV shows together at around this time. In the evenings, Mom loved *Lawrence Welk*, and Dad liked *Hee Haw*, *Sanford and Son*, and *Gomer Pyle*. On the weekends, Dad liked the *Wide World of Sports*, "The thrill of victory and the agony of defeat." He also liked to watch *Looney Tunes* cartoons on Saturday morning, and we kids loved that! We revered any time we got with Dad. He was always the first one up on Sunday mornings, and I would get up right after him just to have him all to myself for a little while. He would read the paper and give me the comics section. Mom watched all the ABC daytime soap operas for years, especially *General Hospital*. I can still remember plot lines from that show as far back as age five. Dad hated most of the situation comedy shows that we all liked to watch and called them "shitcoms," his twist on the abbreviated description. He had an unfair habit of being upset about anyone watching shows he didn't like even if he was just passing through the room and had no intention of staying. He actually forbade us to watch *Carol Burnett* or *I Love Lucy* if he was anywhere in or around the house because he said they were too stupid. I'm not sure what Dad had against funny redhead females.

Us kids especially loved watching the Disney movies and shows along with Mutual of Omaha's *Wild Kingdom* that came on Sunday evenings. We also loved any cartoons, and my favorite Saturday morning show was *H. R. Pufnstuf*. We watched all the popular shows like *Gilligan's Island* and the *Partridge Family*, but my favorite by far was *The Brady Bunch*. There were some great educational shows for kids when I was growing up, like *The Electric Company*, which featured future award-winning actors Rita Moreno and Morgan Freeman. The *Schoolhouse Rock!* commercials were so entertaining and educational that they helped me learn multiplication tables, grammar, how a bill becomes a law, and more. Paula and I also loved the afterschool specials that would come a little later.

CHAPTER 25

"Down on the Corner"

(Creedence Clearwater Revival)

This is where life became full-fledged crazy for our family. I believe it happened because of a combination of things. First, Dad was often gone from home on the truck, running long-distance. He could be gone for two to three weeks at a time and sometimes only spend a few days at home before heading back out. Life began a familiar pattern that would last for many years when Dad was home and when Dad was gone. They were as different as night and day. Second, when John and Dan had arrived from California in July, they were total hippies that fit in out in California but stuck out in Hampton, Virginia, and ended up having a huge influence on the people around them. They had long hair parted down the middle, with low-waist jeans that had holes, sometimes patched. They wore T-shirts with crazy sayings on them and sandals or boots. They had hitchhiked and hopped freight trains from Porterville to come back to Virginia. When they got to Winslow, Arizona, they were discovered, arrested, and jailed for train hopping. Dad called his brother Ellis, who lived in Phoenix, and wired him the money to get the boys out of jail. Ellis took them to the bus station, bought their tickets, and sent them to Hampton. When they arrived, Mom told them that their oldest brother, Don, had died during their trip and that the funeral had already been held in California. The Smith kids had loved Don so much and were all close to him. This was another tragic blow for the family, especially given the way that he died. Don and Dean were both log truck drivers in Northern California now, and Don had an accident in his log truck, causing him to go off a cliff and break every bone in his body when the truck landed at the bottom. There was a rumor that he was lying there alive until they attempted to move his body, and that's when he died. This gave the boys even more cause to be rebels.

When we first moved to Mojer Drive, Sam had a room to himself. Henry was still with us, but he slept on the couch because Sam wouldn't allow him to share the room, in part because of his notoriously stinky feet. He had his foot crushed by a millstone at a mill in Havre de Grace when he was seventeen years old and had to have half of his foot removed. He would stuff a white sock in his shoe and usually kept it changed, but if he didn't, it smelled really bad. He was on the road with Dad most of the time anyway. When John and Dan arrived, they moved into the bedroom with Sam. I'm sure the three boys were happy to be back together in one place. Henry was nineteen, two years older than Dan, and they were both happy-go-lucky and crazy. When the two of them got together, they were like a house on fire. Henry used his foot to his advantage whenever he could. The drinking age at that time was twenty-one, so his favorite thing to do was go into a store, pick up some beer, take it to the counter, and try to buy it. When asked for his ID, he would cause a big scene by throwing his foot up on the counter and bending his shoe all the way back to show that half of his foot was missing. He would then start raging about how he had lost half his foot in Vietnam, fighting for his country, and now this person didn't believe he was even old enough to buy beer? He would tell the cashier, "Not only should you be selling me this beer, but you should probably pay for it too, like I paid my country and my fellow Americans with half of my foot," and saying other things along those lines. He was always able to buy beer after these tirades of his.

Sam started school at Spratley Junior High in the fall. He was fifteen and in the ninth grade. Sam never transitioned very well when he had to move. He was shy and didn't make friends easily. He spent all his time in his room playing records. One morning, John dropped Sam off at school, and while he was walking up to the building, a black guy named Dodo went up to him and punched him simply because he was white. The next morning, Dan, John, and Sam parked in the school parking lot, waiting to see Dodo and confront him. They were never afraid of a fight. Dan said that a white kid saw them sitting there and went over to the local 7-Eleven a block away to tell the black kids that Sam and his brothers were looking for Dodo. Some other white kids were there with the Smith boys as well, but they disappeared when the black kids showed up. The fighting started when one of the black kids swung his belt at John, but John's arms were so long that he caught the belt in the air. At the same time, Dan grabbed a baseball bat out of the front seat of the car, while Sam was reaching for a hunting knife on his belt. The black kids scattered immediately. The Smith kids then went into the school and made their way to the principal's office to talk to him about the situation. They had heard that Dodo was on probation, and if the principal suspended him, he would go to juvenile detention. The principal gave Dodo a warning, and he never messed with Sam again. Later, when we had moved to our next house, Dan, Patty, and one of their friends were at the hot dog stand at the corner of Mercury Boulevard and Mallory Street. Dodo was there with another guy who tried to give them crap. Dodo told him to leave the kids alone because they had backup.

As a family, we had strict beliefs about loyalty. We could treat one another like crap sometimes, but nobody outside our family or inner circle better mess with us. One example of this giving of crap was Dan and Sam picking on Patty all the time, but she fussed at them just as much. They would order her to do things for them, usually making a sandwich or preparing some kind of food, and if she wouldn't do it, there was a price to pay. One quiet night during the week, the family was sitting around the living room watching television. Patty started picking at Sam about how bad his boots smelled.

He had just taken them off his feet and placed them under the living room coffee table. She kept telling him how horrible they smelled and that he should put them in his room so everybody didn't get sick from the smell. He basically told her to shut up and deal with it and that his boots were going to stay right where they were. Patty then started saying that she was going to put his boots outside, and Sam calmly told her that she better not. When a commercial came on the TV, Patty got up, picked up Sam's boots, opened the front door, and set his boots on the front porch. She sat down again, quite pleased with herself. Sam didn't say a word. On the next commercial, Sam went down the hall and came back with Patty's mattress from her bed. The bedclothes were still attached, so she knew it was, indeed, her mattress. He opened the front door and, with Patty fussing at him the whole time, threw the mattress on the front porch. Patty was apoplectic about the situation and was yelling at Sam and pleading with Mom to do something. Mom was used to these sibling squabbles and even found it pretty amusing, as did all the rest of us who witnessed the event. Mom thought this would be the end of the fight, as they were both even now with their personal items out on the front porch.

Sam, however, went back down the hall and returned five minutes later with the pieces to Patty's little single bed. He was experienced at helping Dad move furniture, so it was a quick and easy job for him to disassemble the bed. He put the pieces near the door, where Patty was currently trying to wrestle her mattress back into the house. Sam then took the mattress from her and threw it back outside, then picked up the rest of the pieces and walked out the front door with them. He returned a few minutes later, carrying his boots, which he set down on the living room floor. With Patty yelling and crying the whole time, he picked her up, carried her outside to the sidewalk, where her bed was now reassembled, and set her down on the bed. He came back in the house, shut the door, and locked it. Patty continued to yell and scream and proceeded to start banging on the door, while Sam sat calmly and silently back on the couch and watched TV. We were all so amused by the situation that nobody attempted to rescue Patty, so she continued with the yelling and screaming, which was apparently disturbing Sam's television watching. He got up, went out to the kitchen, and came back with a handful of leftover meatloaf from the refrigerator. He unlocked and opened the front door, where Patty was standing. Before she could move away, he smeared the meatloaf in her face, saying, "Here, dog, stay outside and eat your dog food." Through her laughter, Mom finally told Sam to let Patty back in the house, that she had had enough. Sam was reluctant, but he finally obeyed Mom and unlocked the door, then eventually brought the bed back in the house.

Living on Mojer Drive with the four Smith kids along with Henry and the large group of friends that they acquired would shape the culture of our family life for many years to come. They called themselves the Mojer Mafia or sometimes just the Mob, and my dad was the godfather. The young guys who lived on our street were the first members of the Mob, and Sam had met all of them before John and Dan arrived. Sal was a schoolmate of Sam's and lived down the street from us. He lived with his father and younger brother. We all adored Sal and still do. Another good friend of Sam's was my friend Elaine's older brother Bobby, who lived even further down the street than Sal. Also down that part of the street were brothers Alan and Vernon. Alan was old enough to be out of school and ran around with Dan a lot, but Vernon attended classes with Sam. They lived with their single mother, whom I remember was overweight and always had these diet chocolates called Ayds around the house, which made me think it was a pretty good deal to be overweight if you got to eat this candy! John C. lived up at our end across the street, and Dan ended up dating his sister Stephanie. Tony and his four sisters lived a few houses down from us. Patty was friends with Tony's sisters along with the older sister of my friend, Elaine. There was also brother and sister Bonnie and Mike, who lived beside Tony and his sisters.

The first member of the Mob that didn't live on our street was Bogie, who was a friend of Sam's from school. Mom described Bogie as a not unattractive young man with curly brown hair, khaki dress pants worn high on the waist, a white shirt, and dark, heavy glasses—a total geek. Sam wasn't exactly trendy, but he wore blue jeans and T-shirts, and his hair was longer, and he wasn't nearly as geeky as Bogie. When Bogie met Mom for the first time, he introduced himself as Calvin, but Sam nicknamed him Bogie, and that was all we ever called him. Upon that first meeting, he basically moved in. He was extremely polite and always offering to help. He was very sweet and brought little gifts for us kids. Mom thought he was gay because he was so nice. Bogie had a younger brother, David, who would come around as well. Gary and Wayne were another set of brothers that were part of the Mob, and Dan said they were brought over by Bogie. How and whomever it all started didn't matter because all the boys became a close group of friends, and they grew to be like members of our family as well as the Mob. There were many, many other teenage boys and girls that would come around, but the ones I've introduced were the core of the group.

Most of the Mafia came from typical middle-class backgrounds, and certainly, none had the tragic, nomadic, and chaotic upbringing that John, Dan, Sam, and Patty had. Some of them were from pretty wealthy families, like Bogie. After he moved in with us, unofficially, but for all intents and purposes, and his younger brother was at our house more often than his own home, their single mother became concerned. She decided to drop by our house for a visit. My mother was mortified by her visit as she was a very refined lady, and our house had nothing nice or attractive about it. She looked like movie star Joan Crawford. She had a classy but tough persona, and she drove up in a very nice, shiny car, although I couldn't say what model it was.

Mom invited the lady in the house and was beyond embarrassed when she invited her to sit on our couch, which had one seat cushion missing because Dan had taken it to the beach one night for a girl to sit on so she didn't have to sit on the sand. My mother did the best she could to make Bogie's mother comfortable but also wanted to get her out of the house as soon as possible. She said that she was curious about this place that lured her good sons away from their wonderful home, where they were provided with all the comforts that young men should appreciate. After that statement, she looked around at our very modest home and silently asked the question, "What on earth do *you* have to offer?" My mother told her that her sons were, indeed, good boys and a pleasure for our family to have around, particularly Bogie. She said that they were always welcome and would be provided with food and shelter when they were here. My mother really couldn't make any assurances about their mental, moral, or physical health and safety in our home. Of course, she didn't say that to Bogie's mother. I believe that my mom either invited her to stay for dinner or made an offer for another night, but I don't remember her being there any other time.

Along with hanging out with one another all the time and practically living at our house, the Mob made it a priority to be around when the godfather was in town. When Dad was home on a weekend, the routine was to pile all the family and the Mob into as many cars as necessary and head to John Carey Elementary School a few blocks away to play softball. Dad loved the game and had some pretty good skills. Most of the players were boys, but a few of the girls and Mom played as well. Mom was a good pitcher. Patty didn't choose to play, and we little kids couldn't handle playing with the older teens and adults. We didn't mind a bit because our favorite activity was playing on the awesome monkey bars within sight of the baseball field. The bars seemed as big as a house to me at six years old, and the entire thing was connected, so our favorite game was bar tag. We chased one another, running away from whoever was *it*, and we could touch the ground but had to keep at least one hand on the bars at all times. If you let go, you were automatically *it*. We would play that game for hours, and we loved it!

At some point during our play, we would get called by the softball players to load up and head to our neighborhood store, the 7-Eleven on the corner of Andrews Boulevard and Woodland Road, for refreshments. That 7-Eleven is still there. It was always a Slurpee for us little kids and nonalcoholic drinks for the teens and adults, at least until the games were over and we were back at our house. One time, my brother apparently didn't hear the call to leave from the playground, and nobody noticed he was missing until my dad tried to gather us in the store to pay for whatever we had picked out. The question "Where's Tommy?" circulated in the group, and the store and cars were searched, but he wasn't found. With growing concern, we raced back to the school softball field to find Tommy sitting on a bench, propping his head in his hands, and looking pissed for being left. He asked if we had brought him a Slurpee and seemed to forgive everyone when he was presented with one. That wasn't the last time he would come up missing, and the next time was much more serious.

Another thing we loved to do as a family, especially we little kids, was go to Buckroe Beach less than two miles away to swim. I think the older kids spent a great deal of time there as well. Even better than swimming, however, was going to the Buckroe Beach Amusement Park. It was a little small but certainly adequate for us kids to have a great time. There was a roller coaster, tunnel of love, scrambler, round up, roustabout, and spider rides, and lots of kiddie rides that we started out on until we got a little older. They had a carousel, boats, cars, and airplanes that each only went around in a big circle, except for the airplanes. You could make them go up and down and dip the left or right wing. Maybe that special maneuvering was intimidating to me because one time, I talked my dad into getting on one of the airplanes with me. He was obviously too big for the ride, but I convinced him that I needed him to come with me, and he did. That's the kind of thing that made him my hero. We got on the ride together, and very soon, the difference in our weights became an obvious problem. All of Dad's weight was distributed to one side, so the plane tilted almost sideways and stayed that way the entire time instead of shifting back and forth like all the others. Unfortunately, I was wedged between Dad and the side of the plane, so I was getting squished the entire time. Dad kept asking if I was okay, and I kept telling him that I was, so we stayed that way until the end of the ride. I was never in any pain, but it was definitely not the most fun ride I ever had! The park also had a midway with games of chance and games of skill, like Skee-Ball. They even had monkeys in cages there, which would be very unusual today. I felt so lucky to have an amusement park so close to where we lived and that my parents would take us there pretty often whenever we lived in the area.

CHAPTER 26

"Psychedelic Shack"

(The Temptations)

Playing softball with a bunch of teens might sound like a noble deed, but that wasn't where the activity on Mojer Drive ended. After a few games, we all headed back home, where Mom would cook dinner for this huge group of people, or we would have the only fast food my dad would tolerate for many years to come, Kentucky Fried Chicken. After dinner, the party would begin. Dad or one of the older boys would have gone to buy lots of beer while dinner was being prepared or procured. All the older kids were allowed to have beer at our house, regardless of their age. Dad's theory was that if he allowed the boys to drink, they wouldn't want to do drugs. He allowed them to drink at our house and bought most of the beer. I'm sure this was a big reason for our popularity. The only rule was that they couldn't leave the house once they had started drinking. This resulted in bodies literally lying all over the house the next morning, as I mentioned earlier. Sometimes they weren't immediately recognized, but they had always been invited by someone and were always welcome.

Along with the drinking, there was music. John, David, and Dan played guitar. Dan practiced a lot more here and became a better player. He also made and played bongo drums out of Mom's kitchen canisters. John, David, and Mom would all sing. Dan remembered Mom singing "Little Black Egg," "Different Drum," "Down in the Boondocks," and "Dream, Dream, Dream." She even wrote a couple songs of her own along with some poems. The most interesting instrument, however, was the spoons. Dad loved to play along to Creedence Clearwater Revival records best of all, and they were the Mafia's unofficial band. They were so close to the Smith boys' experiences in California that they had a song named "Porterville," and some of the lyrics in "Who'll Stop the Rain" say, "I went down Virginia, seekin' shelter from the storm." Sam was a really good spoon player too, and everybody had to at least try it. Mom would get so mad at Dad for using all her kitchen spoons to make them. Everyone else I've seen play the spoons would leave them separated and just hold them together in their hand. Dad, however, liked to place them back to back on either side of an object, the most perfect one being a Bic lighter, and then tape the whole thing together. He would put the lighter in upside down so you could still use it even though it was attached to the spoons. He made tons of them over the years, and I still have the last pair that he made me in 2004.

Dan said that the first people he ever saw play the spoons were Don and Dean when he was five years old. He thought that they taught Dad to play them when we all lived on Fourth Street in Hampton when I was a baby. But Dad grew up in West Virginia and learned how to play the spoons as a child. On these music and party nights, we little kids were allowed to stay up for a while, enjoying the music, fetching beers and sodas, and getting lots of attention. This was the second time I knowingly recall seeing my dad drunk, but it wasn't an issue yet. Mom didn't drink alcohol at all until we moved here, and then she would just have a glass of wine every now and then. Dan said she liked Boone's Farm Strawberry Hill, and I remember John introducing her to Liebfraumilch, a sweet German wine. She was often the only sober person in the house along with Patty and us kids. This type of routine partying was the obvious third thing that made our lives crazy. The fourth would be the dangerous and addictive habit that the boys, particularly Dan, brought back with them from California- huffing (inhaling) paint.

Sam ended up dropping out of school before finishing the year and started taking his turn on the road with Dad. John, Dan, Henry, and some of the other members of the Mafia were always taking turns going with Dad as helpers as well. Dad always needed help moving the furniture, which he would have to hire each place he went if he didn't have someone with him. These guys were all hard workers who wanted to do a good job for Dad, and they got to see the country, earn a little money, and drink a little beer when they weren't working. Several of them were also learning to drive the truck as well, so they were even more valuable to Dad. John was a particularly good driver that Dad could always trust.

When sweet Sam went out with Dad that first time, Mom was really worried about him, and sure enough, he came home drunk from his first trip. Other than his drinking, however, he didn't get into any trouble, although Mom wasn't too happy with him when he got drunk one night and peed in the closet at the end of the hallway, thinking he was in the bathroom. Dan, Henry, and even John were a different story. Dan was into huffing paint more than anyone. He would huff anything, but gold spray paint was the favorite. Almost all the Mob tried it at least once. Sal and Sam never did. Mom and Dad were pretty naive about recreational drugs, just as most mainstream Americans were at the time, and this paint huffing was something they had never even heard of before. Mom later said she didn't think the boys were smoking pot or doing acid at this time but would pick up those habits later. Dan said they did smoke pot sometimes and had tried acid, called Orange Sunshine, back in California, but they never did it on Mojer Drive. It might have been because acid was a lot harder to find outside of California at the time. Dan and Henry were the most blatant about their huffing. John did it too but was more covert about his habit, and my folks didn't know he was doing anything but drinking for a long time. When they found out, they were really surprised and disappointed, especially Dad. He was our family golden boy.

It didn't take long before the huffing started to figure prominently in the lives of Dan, Henry, and John—obviously not in a good way. Once, John was stopped by the cops because he was speeding, and he had a bread bag over his face at the time, inhaling something, which was paint, while driving down the road. He was cited for speeding and inhaling a noxious chemical. When he went to court, he told the judge that he had asthma and had placed Vicks in the bag and was inhaling it to help his breathing. Huffing was such an anomaly in Hampton at the time that the judge believed John's story. Another time, Dan and Henry were sitting in a car that belonged to John and were huffing paint. The cops came up to the car and ended up giving Henry a ticket for inhaling noxious chemicals. When he went to court, the judge threw the charge out because there was no law against it at the time. The three of them also got jobs with Orkin pest control, which they liked because they could lie under houses and huff the pest-control chemicals. So it wasn't just paint that they would inhale to get a buzz.

John always kept a job, if not for very long. Dan and Henry seemed to be around the house a great deal and evidently had too much time on their hands. One night, Mom was sleeping in the bed with Dad, and she woke up smelling gasoline. Because of the terrible tragedy of my grandmother and aunt's deaths, Mom was horrified to be smelling gas in her home. She jumped out of bed and went to investigate. She didn't find anything suspicious in the house, so she went outside to see if she could find anything, and it only took a second to find the cause of the odor. The boys' bedroom window was to the right of the front door when you were exiting the house, and under their window stood a can of gasoline with a piece of garden hose coming out of the can and up inside the window, which was cracked just enough to make room for the hose.

She ran back into the house and threw open the boys' bedroom door, where she found Dan and Henry both lying on the single bed under the window, holding a contraption of hose, tape, and an empty bread bag. She yelled, "What are you doing?" to which Dan replied, "Me and Henry are just hanging out." Of course, what they were doing was huffing gas out of the can with the hose. Mom then continued to lecture them about how stupid they were and how they could catch the house on fire, etc. Then she went back outside and grabbed the gas can, carried it to the storm drain in the street, and started dumping what was left of the gas down into the drain. Lucky for Dan and Henry, she then went back to sleep, and she didn't wake Dad and tell him what had just happened. Unlucky for Mom, this wouldn't be the last time she caught the boys huffing.

Another time, Mom was home taking care of Patty, who was sick and had stayed home from school that day. They were in the kitchen together, and they thought they were the only people on the premises until Mom noticed through the kitchen window that there was movement in the backyard. She saw that a piece of clear plastic that Dad had left in the yard was now draped over the clothesline like a tent. Dan and Henry were sitting under this tent, and they were cracking up laughing. When Mom asked, "What in the world?"

Patty looked out the window too. She then exclaimed, "Oh my gosh, they're out there huffing paint!"

Mom was mortified that in broad daylight in the backyard of our suburban neighborhood, these guys were getting high! She wondered, "If I can see this, who else can?" She opened the glass sliding door in the dining room, walked out into the yard, and asked, "Dan Smith, what in the hell do you think you're doing?" Mom didn't curse much back then but would when she was angry. She never tolerated the f-word, however, especially in front of her children. Both Dan and Henry dropped the bread bags that they were holding up to their mouths, looked at each other, and started laughing. Mom was very confused with their reaction. She asked, "Dan, what the hell is the matter with you?"

They continued to laugh, and then Dan said, "Henry, Henry, check her out! Look at that dumb bitch! She thinks she can see us!" Mom was completely perplexed as Dan went on, "That dumb bitch thinks she can see us. She don't even know we're invisible!"

They continued to laugh with each other until Mom said, "Hell yes, I can see you, you dumbasses!"

Dan seemed to ponder this statement for a minute, then said, "Damn, Henry, she *can* see us under here! She must be a witch!"

The two boys continued to laugh and talk about how Mom was a witch. Mom actually started to feel a little afraid at the thought that they really believed what they were saying. At that moment, Patty, who had come up behind Mom, started to cry. She was very sensitive and always got upset when she saw someone abusing drugs or alcohol. Mom took Patty in the house and tried to console her. They were both always a little afraid of the boys when Dad was gone on the road. There was no telling what they might do, and it was pretty scary to witness them hallucinating. What would they see next? Mom was trying to figure out what to do in the situation, and in spite of the fact that they were getting high in broad daylight in front of any neighbor who might see them, she decided not to do anything. With Dad gone and not having John or any of the other boys there to protect them, she didn't want to confront Dan and Henry any further. She wasn't afraid of them sober, but on drugs, she never knew what they might do.

People have asked my mom why she wouldn't call the police in a situation like that. She would have answered that they were always trying to keep Dan *out* of jail and would never put him in there. We had an unspoken rule that you never call the police on the family. They were nothing but the enemy to a bunch of outlaws like us. Also, especially for my mom growing up, the police were not a viable option for help, and that belief continued. Eventually, Dan came in the back patio door and walked up behind Mom, who was washing dishes in the sink. He was snickering and saying, "You're a witch. Heehee. You're a witch." He smelled so strongly of paint that he repulsed her, and she turned around and told him to get away from her because he stank, and she hated it when he huffed paint. He then asked her, with paint around his mouth and stuck on and inside his nose, "How did you know I was huffing?" He continued to talk about her being a witch and how she could maybe make money at that. He was so serious that Mom couldn't help but laugh.

Dan and Henry stayed pretty high for most of the day, and when they finally ran out of paint, they were starving and wanting to eat everything in the house. Mom said that munchies from pot was nothing compared to how hungry they were after huffing paint. This has always been a funny story for our family, but Dad being gone and Mom having to deal with this crazy behavior on her own was beginning to do serious damage to our family.

Dan and Henry were by far the biggest troublemakers, and their obsession with huffing was what got them into trouble most of the time, usually because they didn't have the money for the paint. One evening, they wanted to huff, and they actually had the money to buy the paint, but all the local hardware stores were already closed. There was one that stayed open later by the Newmarket Shopping Center in Newport News, but they didn't have access to a car to get there. They walked around the neighborhood looking for a particular older model Chevy because they had an ignition that allowed you to start the car with a screwdriver. They found one on Andrews Boulevard, which was a block over from Mojer. The car was parked on the street in front of a house, and the owner was sitting inside the large front window watching TV. He could have easily spotted the guys pushing the car away if he had turned his head to look out the window. They pushed the car down the street, got it started, and took off for Newport News. They bought the paint at the hardware store, stopped and huffed some of it on the way back home, and were driving past Spratley Junior High School on Woodland Road not far from the house.

They decided to drive the car around the baseball field behind the school for a while, then they used the car to tear down the brand-new fence that ran from third base to home base. After that, they made their way over to the football field and drove around, then started wondering if they could knock the goal post over with the car. Henry was driving. He got a running start, hauled ass into the goal post, and knocked it over. They were pleased with themselves and were walking away from the car to go home when Dan happened to stumble over a brick. This gave him the idea to wedge the brick on the gas pedal and run the car through the school. Luckily, the car wouldn't start. Disappointed, they wanted to do something else wrong, so they decided to set the car on fire. They turned all the car seats over in the front and back because they knew that they were filled with straw-like material that would probably easily catch on fire, which they did.

After the fires got going well, they went over to the nearby woods to watch, hoping the car would blow up. Then the horn started honking, and the windows started to explode, which sounded like gunfire. The car was engulfed in flames, and they started to hear sirens. After the fire trucks and police cars arrived, they snuck back home to Mojer, where they saw the Mob playing basketball at the hoop down at the other end of the street. They snuck around to the street behind our house, came in the house from the backyard, and got in bed. A little later, the other boys came in the bedroom and told Dan and Henry what had happened over at the school as news had traveled fast. They said they thought it was Dan and Henry who must have done it, but Dan said they had been home in bed for a while. Dan later told John and Sam the truth, but he hadn't wanted the rest of the Mob to know. Law enforcement never suspected Dan and Henry because the car's owner apparently had an enemy, and he told the police he was sure that's who had done it.

John and Henry got jobs at the Holiday Inn in Hampton, moving carts of laundry for the housekeepers. They were each given a pass key for the hotel rooms, and John made two spare keys while he was working there, then he and Henry quit. Dan had gotten a job at the restaurant in the hotel as a busboy, and he stayed on a little longer. He and some of the Mob would use the pass keys to get into the rooms, which had "magic fingers" in the beds that would vibrate the bed for a few minutes per quarter inserted into a box attached to the bed. The Mob would use a big screwdriver to open up the boxes, empty out the quarters, and then put the boxes back together, leaving no evidence of tampering so nobody would be the wiser. They kept those pass keys in the top drawer of the dresser in the boys' bedroom for at least three years, wherever that bedroom might have been located, using them to get access to the boxes filled with quarters when they needed party money. They used the pass keys for a bigger operation at Christmastime on Mojer Drive. Again, Dan and some of the Mob got into a couple of rooms, but this time, they stole everything they could carry out of the rooms, like the bedspreads, curtains, lamps, pictures, etc. They were even able to take the color TVs, which Dan said were hooked up to a light that would flash in the motel office if a TV was removed, but he knew that nobody ever paid attention to it, so they got away with it. One of the guys said he would trade a nice maple coffee table and end tables that he had for one of the TVs, and Dan told him he had a deal. They loaded everything into a car, brought it to our house late at night, and stacked it around the Christmas tree for Mom. She was shocked and had mixed feelings about it but admitted that she loved the nice maple tables.

Dad got upset one time when we lived here, possibly because of all the stolen merchandise that was brought into our house. He opened up the front door in the middle of the day and started throwing everything out of the house and into the yard. It wasn't long before the police came as I'm sure at least one neighbor called due to the disturbance. I wasn't there to know for sure, but he was probably cussing and yelling while the throwing was going on. He wasn't harming anyone, however, just emptying out the contents of our house. When the two officers arrived, one approached Dad, and the other approached Mom, whom I guess was just hanging out and watching what Dad was doing. I don't know if she was particularly upset or not. Dad was never happy to see the cops, but he was cordial, and when asked what he was doing, he said he was throwing his belongings into his front yard. When the officer asked why, he said because he wanted to. When the other officer asked Mom pretty much the same questions, she gave the same answers. When asked if she was concerned about my dad's behavior, she answered no. The officer told Mom that this wasn't normal behavior, and maybe Dad wasn't in his right mind or something, and she didn't agree. She said she knew he was thinking normally. When the officer asked how she knew, she answered, "Because he's thrown everything from the living room out to the front yard except for one thing." When the officer asked what it was, Mom went into the living room and picked up my beloved Baby Tender Love doll off the floor, where Dad had picked it up, looked at it, and gently set it back down. It was eventually determined that my dad wasn't breaking any laws, and nobody was making any complaints, so the officers left.

Not all the crazy adventures that occurred while we lived on Mojer actually happened at that location. One time, Dan went on the road with Dad to Boston, and they had 18,000 pounds of furniture, which took up almost the whole forty-foot trailer. This was the biggest shipment Dan had ever seen. Dad had stopped in Havre de Grace, Maryland, and picked up another helper named Kenny. The three of them had to carry the furniture uphill, and Dan bitched the whole time, so Dad said he wouldn't bring him on the road anymore. He did take Dan again, but Dan didn't bitch anymore. On the trip home from this delivery, Dad pulled over in a shopping center to sleep, and Dan and Kenny took Dad's wallet and got a taxi to a bar. Dad was pissed when he woke up and found the guys and his wallet were gone, but he quickly got over it and forgave them after they got back.

They took Kenny back to Havre de Grace and picked up Henry, who had been there visiting his family. The three of them went to a bar in Aberdeen, where they shut the place down. Dad drank a lot of vodka, and they were all wasted, but they got in the truck for Dad to drive them home. Dan soon passed out in the sleeper, and when he woke up, the truck was stopped, and he saw Dad standing out in front of the truck. He was trying to tuck his shirt in, drunk as hell, and was talking to the cops. When one of the cops walked up and opened the passenger door, Henry fell out of the door and landed on top of the cop as he was also drunk as hell. Dan thought it would be best if he just stayed in the sleeper. Turned out, Dad had stopped his truck at the entrance to the Harbor Tunnel in Baltimore and passed out with his head on the steering wheel because he knew he was too drunk to drive through that tunnel. He didn't tell that to the cops though. He told them that the clutch was going out on the truck, and that was why he stopped there at the tunnel entrance. They ended up leading the truck, with Dad driving, off on a gravel road before the tunnel to a maintenance shop, where the guys were allowed to sleep for the night even though they had to know that Dad was drunk as hell. The three of them thanked the officers and said goodbye to them. After the officers were gone, they drank another six-pack of beer, laughing about what had happened, before they went to sleep and headed to Hampton the next morning.

Probably the worst victim of the Mob was the Buckroe Auto Parts (BAP) store. One time, Dan and Henry wanted paint to huff, and it was late, so everything was closed. They went to the BAP, and Dan kicked out one of the giant pieces of glass in the front of the building. He got his leg cut on a big piece of the window glass, but he said it didn't even hurt. They kept going anyway, got their paint, and left. Another time, on New Year's Eve, they had been partying with the family, but everybody else had called it a night and gone to bed. Dan and Henry wanted to huff, but they had promised Mom that they wouldn't do it anymore and, in a show of faith, destroyed all the cans of paint that they had. So they stole a car, took it to the BAP, and busted another one of the big windows out. Dan broke into that store two more times, taking out one of the giant front windows each time. The store replaced the windows with plexiglass each time so, when all the glass windows were gone, Dan finally didn't break in anymore.

During this particular break-in, they didn't just steal paint this time but also a bunch of tools for Dad. Dan wanted to take all their loot home, but Henry wanted to ride around first. After about thirty minutes, they were pulled over by the cops. Apparently, the people in the house next to the BAP had called the cops and given them a description of the car. They were arrested and taken to jail. Dan was only seventeen, being four days from his eighteenth birthday, so they put him in isolation until his birthday and then put him in with the general population. When he went to court, Dan told the judge that he had stolen the fifty-two cans of paint because he refinished guitars. The theft of the paint and tools, however, was nothing compared to the felony grand theft auto charge he was facing for stealing the car. Henry was nineteen but was charged as a juvenile because he was with a juvenile, so he got off. You can't make this stuff up. Dan was also charged as a juvenile, but the judge was not going to let him off, telling him instead that he could either go in the military or go to jail. Dan chose the Marines and enlisted the next day. He said that he had been planning to marry his girlfriend Diane and join the

Marines before he even got arrested because he thought it would be a good steady job.

I remember the family being very upset about Dan leaving for the Marines, especially Mom. Before he left for basic training, he got his Social Security insurance check from his mother's death because he had turned eighteen. He bought Mom a dishwasher and a router for Dad and had enough left over for a case of beer. After he left for Boot Camp, he would call Mom on the phone from Marine Corps Recruit Depot, Parris Island, South Carolina. When it was time for him to graduate, Mom, Wade, who had surprisingly come from California for the occasion; and Kathy M., a friend of the Mob, attended his graduation ceremony there. Dan sent us his official photo that they made of him, and a more beautiful Marine couldn't be found. I asked him if he was ever concerned about being sent to Vietnam, and he said that he hadn't been worried about it. I knew that there was a war happening at the time, but we didn't know anyone who was serving, so it didn't play a part in our lives.

At any rate, while Dan was in boot camp, the president decided to pull out of Vietnam, which took a long time, but they weren't supposed to send any more soldiers over, so the threat for Dan was over. After boot camp, he went to Camp Geiger in North Carolina for infantry training. He went to his first duty station at Camp Pendleton in Oceanside, California, and was there for two days when he got bored and hitchhiked about 250 miles north to see Wade in Porterville. During their visit, Wade dropped his car key in the dark, and Dan was using a flashlight to look for the key. When Dan accidentally shone the light in Wade's eyes, Wade punched him. Dan didn't do or say a word to Wade. I'll never understand why Wade's children continued to try and have a relationship with him when he still treated them with such low regard. Dan flew back home, and Bogie picked him up at the airport in Newport News. It caused a big uproar in the family because Dan was now absent without leave (AWOL) from the Marines. He was a fugitive. If he was caught, he would be tried in court by the Marine Corps and sentenced to the brig—military prison. This was the most serious situation he had ever been in.

Since he was now AWOL, Dan was around the house all the time and appeared to be keeping his nose clean. He spent a lot of time with Tommy, who was four years old at the time and not in school. He taught Tommy, also known as Bud to the family, everything he had learned in boot camp. Dan would put him through drills, asking him questions and making him answer very loudly, "Sir, yes, sir." He would make him do sit-ups, push-ups, jumping jacks, and all sorts of exercises. One was called praying to the Buddha, which I don't remember specifically except that he had to contort himself on the ground and hold the position until he was released. It looked very uncomfortable. Dan and David decided to take us kids to nearby Colonial Williamsburg one time, and it was total Dan style. Unknown to anyone else at the time, the guys were high on acid. We drove to Williamsburg, and since the guys didn't have money to pay the admission to get into the living-history museum, they helped us kids climb a brick wall to drop down on the side of the museum, then climbed over themselves. We wandered around the outdoor areas for several hours, taking in all the sights, and spent most of our time in the large hedge maze on the grounds of the Governor's Palace. We got hungry after a while, and not having any money for food, Dan found a plum tree with ripe fruit in someone's yard, and we all helped ourselves to plums until we had our fill. We kids had a great day and were none the wiser to Dan's unorthodox way of babysitting and visiting a tourist attraction.

When he got caught stealing a tire from a car in Hampton, they locked Dan up in the Navy brig in Norfolk for twenty days, which he said was really nice, and they would let him come home on the weekends. Then they sent him to the brig at Camp LeJeune, North Carolina. He was only there for half a day until his lawyer got him out. He said it was really rough, and he definitely didn't want to spend three years there, which he expected to once he was court-martialed. He was placed in a subunit waiting for the court-martial, and he said he didn't mind it. He was allowed to leave there and come home sometimes on the weekend, but he still kept going AWOL off and on because he was too bored to stay in the Marines. He would turn himself in sometimes, and one time, Dad talked him into letting him take Dan back to Camp LeJeune. Dad called Mom that night and was really proud that he got Dan back where he belonged. Mom said that wasn't quite true because Dan had already hitchhiked back home to Hampton.

Tommy had an incident with stealing here that ended up creating the family "board of education." One day while Mom was home and we girls were all at school, Tommy wandered off a little too far and found a construction site a few blocks from our house, where they were building new homes. He watched the workers with fascination for a while, then decided he better go home, but not without taking three small two-by-four boards with him when he went. When Dad got home from a local shipment that day, Tommy showed him the new treasures he had found. Dad was calm, but very angry at Tommy for stealing. He told him that tomorrow, when the workers were back on the site again, Tommy was to take two of the three boards back to the site, give them to the workers, and apologize for stealing them. Tommy agreed but asked, "What about the other board, Dad?" Dad told him that he needed to keep that board because he needed to make sure that Tommy never stole anything again. After Tommy went to bed that night, Dad used his pocketknife to carve a handle at one end of the board, then carved the words "Board of Education" into one side of the board and finished up by painting it white. When Dad got home the next night, he asked Tommy if he had taken the two boards back and apologized like he had told him to do, and Tommy said that he had. Dad then got the board from the top of the refrigerator and told Tommy he was going to get a spanking to make sure he remembered not to ever steal again. So Tommy was the first to get spanked by the "board of education," but Mom used it on him and me plenty of times after that. Paula never got spankings, and Dad only spanked me once with the board, but I'll tell that story later. Although the Mob wasn't going to receive any spankings, they got a big kick out of the board and carved or wrote their names on it. Tommy and I would hide it sometimes to not get a spanking, and eventually, it got lost along the way, just like most of our belongings.

Dan was AWOL off and on for three years. He was probably the cutest of all the Mob, and he was extremely confident with his ability to get any girl that he liked. He had the same charm that his father did. He had talked about marrying his girlfriend, Diane, but they broke up before that happened. He wrote a pretty song for Diane, with her name as the title, but she wasn't the one who was meant for him. As for Sam, the first girl that I recall him ever having a crush on was Kathy M., who had gone with Mom and Wade to Dan's boot camp graduation. Kathy lived a couple streets over from us. She was a fun, sweet redhead that everyone liked, and she had a crush on Sam too. They were never really a couple, however, because Sam was so shy with her that he didn't tell her how he felt and wouldn't even try to hold her hand. Kathy wasn't sure that Sam even liked her, so when Henry developed a crush on her and left no doubt about it, she became his girlfriend instead. Sam never expressed how he felt about the situation as he was always tight-lipped about his feelings and held them inside. As far as we know, he didn't have another crush on a girl until he met Faye, his future wife. John was really only ever with one girl, but she wasn't in the picture yet.

There was one other happening on Mojer Drive that had a big effect on our family, especially my folks and my sister Paula, who was now eight years old. Mom's first husband, Jim, who was Paula's biological father, had tracked us down, and he showed up at the house one day. Apparently, he had found out about Paula's birth years ago and had searched for my folks, but we moved around so much that he wasn't able to find us. I'm assuming that Jim had an attorney assisting him, but he was still the very nice and upstanding man that he always was and discussed with my parents that he wanted to get to know his daughter. They agreed, with the caveat that she had a brother and sister, and we needed to participate to some degree because my folks always insisted on equality between us kids; you don't do for one without doing for the others. They thought it wouldn't be fair for Paula to get to go to parks, restaurants, or any other fun places with Jim, while Tommy and I sat at home. This rule also included any gifts that were given. He agreed to the rules and would always give Tommy and me a token gift that we were very happy to get when he began to bestow many gifts on Paula as they began seeing each other on a regular basis. I can vaguely remember going places with Jim and my siblings. I think that he and my parents built up a trust, and Tommy and me really didn't want to participate, finding more fun elsewhere, so Paula and Jim were eventually allowed to have visits on their own.

At some point, Jim told my folks that he wanted to have custody of Paula. The whole family had been anxious about Jim's presence from the start, and when he said this, everyone became very upset and protective over Paula. The matter was apparently settled by Paula herself. When informed of Jim's wishes, she said that she understood Jim was her actual father, and she really cared for him and wanted him in her life but that Tom Stanley was her Daddy, always had been and always would be, and she wanted to stay with him. Paula was a very intelligent and mature child, and her opinion was honored. Paula had stated this to Mom, Dad, and Jim in our living room one evening, and while they were having this discussion, Dan was outside slicing Jim's tires on his car. When the group of four came outside after their discussion and discovered the tires, Dad was really upset, knowing that Dan must have done the deed. Dan didn't realize that everything was getting worked out amicably and that we weren't losing Paula. Shortly after, my dad legally adopted her, and they adored each other until he passed. She also continued to have a close relationship with Jim until he passed, except for the separations they endured with our moves and his Navy duty stations changes.

Now summer was almost upon us, and we kids finished our school year. This would be one of only two school years that I completed at one school for the entire year without moving. I loved my life on Mojer Drive, and I didn't want to leave it, but we were moving again.

CHAPTER 27

"Brand New Key"

(Melanie)

Two of the Mob brothers, Gary and Wayne, were from a prominent real estate family. When they found out that we wanted to move from Mojer, for what reason I don't know, they found us one of their parents' homes to rent. It was located on Mercury Boulevard in the Phoebus section of Hampton just outside of Fort Monroe. I thought this house was a mansion! It had a small, unfinished basement and a large attic, which meant it was three stories, and anything more than one story was considered huge and fancy by me. I thought it was a very large house, but looking at it now, it's more like a cute cottage or nice starter home. It had a built-in breakfast nook in the kitchen, which felt so special. The built-in hamper in the bathroom also felt special. There were two bedrooms on the main floor, one for my folks and one that Paula and I shared, which had built-in bench seats with storage underneath. More special! I had started playing 45 records on the portable record player that we had, and my favorite one was "My Guy" by Mary Wells. It was my song for my dad. "Go Away Little Girl" by the Osmonds was a current favorite of mine, and we kids all got a kick out of one of the new songs on the radio, "Ding-a-Ling" by Chuck Berry. Even at five, seven, and eight years old, we knew what he was singing about and couldn't believe we were hearing it on the radio!

Back to the house. The upstairs belonged to the older kids. There was a large open room, where all the boys slept and hung out. Sam made himself his own room out of the large closet, complete with black lights and posters, and I believe he had a flashing light from a construction site in there. He loved to listen to his music really loud in there, and I remember "In-a-Gadda-Da-Vida" by Iron Butterfly being one of them. Off the large boys' room was a separate smaller room that belonged to Patty, and the most amazing thing about it was that she had her own powder room with a toilet and tiny sink! Her room also had a little crawl space housed behind a miniature door. I might have thought it was really cool under other circumstances, but it was dark and musty in there, and most of the space was taken up by a large roll of carpet. I loved to explore in Patty's room, namely her record collection, which contained "Everybody Plays the Fool" by The Main Ingredient, "Build Me Up Buttercup" by The Foundations, and "Knock Three Times" by Tony Orlando and Dawn. There was also her jewelry box, which contained more strange souvenirs than jewelry. She had a collection of wishbones, both broken and unbroken. She also kept locks of hair, fingernails, and toenails that belonged to her family members and loved ones. Ewwwww. My favorite thing, however, was her strawberry perfume, which I would smell and steal just a tiny dab of to put on my neck. It smelled so wonderful that I knew it must taste just as delicious, so I tried tasting it one time. Wow! That was a rude awakening! Once again, Tommy had no room of his own, and this would occur often throughout our childhood, but he never seemed to be bothered by it. Maybe it's a boy/girl thing because I sure wanted a room for myself even if I had to share it with someone else.

The location of this house was very different from the Holly Homes neighborhood, where Mojer Drive was located. Mercury Boulevard was a four-lane road and very busy with traffic. We kids were warned to never try and cross that street as it was very dangerous. That was fine with me until I met a girl after school started who lived across the street, and I wanted to be able to visit her. I had a discussion with Dad about it, and in spite of his warning about the rule, I told him that I was going to cross the street anyway. He said that he couldn't possibly watch me all the time and that I could break the rule and cross the street if I really wanted to, but I had better be prepared to pay the price for breaking the rule. I could be caught and punished, or I could be injured and possibly killed if I were hit by a car. That was a huge life lesson for me. I was very headstrong and passionate about what I wanted, but that lesson taught me to stop and think about what price I would have to pay every time I did something reckless. There were many times when I decided to do what I wanted and damn the consequences, but I suffered those consequences as my own responsibility. Other times, I decided to follow the rules, as I did in this case, and I never crossed that street. We learned all too well how dangerous it was when our dog, Cotton, a large mixed-breed dog with long, fluffy white hair, was hit by a car out front and ran off. Somehow, we got him back again, and Patty nursed him back to health down in the basement, staying with him constantly on some old blankets until he was well.

On our side of the street, however, we were allowed more freedom to roam as it was just small residential streets on that side. One day, I was walking down the sidewalk by myself about two blocks from our house. I had found a piece of paper, and I was tearing it up into little pieces and leaving a trail, like Hansel and Gretel. I would never litter like that now, but I thought it was great fun to live out the fairy tale at the time. My innocent fun was interrupted when I saw a man in his backyard, across the street from me. He was an old man with a beard and cap, dressed in rather shabby clothing. He waved to me, and I waved back but kept walking. He motioned for me to come over to him, and I stopped and shook my head. He motioned a few more times, and I just kept shaking my head. He then pulled his pants down to his knees, exposing his naked groin. He started touching himself with one hand and kept motioning for me to come over with the other. At that point, I started to run toward home. I stopped at the corner and turned around to make sure he wasn't chasing me. I didn't see him behind me, so I assume he stayed in the yard, which

I couldn't see any longer. I don't remember anything that happened after that, if I told my parents or if they did anything about it.

There was a beautiful, old brick Baptist church one street over from ours, and Patty took us kids there a few times. We sat in the balcony, and I remember singing hymns, which I always enjoyed. This is the first church I can remember attending, but there would be many more in my future, especially on Easter. We would usually only attend once and just with Mom, never Dad. We moved around so much that being a regular attendee anywhere wasn't a consideration. Dad considered himself an atheist at the time, and Mom had an ambivalent relationship with the Lord. She would say that you cannot love and fear God at the same time, and she was very bitter about my grandmother and aunt's deaths and how God could allow such a thing to happen, as I've mentioned already. Still, we continued to attend church here or there throughout my childhood, and Mom read Bible stories to us, which we loved.

While it was still summertime, my folks bought us kids a three-foot, above-ground swimming pool that they put up in the backyard. It was awesome having our own swimming pool, and I have good memories of playing in it. My favorite one is how Paula and I liked to "go to the beauty parlor," meaning we would plug our noses and dip our heads back in the water, leaving our hair perfectly slicked back and out of our faces. We also loved to crawl around the inside edge of the pool on our stomachs as fast as we could, creating a whirlpool effect that we would then ride until the water calmed. The boys also had a basketball hoop out back, attached to the garage, and they would play games in the driveway. One time, Patty was walking near the makeshift court during a game, and Dan suddenly picked her up, ran over to the pool, and dropped her in. Just for fun. Of course, Patty was furious and yelled and cried out of frustration.

Apparently, Sam thought this was a great idea and made a habit of throwing Patty in the pool whenever she pissed him off or didn't do what he told her to do. It was especially upsetting to Patty because she wasn't a little girl anymore. She was thirteen years old and had her first boyfriend, one of the Mafia named Ernie who was probably the sweetest of all the guys in the Mafia. She felt she was too old to be humiliated by her brothers. The worst time was when Patty was dressed up to attend the funeral of a girl she had gone to school with on Mojer Drive. The girl had been swimming at Buckroe Beach, got caught in an undertow, and drowned. Mom said that people formed a human chain to rescue the girl but were unsuccessful. Although it was a solemn occasion, it was still a social one, and Patty had taken great care to pick the right dress, wear nylons, and curl her hair for the event. When her friend, Kathy M., Henry's girlfriend, arrived to pick her up, they walked out back to where all the family was gathered to tell my folks that they were leaving. Sam, who was shooting hoops in the driveway, told Patty to go in and make him a sandwich before she left. She told him absolutely not, that she was getting ready to leave, and to make his own sandwich. He said, "Girl, you better go make me a sandwich." Again, she refused, and started down the driveway to the front of the house. Sam ran up behind her, picked her up, and walked over to the edge of the pool. Patty was surprisingly calm and quiet and pleaded softly to Sam not to throw her in the pool. Sam looked over at Dad, and Dad shook his head, but after a moment of consideration, Sam dropped her in anyway. He then apologized to Dad for the deed but didn't bother to apologize to Patty. She was obviously devastated and refused to speak to or look at Sam for quite some time after that.

We kids started school in the fall at Jane H. Bryan Elementary. Tommy started kindergarten this year. I was in second grade, and I got into trouble in school for the first time. I was sitting at a table with my class at lunchtime, and some kid decided to tell another kid, "Say *eat*, pass it down." So when the command got to me, I passed it along just like every other kid at the very long table. The command was passed to each one of us, and we all started saying, "Eat!" It was a little quiet and random at first but turned into a loud chant of twenty-plus second graders yelling "Eat, eat, eat!" It felt so powerful and fun until our teacher walked up and quieted us instantly with just a look. After lunch, instead of going outside for recess, we all sat in class with a piece of paper, writing over and over again, "I will not say 'Eat' at lunch." I felt the punishment was totally worth the crime!

Dan got himself into some trouble here one night, which was a little more serious than saying *"Eat"* at the lunch table. He decided to steal some plywood and two-by-fours from Cavalier Cabinets, where he was working at the time, to build Tommy a little fort in our backyard. He had installed some cabinets for the company in a nice house in Fox Hill that day, and while on the job site, he spotted the lumber and thought a fort would be a cool thing to build for Tommy. That night, he and some friend took the family Plymouth Station Wagon over to the house and got the lumber all loaded up in the car. They could have left then, but Dan wanted to show his friend the beautiful cabinets he had helped install earlier in that day. While they were admiring the work, a cop was doing a routine patrol outside. He noticed the loaded station wagon sitting in the driveway of an unfinished home and decided to stop and take a look. Dan and the other guy spotted the cop in time to run out the back of the house to a nearby shopping center and called Mom on a pay phone to report the car stolen. The car was kept for three days in impound, being checked for fingerprints and other evidence, but was eventually returned to my folks without finding the thief.

Dan had another little mishap when we lived here, but it was totally innocent and unplanned, and he was not looking for trouble but maybe for love. He and David were driving along four-lane Mallory Street in the Plymouth Station Wagon, heading toward Phoebus. They were in the right lane, while a carload of cute girls was in the left lane beside them. Dan and David were both big flirts and very cute too. They were looking at the girls and waving to them, but the windows weren't down, so there wasn't any talking back and forth. At some point, Mallory curves pretty sharply to the right, so the carload of girls curved appropriately, but Dan didn't. He wasn't paying attention and ran into the girls, side-swiping them until the road straightened out again. He then got the heck away from the scene and headed back home.

Patty got into some trouble in school here also. Mom got a call at home one day from Patty's junior high school. They informed Mom that she needed to come to the school to have a conversation with the principal about an incident with Patty. Mom went directly to the school, joined Patty in the principal's office, and was told that Patty had been caught smoking cigarettes in school, and she was suspended from school. Mom was shocked, and Patty was crying. They got into the car and left the school to go home. On the way, Mom asked Patty what had happened, and she said that she was not smoking and that she didn't smoke at all; she was merely holding a cigarette for another girl while she tied her shoe. She was caught with it in her hand, so she was the one blamed for smoking. Mom believed every word Patty said because she was a good girl and was not known to lie. By the time they got home, Mom was furious that Patty had been wrongly accused and punished, so she called the school and got the principal on the phone. She said that now that she knew what really happened, she believed in Patty's innocence and demanded that she be admitted back to school and not be punished. The principal relented, and she went back to school the next day. Unfortunately, a few weeks later, Mom walked into Patty's bedroom and caught her smoking at her open bathroom window. Patty admitted that she had lied about the incident at the school and that she was, indeed, smoking. Mom was humiliated and disappointed, and Patty smoked openly from that point.

We had a fun New Year's Eve at this house. We kids were allowed to stay awake until midnight, and we hung out with all the Mob, except for Dad, who was on the road. I remember that just before midnight, we all went out into the front yard, and Mom gave us kids sparklers to play with. We had a countdown, and at the stroke of midnight, we all yelled and hugged and kissed one another. The guys shot off some fireworks, and they picked up the ladies and us kids and swung us around in the air. We played in the yard with sparklers a little longer, then Mom said that we kids had to get ready for bed.

We continued to have the fun we had really started together as a family of nine on Mojer Drive. It wasn't all parties, softball, basketball, or the swimming pool. We played board games like Monopoly Sorry, Trouble, and Aggravation along with all the card games we knew, like Rummy, War, Slapjack, Old Maid, Go Fish, Crazy Eights, and Two-Hand Solitaire. Dan taught us to play several solitaire games as well that he had learned when he was in jail. Sometimes it was everyone in the house playing, including the Mob, and other times it was just some of us, but there was always some sort of game playing going on in or outside of our house. We little kids loved playing four square, hopscotch, and wall ball outside, and my sister and I played Chinese jump rope, cats in the cradle, pickup sticks, and jacks. Dad would play poker and blackjack with us when he was home, but he played very strictly by the rules in his handy book of Hoyle, and it was hard for us little kids to maintain his standards. He would even get upset with us and say, "You have to play by Vegas rules!" to which we might reply something like, "But, Dad, I'm just a little kid!"

Someone had given us a small organ here that Mom placed in the living room. She bought beginner books with classic songs like "Little Brown Jug" and "Camptown Races" for us kids to learn to play. It was great fun for Paula and me, and Mom played it as well. Her favorite song to play was the more current "96 Tears" by Question Mark and the Mysterians. That's one hell of a name for a band, but it was a cool song, and she played it well. We had a mulberry tree that we loved picking the berries from in the backyard, and Mom's little Valiant car was parked in back, broken down at the moment, so we were allowed to play in it as long as we didn't mess it up. Tommy especially had a great time playing in the backyard in the fort built by Uncle Dan. It's the first thing I remember Dan building, but it certainly wouldn't be the last as he became a talented and creative master carpenter eventually.

We had a shooting while we lived at this house, which caused great injury and was very unusual. What led up to the incident was Dan dating a girl named Sylvia, whose mother was giving him a hard time about dating her daughter and put a lot of restrictions on Sylvia to keep her and Dan apart. Dan was really upset about it and very vocal about his feelings, which went on for some time. At the same time, Sam had hand-built this gun out of a piece of galvanized pipe and wood. It was called a zip gun, and they were apparently popular at the time. He and Bogie were out driving around with the gun one night, and Sam decided to shoot at Sylvia's mother's house to teach her a lesson. He didn't expect the shot to harm anyone or even any property but just to startle the people inside. He had built several of these guns and shot them successfully when he was still in California, and he felt confident about what he was doing. He had stuffed the gun with rolls of gun caps and match heads and used a shaving styptic pencil for the bullet.

Bogie was driving, and he pulled over close to Sylvia's house for Sam to prepare the gun. Sam was packing the gun into his wrist several times when it accidentally went off and shot a hole into Sam's wrist. The styptic pencil was protruding from the other side of his wrist but didn't break the skin, meaning all the gun caps and match heads were still inside his body. Bogie brought him home, and my folks took him to the hospital, where they lied and said they were his parents as he was technically still a ward of the state of California. He was in the hospital for about a week, where they were very concerned with infection and Sam keeping the use of his hand. There's a picture of him lying in the hospital bed with his long, hippie hair, his hospital pajama shirt unbuttoned, and a transistor radio on the table beside him. One of the Mob, probably Bogie, is behind the bed with his arm sticking out, giving the peace sign. Sam came home with a tube in his arm that Mom had to suction out several times a day to keep getting the gunk out and try to avoid infection. In spite of the good job Mom performed as caretaker and everything that Sam's medical team did for him, he ended up being disabled for the rest of his life, with his fingers permanently bent up, but it didn't stop him from having a successful career as a pipe fitter eventually and continuing to play the guitar.

CHAPTER 28

"Playground in My Mind" (Clint Holmes)

Mom was still taking care of Sam's arm when we moved to our next house. It was sometime between New Year's and school getting out because we finished up that year at the same school but from the new house. Dan wasn't going to be making this move with us. Instead, he went to California to stay with Dean. He got back together there with a former girlfriend named Debbie. The girl was married now but left her husband when Dean told her that Dan was back in town. She called and asked Dan to meet her at a motel, where she showed up with everything she owned in her truck, including her baby. She, Dan, and the baby ended up living in that motel for the next six months until Dan came back to Hampton.

I didn't want to move again, as usual, because I loved our house on Mercury Boulevard, and it continued to be my favorite of all the houses we ever lived in with a couple of close seconds. As usual, I don't know why Mom and Dad wanted to move. Our next house was on Grove Street in a smaller neighborhood of tract homes, heading back toward Holly Homes. It was originally a small two-bedroom house. Paula and I shared one, and Patty and Tommy had bunks in the other. There might have been two sets of bunks in that room because John and Sam were still living with us, and Dan came back as well. Another bedroom had been added onto the house off the living room, and that was Mom and Dad's room. Our house also originally had one bathroom, but a powder room and laundry room had been added on to the back of the house from the kitchen as well. It was such a luxury to have a second toilet in the house. It would have been great back on Mojer when we had as many as twenty people spending the night. The Mob would still come around often, but I don't recall having any parties like we did on Mojer and as many people spending the night.

When Dan came back from California, he ended up back at Camp LeJeune at some point, and he decided to walk home to Hampton one night. He got about eighty miles north to the town of Washington, North Carolina, when he came upon a mobile home sales company. He noticed that a truck was connected to a trailer with a mobile home on it. He was tired of walking. It was dark and late, and nobody was around, so he unhooked the trailer and drove the truck the rest of the way to Hampton, about 150 miles. He kept the truck parked at the beach for three days, taking it out off and on with all his friends piled in it. He didn't want to park it at our house, in case it was discovered that it was stolen. On the third day, he decided that he wasn't going to drive it any longer, but he asked John to take him to the truck one last time to get the fireman's axe that he had found in the toolbox. When they got near the truck, they saw what looked like a police detective there, who was writing down all the numbers on the truck, so they left. That night, the guys all went to a local McDonald's, and Dan spotted the stolen truck at a garage next door to the restaurant, so he walked over and got the axe out of the toolbox. Nobody ever found out how that truck got from Washington, North Carolina, to Hampton, Virginia, or what happened to the axe that had been in the toolbox.

My time on Grove Street started out great, but this was where ugly slithered into my life like a snake, showed itself, then left and then came back to stay, lurking in the shadows of my life. But let's start with the good stuff. There were two brothers across the street around our ages, and all us little kids had some of the best fun ever playing cars in our backyard on a dirt pile that was left there by the previous owners. We built tons of roads and some tunnels, and it was one of those activities that Mom had to make us come in the house for lunch, dinner, and bedtime, which came after a bath to remove the literal layer of dirt from our bodies. I thought it was neat when a spot of water would disturb the layer and create an anomaly, then I would add them on purpose and make myself look like a spotted cheetah or a zebra with stripes. So funny, the things that amuse kids.

We also had an unused clothesline bar in the backyard, which my sister and I utilized as a high bar for our gymnastics tricks. We balanced on top of the bar with one leg over and the other wrapped behind it to lock us in, then we spun around and around, forward or backward, as many times as we could. As usual, Paula was always more adept at athletics than I was, and she performed much better. Our favorite move was called a penny drop. We would hang upside down by our knees and swing ourselves forward out high enough to let go and land on our feet. I'm not sure who named it or how we even learned it, but it gave me such satisfaction to accomplish!

The older boys played some mean basketball games at the hoop in the backyard. Someone also had a mini bike and rode it around the yard and neighborhood a lot. It was fun to watch them looking like big clowns on this tiny little bike, fitting as many people as they could on it. We little kids weren't allowed to ride on it, but I didn't mind just watching them being silly. The older boys usually got along great, but like brothers, they had some heated moments too, and Dan told me about one that happened on Grove Street. Mom was driving the Valiant that had been broken down on Mercury Boulevard and was now up and running. She had Dan in the front passenger seat, and John was in the back. Dan made a rude comment about John's girlfriend, so John made a rude comment about Dan's girlfriend. Dan got mad and picked up an electric can opener that was in the floor and was going to turn around and hit John with it. I have no idea why there was an electric can opener in the floor of the car. Just then, John used both feet to kick the back of Dan's seat and smashed Dan against the dash. Mom stopped the car in the middle of the road, and they, all three, jumped out. The boys went at each other to fight, but Mom got between them and calmed them down enough to get back in the car and get it out of the middle of the road. John never hit Dan in his life but would usually just hold him and pin him up until he calmed down.

Patty had a boyfriend who would come visit her on Grove Street and bring his huge Saint Bernard, Brandy, with him. I remember loving the dog and having no fear of him, but he ended up biting the cheek of one of the boys across the street one day, and then he wasn't allowed to come over anymore. Patty wasn't with this boyfriend long. She had met a couple of guys named Keith and Dusty in the alley at Buckroe at this time, who had just gotten out of jail for breaking into a place and stealing. Patty took a liking to Keith and started dating him. Everyone seemed to like Keith, who was goofy and sweet with us kids.

One time when we lived here, we had a flood due to torrential rains. Once the rain stopped, the end of our road was filled with several feet of water at its highest. A bunch of neighborhood kids went down there and were swimming in the water, and we kids wanted to go too. Mom threw down an emphatic no on that and said that flood water was full of germs and you should never go in it. We were disappointed for missing out on the fun, but that wouldn't be the last time that happened. Most of the time my folks had strict rules about things, but others, we were left to do some pretty dangerous things.

I figured out on my own that we chose the house on Grove Street because the same friend of Dad's from West Virginia that brought us to Hampton for the first time lived just a few houses down. Dad really liked this guy, who was married and had two children. They made beautiful wooden shelves together in the friend's garage, and it was nice to see Dad do something creative. The friend and his family would come over to visit, and I remember we kids would be locked in mine and Paula's bedroom while the adults watched stag movies on our new 8 mm projector. I snuck and looked at the films once, unreeling them and holding them up to the light. I could tell that there was nudity but didn't really get what was going on in the films and just thought the naked people were gross. My folks had bought an 8 mm camera to go with the projector, and we started taking home movies. The first one was taken at a skating rink, with Mom and us kids skating and Dad taking the movie. Patty was with us but hated being on camera, so there's only one shot of her quickly turning her head away.

We left the skating rink and continued to film at what we called the NASA Space Park, which is actually named the Air Power Park. We kids loved to go there and see all the planes on display in the big outdoor park. There was one hollowed-out plane that we could crawl through, but our favorite was a huge white statue of a plane made out of concrete, I think, that rose about thirty to forty feet in the air. I don't know if you were even supposed to be on it because Dad had to lift us kids up to even reach it. Once we were on, we climbed up really high and could have been seriously injured if we had fallen. Paula and I climbed about halfway up, but Tommy went all the way to the top. One example of the crazy stuff we survived as kids that people would never let their children do now. We continued to take movies of the family for years, all without sound. I still have all of them but have converted them to digital form as well. One consistency with the Smith boys or any of the Mob on the movies is flipping the bird at the camera, so that's on just about every movie we made.

As I mentioned, Dad's friend would come over often with his wife or family, and he would sometimes stay after they went home and Mom and we kids went to bed. He and Dad would stay up drinking and talking about old times. One night, the friend got really drunk and eventually passed out on the couch, so Dad went to bed. Sometime during the night, the "friend" woke and came into my bedroom, where I was sleeping next to my sister. He quietly molested me without waking my sister, and I was too terrorized to move or say a word. I can't say exactly how long it lasted, but he eventually left the room, crossed the hall, and went into Patty and Tommy's room. He tried to kiss Patty and touch her breast, and she woke from her sleep screaming hysterically, as I only wish I had done. The "friend" ran out of the house, and everyone in the house was now awake and alert. After Patty told her story, Dad and any of the other Mob left the house to find the molester and do him harm; how much we'll never know.

After all the men were gone, everyone was ordered back to bed, and Mom was left awake in the living room, waiting and worrying. I lay in my bed awake, thinking about what happened and wondering if I should tell my mom because they only knew what had been done to Patty, and it might be important. I decided that I should, went out to the living room, and told my mom that something had happened to me too. I told her the story, and I remember that she eventually told me to go back to bed, but I don't remember her saying anything significant or having a particular reaction. Dad was already after the friend for what he had done to Patty, so maybe my addition didn't really matter. That "friend" disappeared, and my dad was never able to find him again. We didn't call the police this time. Nobody talked to me or asked me about it, and life in the family moved on like nothing had ever happened. Unfortunately, I was mentally and emotionally scarred from the incident, blaming myself and beginning to feel what would be a lifetime of self-loathing. It didn't help that the only explanation my mother ever gave me for a man doing things like that to a little girl is that I was "sexy." I was seven years old.

I developed very confusing feelings about sex as I got older and couldn't understand why its desire made people do bad things to people that didn't want them to. The incidents never stopped until I became old enough and powerful enough to fight off most of the advances. I was never able to have a fully healthy sex life even after several rounds of therapy as an adult until my current marriage. After fifteen years of marital happiness, however, my mother was able to rip open the scars of this incident by telling everyone in my family what a great guy the "friend" had been and how much he had helped our family—yes, the one who molested me. Sadly, it was only a short time before I experienced another inappropriate and potentially dangerous encounter with another child molester at this place.

I was friends with a girl who lived one street over, and I was allowed to go and visit her on my own. She had a very nice two-story home that was unlike the others in the neighborhood. She had a playhouse in the backyard, and her sister had a pet baby skunk, which I thought was incredible! Her mother also had a mynah bird that talked, and that was pretty amazing too. One day, my friend wanted to walk down her street to visit another friend, so I went with her. We ended up in a little cinder block house that was dark and somehow creepy, although I can't say why. Her friend was a grown man who was wearing a bathrobe, and we were the only ones there. I was very uncomfortable and wanted to leave immediately, but my friend seemed very comfortable and cheerful to be there. They chatted with each other for a minute, while we girls took a seat on the couch. Then the man sat on a barstool in front of us and let his robe fall open, fully exposing his penis. I immediately ran out the door and back down the road. My friend caught up to me, frantically asking me what was wrong. I tried to explain that her friend shouldn't be showing us his penis, and I don't remember exactly what she said, but she seemed completely unaware or okay with that man's behavior, and I certainly was not. I never played with her anymore, but it was time to move again anyway.

My mom had become friends with a neighbor named Juanita, who encouraged Mom to go out for drinks while Dad was gone on the road. During one of these outings, Mom met a military officer named Frank, and they developed feelings for each other. I don't know how serious or physical their relationship became before my dad found out, and Dan and I have differences of opinion on when he found out. We got moved out of the house before school started, and Mom was extremely excited about where we were moving to next. I wonder if it was because she thought the move would put her marriage back together and protect it from this new intruder. We have a home movie of us moving out of Grove Street. The older boys are moving the furniture out, taking time to flip off the camera when they can, and then Mom is locking up the house to leave for the last time. That's the last thing that I remember about Grove Street and continued on with what was to be the first worst year of my life.

CHAPTER 29

"Don't Pull Your Love" (Hamilton, Joe Frank & Reynolds)

We moved to an apartment complex on Cunningham Drive by the Hampton Coliseum about six miles inland from Grove Street in a different part of town than we had ever lived in before. They were the Riverdale Apartments at the time, but I believe they are called the Peninsula Grove Apartments now. We spent the day getting moved out and in, and Mom had a new living room suite delivered to the new apartment that day, perhaps another way of starting anew. The couch was a large sectional that was gold crushed velvet, with back cushions that had a floral pattern. There was also a matching oversized chair and a huge square coffee table with a black top being the only part not covered in the same crushed velvet. It's the kind of style that we laugh at now as being part of the tacky, wacky 1970s, but it was good quality and at the top of the popular chart at the time. Furniture was a big deal to my folks, and they liked to have nice pieces when they could afford it. They would never leave the plastic on to keep it nice, like many people did in those days, but they would keep us kids off it or make sure everyone was on their best behavior when they used it. I still cringe when I see people putting their shoes on furniture or not using a coaster to put a drink on a table due to my folks' strict rules growing up.

We hadn't even put the beds together or unpacked much on that first day, so I was sleeping on a mattress on the floor in my bedroom along with my sister. My brother and my folks were doing the same in their rooms. John was spending the night, but I'm not sure if anyone else was there, and I don't know where they would have been sleeping. I awoke to a strange noise and lay there trying to figure out what it was until I realized it was Mom saying "John" over and over again in a very hoarse voice. Apparently, my mom needed his help. I didn't see or hear anything else that night, or if I did, I don't remember. Apparently, my dad had his hands around my mom's neck because he was angry about her relationship with Frank. I can't say how he found out or when. Maybe my mom had just confessed to him. Dan didn't think that Mom was dating Frank yet, and that wasn't why Dad was choking her, but I can't imagine what else it could have been. I don't think he was truly choking her, or she wouldn't have been able to speak, but obviously he had his hands on her throat in a very menacing way. John somehow intervened, and the incident was over. The next day, Dad was gone on the truck, and the mood among the adults was very tense.

Nobody said anything about what happened, except for me, apparently. I must have said something to the kids in my new neighborhood about what happened because I was told by my parents not to ever speak about our family matters or anything that happened in our home. My guess is that my sister found out or overheard me and told my parents what I had done. In spite of all the craziness I could have talked about to anyone outside our home, this is the first time I remember being told not to and being made to feel bad about it. It brought a great deal of guilt and shame to me, which began to make me very angry, although I didn't realize it for many years. It also started my behavior of being two different people—the good girl to the outside world, who didn't have anything wrong with her or her life, and the angry girl at home living her real life, which was full of problems.

Dan showed up that day, and Mom told him that my dad had left the order that he couldn't stay with us because he hadn't helped us move. Mom had sold the dishwasher Dan bought her with his Social Security money because this apartment came with one, so he asked if he could have that money so he could get a place to stay, and Mom gave it to him. He rented an upstairs studio apartment on Buckroe Avenue by the beach. Sam moved in with him about a week later and Patty about a week after that. John stayed with us at our new apartment for a little while, then moved to Buckroe himself. Sam got a pet boa constrictor snake that he named Acid and kept in a large tank at their apartment. Dan didn't want the snake to stay there at first but then got used to it. He said that the snake loved to smoke pot and would crawl up to the top of the tank every time they were smoking it. They would hold a joint up to the snake, and he would breathe in the smoke. Dan said this was where they lived when he got the nickname Alice, which I don't remember. Two of the Mob brothers Wayne and Gary's dad took all the guys to see the movie *Dirty Harry* at the New Market theater in Newport News, and when the character, a guy named Alice, was on the screen, Wayne yelled out that Alice was Dan, so that became his nickname.

The kids were in their apartment on Buckroe Avenue for two months, and then they moved around the corner on Fourth Street to another upstairs apartment. They moved the snake with them, but Dan came home one day and found him dead after he had been sick for a while, so he skinned it and tacked it to the wall. Patty brought a girl named Faye to the old apartment the night they were moving out. Faye and Sam hit it off right away. Then the boys didn't pay their rent at this apartment, so the landlord put a lock on the door. Dan, Sam, and Patty moved in to the place John was now renting with a friend, located in the alley between Fourth and Fifth Streets. Sam wanted his footlocker full of his precious record albums that was now locked in the apartment, so Dan, Mob member Alan, and another guy broke in one night, got the footlocker out, and put it in John's car that they had borrowed. The cops showed up, and Alan and the other guy parked the car right next to John's house and took off running, while Dan ran and hid in a magnolia tree, watching the cops look for the thieves. They knocked on John's door, and Sam answered it. He had obviously been sleeping, but when the cops asked who broke into the apartment, Sam knew that Dan had been planning on breaking in, so he covered for him and said he did. They took him to jail but didn't charge him and let him go.

I started the third grade in school, and the only thing I remember about this school is when our class had a special visitor one day, who told us we would be living in space by the time we were adults. He showed us a model of the spacecraft we would be living in, which reminded me of the carriers they use in the pneumatic tubes at the bank drive-through. Fifty years later, we're still trying to figure it out.

After only a month or two, my parents separated, and my mom moved in with Frank, leaving our family for the first of many times. We kids were devastated about Mom leaving. We had never been away from her before. Dad wouldn't let my mom have custody of us kids and even threatened to kill her if she ever tried to take his kids. However, he couldn't take care of us himself, being a long-distance truck driver, so he packed us up, and we headed about five hundred miles north to Groton, Connecticut, to live with my aunt Ruth, her husband, Paul, and my cousin Vickie. Paul was stationed in Groton in the Navy, and they lived on the naval base there. I remember that the houses were one-story row houses, all white with black trim. The neighborhood was laid out with sidewalks and a lot of common green space. I adored my aunt Ruth, and she was always good to me. She made us hot chocolate from scratch, cream puffs, and cinnamon toast, which were all things that Mom didn't make, so they were novel and special. Her daughter, Vickie, did not get along with us kids. She did better with my sister than with my brother and me, but even their relationship was tenuous. I have to say, though, to the family's credit, they always made me feel welcome in their home and not like I was a burden that had been placed on them. I will always be grateful to them because it was a painful situation for us kids to be in, and we needed all the love, kindness, and acceptance that we could get at the time. We enrolled in school there, but I don't really remember anything about it.

It just so happened that Paul was getting a new duty station in Mystic, Connecticut, about eight miles east, so we were only in Groton for a short time. Aunt Ruth found a big Victorian house for us all to live in that was much more spacious than the Navy housing in Groton. I thought this house was so beautiful, and I always felt like a wealthy princess when we lived in a two-story house. Looking back, I realize that the house wasn't the mansion I thought it was at the time, but it was very nice. It had a large front porch, living room, dining room, and kitchen on the ground level, and the second story had four bedrooms. One for Ruth and Paul, one for my dad, one for my brother, and the largest room for us three girls. We girls' favorite indoor activity was playing with paper dolls. We got an allowance every week and bought as many new paper dolls as we could find. Before long, we had enough to allow all the dolls to hold hands across the entire length of that bedroom. There was also a partially finished basement in the house, but I didn't like going down there because it was creepy. There was a small tree in the backyard just big enough for us to swing from a branch and do our bar acrobatics.

I remember the school here fondly. The cafeteria had wonderful food, including yeast rolls, which were and still are one of my favorite foods. At recess after lunch, we could buy an ice cream bar. The building was a large, old stone structure that I loved, and the library had lots of nooks and crannies and even a small, somewhat hidden staircase up to another level. I remember gathering in that library and sitting on the floor while they wheeled in a television set for us to watch whatever space mission was occurring at the time.

I had no knowledge of this next incident at the time, but it would become a family legend. At some point during my parents' separation, while Mom was living with Frank, John and Dad were on the road together and got into one hell of a fight. In a roadside bar in Crossville, Tennessee, that offered semi-truck parking, John was trying to find the song "Satisfied Mind" on the jukebox for Dad, which was one of his favorites. John and Dad had been playing pool in the hall separated from the bar by batwing doors after having to win the table from some jerk. He obviously didn't take losing well because now the jerk was at the jukebox giving John crap and telling him to hurry up and get out of his way.

When John returned to the pool table, Dad asked him what happened, and he told him, so Dad went up to the guy and asked what his problem was. He said he didn't like hippies. Dad said John took a bath every day and worked hard, so he wasn't really a hippie. The jerk then said, "I think he's a queer." When John heard that, he jumped for the guy, who took out a knife and sliced across John's stomach, luckily only cutting his shirt. Dad broke a pool stick over the guy's head, and the guy's brothers and father came in the room, so Dad started hitting them with the pool stick too.

When the father took out a gun, Dad took the gun out of the guy's hand and threw it across the room and then beat the crap out of the guy, not realizing that he had been shot. John was fighting too and had his nose broken. Another guy picked up the gun from earlier and held it on Dad, who told him he was stupid, and the guy decided to put the gun down. Dad and John then tried to leave the bar, but the original jukebox jerk started throwing pool balls at them. Dad told him that he would eventually run out of balls, and then Dad was going to kill him, which Dad proceeded to do by repeatedly banging the guy's head into the wall, but John talked him into stopping, thank God. Dad and John then left the scene and headed to the hospital, where Dad got stitches in his head from some blow during the fight, and John had his nose set.

Seven of the people they were fighting ended up in the hospital, and the father was in critical condition. While Dad and John were still at the hospital, the cops came to take them to jail, but while en route, John noticed blood on Dad's pants from a wound on his leg, and they were taken back into the hospital, where they examined the wound more closely. They said Dad had taken a bullet, which had gone right through, and treated it with antiseptic and a bandage. They were then taken to jail and held to see if the man in critical condition was going to die, at which time Dad would be charged with murder. Dad said, "If he don't die, it ain't my fault, because I damn sure tried to kill him." They were allowed to shower and were treated well and were eventually released. Apparently, this group of guys were real troublemakers in the area. The cops advised Dad and John to file charges against the shooter, which they did, and Dad's pants were taken for evidence. Dad didn't get charged with anything. Instead, he was praised. We don't know what ever happened with the bad guys and the charges that were brought against them.

The Smith kids were living the Buckroe Beach Alley life the whole time we were in Connecticut. Dan met a gal named Alice there, who was dating a guy about two houses down from his place on Buckroe Avenue. Patty and Alice became fast friends, and the two of them ran around pretty wild. They hitchhiked everywhere and got in cars with guys, and they also broke into houses and stole things, but they got lucky and never got into any trouble. When Dan started dating Alice, they rented a trailer together with Patty and her boyfriend at the time, Brian. Dan and Alice had a volatile relationship for a few months mostly because Alice liked to hang out with other guys and was very independent, although she was still a virgin. Dan said that he left her virginity intact and that it was one of the few times he was a gentleman.

Meanwhile, it wasn't a bad life for me there in Mystic, but after a month or so, I was getting really sad and depressed from missing my mom, much more so than my brother and sister were. I finally got up the courage to ask my dad if I could go back and live with her. It was really difficult because I had a strong sense of loyalty to my dad, and I didn't want him to think that I loved Mom more than him. If I could have had Dad around all the time, it might have been different, but he was always gone on the truck, and I guess I really needed at least one parent at the time. He was understanding and arranged to have my uncle Paul take me down to Hampton. The only thing I remember about the trip was stopping at a travel center, much nicer than the usual truck stops I was used to, and getting a toy out of a machine. It was a little pink plastic elephant, whose legs walked when you pulled a string attached to the front of his head. I don't remember staying at a motel on the trip, so he probably drove the ten hours straight through, which was always the custom in our family.

Mom was living in the same apartment complex we had been in, only this time with her boyfriend, Frank. I don't remember much about Frank or living there this time, except that he was nice, and he let me eat a whole can of peanuts once, which made me throw up. I went back to my old school again, which was number four for this third-grade year. Once, Sam came over to visit, and he brought his now girlfriend Faye to meet us. This was really significant because Sam didn't have a lot of girlfriends. Sam was eighteen at the time, and Faye was fourteen. Shortly after, they convinced her parents to let them get married. They found out that a girl could be married in the state of South Carolina at the age of fourteen, with her parents' permission. Had she been pregnant, they could have been married in Virginia without her parents' permission. I don't know any of the details, especially because we weren't around at the time, but they got married, and she became Aunt Faye.

Mom and I only stayed there with Frank for a short time, and one day, she told me that Dad was coming to pick us up in a couple of hours and that I needed to pack all my things. I was shocked but so happy that my parents were reuniting. He came to get us in a car, and we must have been short on space because I had to leave behind my Easy-Bake Oven. I can still remember how sad I was, looking out the back window at my little oven sitting next to the patio all by itself. But I had more important things to think about on the long drive back up north because we were going back to Connecticut, this time with Mom.

We stayed in the big house with everyone through at least Christmas. I enrolled back in school, which was the fifth one for that third grade, and we were only halfway through the school year. We had the best Christmas of my life that year, probably due to my aunt Ruth. My parents had never cared about or honored holidays much, so they never tried to make them really special. This year, however, was awesome, and we captured it with our home movie camera. Mom put all of us girls in pin curls on Christmas Eve, so we had beautiful, bouncy curls the next morning. We four kids sat at the dining room table and were each given one of those plastic stockings with stuff already inside to keep us happy until the adults drank their coffee and finished watching *Jeopardy!*, one of my dad's favorites. We finally got to open our presents, and we each got tons of toys, my favorite being a Barbie Beach Bus. We played a lot with Barbie dolls, and each of us girls got a new one. Paula got a Barbie Townhouse, and Vickie got a Barbie Airplane. We were very blessed and very grateful.

Back in Hampton, Dan decided he didn't want to be with Alice anymore, and he wanted to come up to Connecticut to stay with us for a while. He and John were at a party at Gary's house, one of the Mafia, and Dan told John he was leaving. At that same time, Alice was talking shit about Dan in the other room, and Dan went in the room where she was sitting on an ottoman, kicked her in the head, and left. He obviously really needed to get away from her, so that night, John took him to the bus station and put him on a bus to Connecticut. He stayed in the basement at the big house we all shared for a little while. He said he used to watch those old stag movies that my dad had while he was down there.

One night, while he was in the basement and was huffing paint, he heard Ruth and Paul come home. He overheard them arguing in the kitchen because Paul found out Ruth hadn't been paying the bills while he was gone. Ruth told Paul that Mom and Dad hadn't paid the rent, which Dan knew wasn't true. Dan came upstairs and told Paul that Ruth was lying. Mom and Dad heard the argument and came downstairs to join the discussion. Things got heated, and Paul acted like he was going to fight Dad, which would have been laughable. Paul put his fists up and told Ruth to hold him back, like he needed to be stopped from hurting Dad. When she didn't respond, he looked back at her and asked again, with more urgency to hold him back. Dad, Mom, and Dan just laughed at him, and the situation calmed down, but we ended up leaving the house the next day after Mom found us an apartment in Norwich about fifteen miles north of Mystic.

We learned from Aunt Ruth after we had moved away that one of the boys we used to play with fell through the ice at the pond that all the neighborhood kids would skate on down at the end of our road, and he drowned. That tragedy stuck with me and taught me a lesson. My folks had forbidden we kids to skate on any frozen ponds, which was a common activity in Connecticut but one that we weren't used to. We three kids were often in the position of getting left out of potentially dangerous activities that other kids were doing, but I'm grateful that my parents protected us in some ways at least. Mom and Dad were also really strict about letting us go swimming with anyone, which was also probably a good thing since I almost drowned once when John took us kids to some muddy swimming hole at some point in the future.

CHAPTER 30

"Seasons in the Sun"

(Terry Jacks)

Dan helped us move into our new apartment close to downtown Norwich. It was so different from any place we were used to living, and we all loved it! The apartment was on the second floor above an appliance store with a staircase up to the place at the front and direct access at the back because the building was built into a hill. There was another apartment above us, which was accessed from a staircase in the back. It was a turn-of-the-century building with lots of character. Our apartment was very large and had pocket doors opening into a formal living room, where Mom was so happy to display her beloved crushed velvet furniture and relegate it to special occasions, like she had always wanted. She would call us kids in there at night before bed and read to us from a book of Bible stories. We loved it.

The apartment had four bedrooms, so each of us kids had our own room for the first time in our lives. I guess the place needed some TLC, including new paint, so Mom let us pick our own paint colors for our rooms. Each bedroom had a fireplace, but we never used them, and my sister and I had an adjoining door between our rooms. I thought all these architectural details and idiosyncrasies were magical! We had a boy who lived on the third floor that was close to us in age. We played with him, and we walked to school together in the cold wind, ice, and snow; and yes, it was uphill. There weren't any other kids close by, but the four of us had a great time playing in the empty lot next to our building, which had a steep incline. It was completely iced over while we were there, and we loved to slide down that hill on pieces of cardboard and other stuff. We would start at the top of the hill from the back of our building, slide down, then use our front stairs and cut through our house to get back out back again. Fun times! There was a little pizza joint across the street, and we kids were allowed to go there, if we were together, to play pinball and listen to the jukebox. There was also a library a couple blocks away in a beautiful, old, ornate building, and Mom would take us there to pick out books. I don't remember my school here, which was number 6 for this year, but I really loved our apartment, our neighborhood, and our way of life. As always, it wasn't meant to last.

CHAPTER 31

"I Fought the Law"

(The Bobby Fuller Four)

Dan was still staying with us in Norwich when he decided to make a trip on the truck with Dad because Dad was going to Hampton. Faye's parents, Bess and Sarge, happened to be taking Sam and Faye to get married in South Carolina while they were there, so they offered to let Dad and Dan to stay at their house while they were gone. Before they got to Hampton, they had stopped in Yorktown at the home of Susanne, Faye's sister, and her husband, Rick. Dad had let Dan drive the truck all the way from Connecticut to Yorktown for the very first time, and they were both pleased with his performance. They decided to leave Dad's semi at Rick and Susanne's house and rode back to Hampton with them since they were going anyway. When they got to Hampton, they started partying with Rick and Susanne at her parents' house, and Dan gave Dad a joint laced with angel dust. Dad never did this type of drug, and he ended up passed out at Bess and Sarge's house, and nobody could wake him when it was time to go back with Rick and Susanne to Yorktown and get his truck. Dan decided to go with them and bring the truck back by himself, even though he had only driven it once before, and left Dad there passed out.

He made it back to Hampton in the truck just fine, picked up some of his friends, and was on his way to Bess and Sarge's house when the truck began to spit and sputter. He ended up pulling it into a parking lot, where he got the truck started again. He couldn't back the truck to get it back out of the parking lot, so he decided to pull it forward instead into someone's yard, where he stopped it between a telephone pole and their house up against the front steps. When the man came out of his house to see what was going on, Dan told him that the truck was out of fuel, and he would go get fuel and come back. Dan wasn't worried about the guy calling the police because he had torn the phone lines down with the truck. Dan didn't have any money and didn't know what to do, so he and his friends walked back to Buckroe and partied some more. He somehow met up with Gary, one of the Mafia, and asked Gary to drive him by the man's house to see if the truck was still there, and it wasn't. Dan finally went back to Bess and Sarge's house, where Dad was still passed out, so he slept too until Dad woke him up and said, "Let's go get the truck." Dan told him the story of what he had done with the truck, and Dad called the police and reported it stolen. The police were skeptical that the truck had been stolen. They thought that Dad must have been the one to leave the truck where it was found because only a professional could have put the truck where they found it. The cops did allow them to get the truck out of impound with Dan's last paycheck that he had picked up from his last job in Hampton, and Dad went back to Connecticut, while Dan stayed in Hampton.

Dan was staying in Buckroe with a friend named Steve, who had a place on First Street. One night, they had been huffing paint all night. They were hungry and didn't have any money, so they broke into Sarge and Bess's house, who were still in South Carolina getting Sam and Faye married, to get some food. They got the food, Steve grabbed some guns out of the house, and Dan took Sarge's boots that were sitting on the back porch. They had the guns at Steve's place, about three blocks down from Sarge and Bess's. When they got home from the wedding and discovered the robbery, they went right to

Dan; even Sam questioned him. Dan denied it, but later that day, he tried to sell one of the guns for some weed and discovered that they were all gone. Steve had given all the guns back to the cops after he, as a redhead, had been identified as one of the robbers. He told Dan everything was going to be okay since he gave all the guns back.

The next day or maybe the same day, Dan decided he better get out of town, so he and another friend, named Terry, stole a car in Hampton and took off for Maryland. They stopped at a gas station on Route 17 outside of Fort Royal to get a soda out of a machine and decided to break in and take the money out of it. They were seen by someone, so they took off in the car. Driving away in the dark, a car was coming up behind them, so they assumed it was a cop and accelerated up to 100 mph, then tried to turn down a road and missed it, so they stopped and ditched the car and took off running. It was the cops after them, and they gave chase along with a dog. Dan was a crazy fast runner with a long endurance, and he outran them. After several hours, he finally got tired and lay down in a field. He woke up with the German Shepherd licking his ear and an officer standing by. He was taken into custody. He and Terry were both in jail in Bowling Green for two weeks. Since Terry stole the car, Dan was only charged with joyriding.

Back in Hampton, however, Steve had turned Dan in for Sarge's theft, so he got sent back to Hampton to face those charges. Since he thought he was going down for stealing from Sarge anyway, he confessed to stealing the car rather than letting Terry get the charge. So he was locked up for grand theft auto and for stealing from Sarge. After serving twenty days, Dan was approached by a detective who told him he could get out of jail if he would agree to snitch for him. Although he had no intention to snitch, Dan agreed and went to trial for grand theft auto for the second time in his life and was sentenced to his twenty days served because the authorities thought they had a bigger fish with the gun theft.

Sometime after he was released, he was walking on the beach and saw Sarge in his yard. Dan was trying to ignore him, but Sarge kept yelling for him to come and talk to Sam on the phone from California. Sam and Faye had moved to Porterville at about the same time Dan went to jail. They stayed with Dean until they got on their feet and were only there for probably six months. Dan went over to the house and talked to Sam on the phone. Bess then served him a meal, and she and Sarge were both real friendly to him. Dan then decided to hitchhike back to Maryland and take his chances with the trial there instead of sticking around and snitching for the detective in Hampton. He stayed with us in Aberdeen, where we had relocated to from Connecticut. He did go back to Hampton after about two weeks for his trial, however, where he was admonished for leaving and not helping the detective. He was accompanied at his trial by Alice, with whom he stayed in the alley for the two days before his court date. He was convicted of the theft at Sarge's and put in jail for two months to wait for his sentence. At the trial, Sarge was asked how he knew Dan was the one who broke into his house and stole from him. Sarge replied that Dan was actually wearing his boots from his house at the time.

CHAPTER 32

"The Happiest Girl in the Whole USA"

(Donna Fargo)

We had moved from Norwich back to my folks' old stomping grounds of Aberdeen, Maryland, roughly three hundred miles south. Mom and I traveled in the car together and rented a two-bedroom house in Swan Meadows because there were no three-bedroom homes available at the moment. Swan Meadows is a neighborhood of tract homes built in the 1940s to house soldiers stationed at the Aberdeen Proving Ground, the front gate to which is about one mile away. It wasn't as nice and middle class as Holly Homes back in Virginia. The homes were more military-style housing with a mix of free-standing two-bedroom houses and mostly duplex two or three-bedroom houses. They all looked exactly alike and attracted more of a lower-middle-class population. Everybody called it the Projects, but we kids called it heaven! Dad, Paula, and Tommy followed Mom and me down in the truck with our household goods, and Mom got us enrolled at Halls Cross Roads Elementary, which was just across the street from Swan Meadows and close enough to walk. I spent the last couple months of my third grade year there, which was the seventh school I attended that year.

Our friends Ersel and Shirley and their kids that we stayed with at the boarding house a few years earlier lived across from our little house on Liberty Street. We were close to them any time we lived in the area. There was another good family that lived a few houses away, Lawrence and his wife, nicknamed Beanie, and their six children, I believe it was. Beanie always talked about being a Pollack and told Pollack jokes. Nobody ever uses that word now. She and Lawrence and all their kids were always good to us. They had one boy and twin girls who were quite a bit older than me, about like the Smith kids. I thought he was so handsome, and the girls were beautiful, all with blonde hair. Then they had three girls around mine and Paula's ages, one of whom was in my class.

There was something very distinctive about one of the older twin girls. She was in a romantic relationship with a young man who was black, making theirs the first interracial relationship I had ever witnessed. I think it was a fairly new relationship when we moved there, and Lawrence was having a really difficult time dealing with it, sometimes raging about it when he was drunk. There was a lot of talk about it among the neighborhood adults, like what they would do if it were *their* daughter who did something like that. I don't think we kids really cared about it. As for me, I found it interesting more than anything. The young man in question was a really good guy by everyone's account, who managed to keep the peace with all involved without losing his self-respect. He eventually won the day and won the girl, and they got married, then started having children.

I wasn't conscious of it at the time, but I was beginning to show pent-up anger at everything that had happened to me since the molestation on Grove Street. I had been through hell with the abuse, relocations, living with another family, being separated from our mother, and the insecurity of not knowing whether our parents would get back together again. My folks never seemed to understand how their behavior and actions affected us, so life just went on as if nothing traumatic had happened. My anger came to light in a disturbing way right at the end of the school year, but first, I have to explain how I acquired the weapon I used.

During the few months that we were in the two-bedroom house on Liberty Street, waiting for a three-bedroom to open up, we went to visit my dad's older brother, Emmett, who lived about twelve miles south in Joppatowne, Maryland. Emmett was married to Gaye, and they had one daughter, Sharon. Sharon had one child at the time, a daughter named Alyce. Dad really looked up to his older brother Emmett and Gaye as well. I've already spoken about how they had been good to him when he was a child, buying him his one and only Christmas gift and showing him a better way of life to look forward to once he could leave his parents' home.

This was the first time we kids had met these family members, at least that we remembered. We loved this family, and we always enjoyed going to their house. Aunt Gaye had fun toys, like a giant dollhouse, and they lived on several acres out in the country, where we loved to run around. Emmett had a large concrete porch in front of his house, which was four feet high and didn't have a railing. We kids were always running, tumbling, and doing gymnastics, and I had recently seen some girls doing cartwheels off a porch, which I wanted to try. They put their hands down near the edge of the porch and let their legs fly over and onto the ground. I should have run it by my sister first. With my dad and uncle sitting on the porch, watching us kids run around the yard, I decided to try that move, but I had forgotten exactly how the maneuver was performed and really didn't think it through. Before anyone could stop me, I threw myself hands first off the porch, straight into the ground, and landed hard, primarily on my left wrist.

I lay on the ground in a bit of a heap with my left arm beneath me. My bewildered dad and uncle commented on how crazy my stunt was and then began to ask if I was okay when I didn't get back up. I told them I was fine and that I just wanted to lie there for a minute. They gave me a minute or two, and then Dad came over and lifted me up off the ground. When my left arm was revealed, it shocked everyone who saw it, including me. Dad said, "Sis, it looks like you broke your arm, honey."

I asked, "Are you sure?"

To which he replied, "Oh yes, I'm sure."

There couldn't be any doubt. Dad best described how my arm looked when he said it looked like a motorcycle tire ran over it. It was elongated, and a section of my wrist hung down below the rest of my arm. It was really grotesque.

I was a tough-as-nails kid, as were my brother and sister. I rarely went in the house after a long day of playing without some sort of injury. I could take a strong punch or kick and had a high pain tolerance. I don't remember my arm really hurting at all, and I didn't cry until Dad said I would have to go to the hospital to have it fixed. I didn't like that idea at all. They made a sling for me with a dish towel, and I rode on Dad's lap while Mom drove us to the hospital emergency room. We didn't have to wait long to be seen, and we were taken to a room where I laid on the bed and noticed the Disney character stickers on the wall. I can remember Bambi, specifically. After the examination, the doctor told me that he was going to fix my arm and put it back where it belonged. He held my left wrist and told me to look at the characters on the wall to my right. He then snapped my arm back into place, which hurt tremendously, but the pain was over so quickly that I didn't even get upset. They put me in a cast that went from the top of my fingers to over my elbow and about halfway up my arm and sent us home.

I had trouble trying to learn to write and eat and do everything with my right hand given that I was left-handed. I became pretty good at it, and as a result, I am partially ambidextrous to this day. I eat and write with my left hand now, but I bat, bowl, and throw with my right. However, I play a guitar with my left or have at least attempted it. I finished out the school year wearing the cast, and people had to help me carry things like my lunch tray until I became more adept. I had a little boyfriend in my class named Denny, whose hair was almost as long as mine, which fell to my waist. He was kind of a troublemaker but was really a sweetheart.

Denny came to our house to visit me one day after school, and we talked and played in the front yard. At some point, Mom looked outside and found me wailing on Denny's head with my cast, while he just stood there and didn't even run away or defend himself. She ran outside, yelling for me to stop. I didn't stop until she grabbed my arm and pulled me away from Denny. She was asking me things like, "What are you doing, and what is wrong with you?" She asked Denny if he was okay, and he said he was. She apologized and sent him home, then took me in the house and began to question me about my behavior. I remember being furious and having a hard time calming down. I gave her some explanation about something Denny had said to me. I don't remember what it was, but it didn't make any sense. He hadn't insulted me or said anything to warrant my behavior. I believe that I had latent anger at my parents for the situation they had placed me in for the past nine months, and I took it out on poor Denny.

From that point on, I had a real temper and developed a dual personality, which my mom equated to the "little girl with the curl in the middle of her forehead," from a poem by Henry Wadsworth Longfellow. I was usually very, very good and the sweetest kid that Mom had. Sometimes, however, I was very, very bad and the worst kid that Mom had. It took me until I was sixteen years old to make a conscious decision to change that behavior, and since that time, I have only been really angry a handful of times. When that anger surfaces, however, it is lethal, and I feel quite out of control, but it is always a verbal response and never physical.

You would never guess that I had that temper if you saw me in a home movie we took right after breaking my arm. I look like a sweet girl, smiling for the camera, then getting a drink of water from a fountain by the baseball diamond at the front of Swan Meadows. The real purpose of the movie—taking place that day was the baseball game Dad was playing in, with a team of all his buddies from the Village Hut Bar and Restaurant. They were taking on a team from another local bar. We have lots of shots of the game, which I think they won, along with all the family members on the bleachers cheering them on. John was in town and playing for the team as well. The Hut, as it came to be known, was an old hangout of Dad's since it was the Aberdeen Restaurant back when my folks first got together. Now it was owned by one of Dad's best friends in life, Wendell. It was located on Route 40 right next to the railroad tracks. It had a strong, loyal crowd but also attracted a lot of soldiers from the Proving Ground along with people passing through town on Route 40. It wasn't fancy, but it wasn't terrible either. Mom and especially Dad would spend a lot of time in that place from then on anytime we lived in Aberdeen.

Wendell was divorced from a wealthy woman who lived in Delaware, and they had three children. The eldest was a girl that we would not see as often, and the two younger ones were boys, who liked to visit their dad on weekends on a regular basis. They were Jeff and Eric, and we kids loved them. Jeff was Paula's age, and Eric was a couple years older. I think they welcomed having a somewhat normal family with kids around in their father's world when they were visiting him, rather than just the adult bar scene. From what I could tell, everything revolved around the bar, with Wendell even living in the apartment upstairs. It seemed crazy exciting to me, but I can see where it would get old after a while. We would end up spending a lot of time together with Jeff and Eric, and I have such fond memories of them. The three gentlemen hold a special place in my heart, and I have had a lifelong friendship with them. Kids were allowed in bars in Maryland, if accompanied by a parent, and we kids spent quite a few days hanging out there at the Hut with the boys. There was a shuffleboard game we could play, and we could eat bar food, like burgers. It was really tame in the day but was a totally different story at night.

I only went in there once at night myself. It was actually a couple years later when we kids and the boys went into town to check out the traveling carnival. We had a lot more freedom when we were with them because they were older, and Eric was very responsible. The boys walked to our house and got us, then we stopped in the Hut for spending money from the parents and continued on into town to the carnival. When we had our fill, we walked back to the Hut to tell the parents that the boys were walking us kids back home. We all walked in together, looking for our folks in the crowd, but couldn't help but notice a topless dancer on a little platform behind the bar, gyrating to Elton John's "Bennie and the Jets." Whoa! Wendell didn't always have dancers in there, but he did that night. Eric and Jeff seemed pretty indifferent to the pretty brunette. Tommy and I were both fascinated, and Paula was offended and wouldn't look. My mom found us right away and hustled us back out the door and onto the sidewalk, and we left to go home. That was the only experience I had in person in the Hut, but I feel like I know it so well from the tons of stories I heard all during my childhood and beyond.

CHAPTER 33

"The Streak"

(Ray Stevens)

I can't stress enough how much we kids absolutely loved living in Swan Meadows. That summer was some of the most fun I've had in my life and is what I would call the quintessential perfect childhood for the most part. We would wake in the morning, have breakfast, get dressed, and then head out to play. We had the freedom to roam the neighborhood of about half a mile by a quarter mile on foot or on a bike as long as we weren't alone. We had access to a playground, baseball diamond, basketball court, and tons of green space in the backyards of the homes, where we could play ball games and others like Red Rover, Simon Says, and Red Light Green Light. We had all the playmates we could ever want, and we stayed out for hours, with instructions to be back at noon for lunch. After lunch, we were right back out for more fun, and we knew we had to come home before dark. It got scary when it was getting dark anyway because bats would come out and fly around, threatening to get too close and get tangled in our hair. After returning home to our own yards, we chased fireflies until Mom called us in for dinner. After dinner, we would wash off the layer of dirt we always acquired in the tub and then gather in the living room for TV watching. Our neighborhood was also perfect for the ice cream man, because we could hear his bell and the music that he played no matter where he was or where we were. Whether we were home or out and about, our reaction was always the same- we made a beeline for Mom, yelling "*Mom*, it's the ice cream man!" the entire time. Mom almost always indulged us and gave us money, along with her order. Then sometimes we had to *find* the ice cream man, because he may have relocated while we were getting money. We might have to run after the truck, praying he didn't leave us and our neighborhood behind before we could get our ice cream. We ran as fast as we could, with our arms flailing, yelling "Ice cream man!" as loud as we could, so he could hear us over his music.

As I mentioned earlier, Dan was released from jail in Hampton, and he hitchhiked down to Aberdeen, where he stayed with us for a few weeks. He met and became good friends with a guy named Charlie from the neighborhood, and the two of them spent a lot of time together. He decided to be in Hampton for his trial date, however, so he hitchhiked back down there but not before helping us move a little more than a stone's throw away to 7 Aberdeen Avenue, which had three bedrooms, so Paula and I didn't have to share a room with Tommy any longer. The family that shared our duplex had some sweet girls mine and Paula's ages, with whom we liked to play Barbies.

Although we were having great fun, us kids' behavior definitely began to change for the worse at this point. I literally got spanked every day that summer vacation, and it was usually because of something I said, not what I did. I had developed such a smart mouth and was always talking back to Mom, although I never tried that when Dad was home. Mom actually told me once that "I could spank you over and over. Heck, I could beat you into the ground, and as long as I left your lips hanging out, you would still be talking *shit*!" Although we had a great deal of freedom, Tommy would run off alone and stay gone rather than being in a group and checking in, and he got lots of spankings from Mom for that. I know she really worried when she didn't know where we were. Paula never got a spanking because she didn't get caught at what she did wrong. One time, she wanted to try smoking cigarettes, and her idea was that if she convinced Tommy and me to do it too, then we wouldn't tell on her, or we would get into trouble too. I remember that we waited until Mom left the house, then the three of us locked ourselves in the bathroom, at the open window, and tried a puff on a cigarette that Paula had stolen from Mom. I didn't like it at all. If only that feeling had lasted. After we each tried it, Paula sprayed a can of Right Guard deodorant to get rid of the smell.

One of the craziest things we three kids did a few times was to sneak over to what we called the jungle or the school woods. It was quite an adventure that took a lot of time, so we had to make sure we had plenty of time on the play clock. Tommy was usually the only one to run off without our parents knowing where we were, and I don't know how they would have found us if they tried.

We would walk to the edge of the Projects to Bel Air Avenue right across from Sid's Market. We had to sneak down the embankment next to the road to get access to the five-foot water drain pipe that went under Bel Air Avenue and sloped downward about one thousand feet long to the southeast. We always went in a good-sized group, maybe six to ten kids, and we didn't want to get caught because we obviously weren't allowed in there. It was considered *very* dangerous around the neighborhood, and it was said that bad people hung out down there, although I only ever saw maybe a teenaged boy down there sneaking a cigarette or a joint near the entrance. It was just a steel pipe with some kind of rocks in the bottom to slow down the water, which we found a little off, but nothing above ankle height. There were some rivets jutting out on the sides of the pipe that you could hit your head on if you lost your footing, but we never really got hurt. There was pretty good light in there because every so often, you would come across a grate in the ceiling. Somebody would usually have a lighter too, just in case. There were supposed to be rats in there, but I can't remember if I ever saw one or not, so there probably weren't because I wouldn't have liked that. The pipe traveled under the neighborhood, then down under Route 22 (the Aberdeen Throughway), and ended in the area we called the jungle or the school woods. There are some city industrial buildings there now, according to Google Maps, but I don't know if they were there at the time. If they were, we avoided them and headed through the mostly wild growth of about eight acres that we loved to explore. Some was woodsy and some marshy, and there were even cornfields for free food.

One time, in the marshy area, we came across tons of little bitty baby frogs, some as small as one-half inch. I have always, and still do, love frogs, and I also used to love miniature things, so these frogs were irresistible to me. I asked Paula if I should try and take one home, and she said it was worth a try, so I found a tiny one and held it in my hand for a while during our explorations. Then it occurred to me that the frog was taking up hardly any space in my hand, so I could fit a few more to take home with me as well. I started collecting them one by one and adding them to the others, trying to be sure and keep my hand loose enough to give them room but tight enough not to let them out. Probably an hour later, we decided to end our adventure and head back home through the jungle, through the tunnel, through a bit of the neighborhood, and to the house. When we were within sight of our house, I checked on my frogs, which I admit I had probably been neglecting, and I carefully opened up my hand. Paula looked with me, and what we saw was roughly the shape of a ball, with heads and hands and feet sticking out of it here and there. When I very carefully tried to separate them from one another, I wasn't having much success. I was crying and asked Paula if she thought we could save them, and she said she didn't think so. She convinced me to throw them in a trash can on the side of the road. I mourned those frogs and cursed my stupidity and cruelty for many years. My daughter likes to pretend to torment me for my evil frog ball incident because she says it's the total opposite of my nature to ever hurt another creature or even be thoughtless and irresponsible. I guess those poor frogs didn't die in vain.

Paula and I made friends with what ended up being a very special girl across the street named Tammy. Mom thought that Tammy's mother looked familiar when she would see her across the street, and one day, she finally asked Tammy what her mother's name was. When

Tammy answered Carol, Mom knew that her hunch that she knew her must have been right. We all went across the street for Mom to talk to Carol, and they rekindled their friendship from back before my parents had ever gotten together. This was the beautiful Carol that befriended the awkward teenage Mom and taught her how to dress, fix her hair, and dance. Mom was so, so excited to reunite with her old friend, and they spent a lot of time together.

Us kids had another adventure one afternoon when Mom had gone bowling with family friend Shirley, and Shirley had suggested that her teenage son Georgie babysit us kids. We had loved Georgie since we all lived in the boarding house together, so we were happy. We were hanging around the house, and at some point, a beautiful teenage girl named Anita showed up at our house to visit Georgie. I'm not sure if he had called her from our house or told her where he would be in advance or if it was complete coincidence that she spotted Georgie playing with us in the front yard while she was passing by. Georgie was not the most physically attractive guy, and he must have been over the moon to gain the attention of this beautiful girl.

I don't know how the subject came up, but after hanging out and playing in the yard for a little while, it was decided that we would all go streaking. It sounds totally crazy now, but streaking was really popular at the time. There was even a hit song written about it, "The Streak" by Ray Stevens. We ended up naked, the five of us, and wrapped in blankets. We went out back to the middle of the greenspace between the backyards, which offered a little more privacy than the front yard. I can't remember if we actually threw our blankets off or if we kind of held onto them like capes flapping behind us as we all ran through the field. I think we only did it once.

The next thing I remember, some of Georgie's teenage guy friends showed up at the house. Just as with Anita, I'm not sure how they arrived there. The teenagers all decided they were going to streak again. Tommy might have joined them, but Paula and I weren't going to be naked in front of Georgie's friends. Georgie was a different story; he was like a big brother. The teens all got naked, leaving separate piles of clothes on the back porch. While they commenced with the streaking, I thought it would be funny to hide their clothes from them. I took two piles, which belonged to two of the teenage guy friends, and searched for a place in the kitchen to hide them. I decided on the crisper drawer in the bottom of the refrigerator since it happened to be empty at the time. They would never think to look in there!

The next thing I knew, Mom and Shirley arrived home, and when they saw what was happening, they were shocked and livid. There was pandemonium as the teens all struggled to get back into their clothes while Mom and Shirley screamed at them. The friends that could find their clothes, including Anita, put them on and beat a hasty retreat. The other two poor souls searched all around the yard for theirs, and when it became obvious that this wasn't fun anymore, I went inside and got their clothes. While they were dressing and hightailing it away from the scene, Shirley had started to beat on Georgie while screaming obscenities at him. We had all heard stories about her beating him with belts, including the buckle end, and any other object that was handy to her, like a hairbrush. Mom pleaded with her to stop, telling her it wasn't that big a deal and not to punish him. We kids pleaded as well and kept saying it wasn't his fault, although it technically was, but he certainly didn't deserve this beating for it. She stopped long enough to get both of them in the car, but we saw her continuing to hit him as they drove away. I don't remember getting into real trouble for what happened, perhaps because Shirley's behavior had left such a sad, ugly pall over all of us.

CHAPTER 34

"The Boys Are Back in Town"

(Thin Lizzy)

Eventually, we were reunited with all the Smith kids here again. Patty had married Keith while we were still living in Connecticut. Dan hadn't made it back to Hampton from Connecticut in time to meet the groom or attend the wedding, but he heard rumors that Dusty tried to stop their wedding, telling Patty that she should marry him instead of Keith, and then later Dusty kicked Keith's ass. At any rate, the newlyweds were now at our place. Dan thought they might have gotten their own place in Maryland for a little while. Sam and Faye had come back from California to Hampton, and they were living in a trailer near Langley AFB on King Street. John had a trailer there as well until he decided to come to Maryland too, along with Alice.

Apparently, Alice and John became a couple while Dan was serving his two months in jail, waiting for his sentencing for stealing from Sarge. Sarge loved Dan for some reason and told the court that he wouldn't see Dan go to prison for the crime and the other guy,

Steve, get off scot-free when Steve was the one who actually took the guns. As a result, Dan was sentenced to seven years suspended and eighteenth months of probation after which he hitchhiked back to us in Aberdeen. When he saw Alice, he took her in the bedroom and started kissing her, and she kissed him back, but then she pulled away and said she should probably tell him that she was with John now, and Dan said he was cool with that.

Sometime while we were living here, John and Dan wanted to go out and huff some paint. Alice was always jealous of John spending time with anyone but her, so as the guys started walking down the street, she went out on the porch and yelled for John to get back to the house. Dan said something smart back to Alice, and she called him a simple bastard. Mom heard what Alice said from inside the house, and she knew Dan wasn't going to stand for it. She came out of the house just as Dan was walking over to confront Alice. Mom got between them and told Dan to cool it, but he was able to raise his foot up and kick Alice in the head, knocking her onto the ground. Nobody, not even John, would say anything to Dan about his behavior at that time because he was crazy. John just stayed in the road and didn't say a word, and then they went off and huffed their paint. I'm sure he had to pay for it with Alice later. John and Alice got a little apartment in Maryland for a while, and he was working at a boat-building place with family friend Lawrence.

While Dan was staying with us, our love/hate relationship became a little more hate, probably because of the newfound anger I was feeling. Mom used to ask him to babysit us, and he and I would fight a lot. I remember once that he picked me up by my arms in anger and swung me down off the porch, and I embellished to my folks that he pushed me off the porch. Nobody was ever allowed to hit us kids, but my parents didn't punish Dan for that act.

Another night, when Dan and Keith were left to babysit us while Mom was out, they decided/allowed me to get me drunk on beer. I really don't remember the exact circumstances, and Dan didn't either, but I was eight years old at the time. By the time Mom got home, I was wasted and out of control. She was really upset, but I don't remember there ever being any fallout for the guys, just me. It was past my bedtime, so she ordered me to bed, but I wouldn't stay there. I kept coming out to the living room and taunting her. I was having a great time, but I apparently called her ugly names. The next morning, I was throwing up and had a horrible headache. I tried more alcohol over time after that but usually in small quantities, and I've only been drunk a few times in my life, none anytime soon after this incident. I can't imagine this same scenario happening with my own daughter at eight years old, but the family treated it like it wasn't a big deal. Tommy was always stealing drinks of beer, but he only had a few sips at a time.

For some reason, my grandfather, Wade, came to visit us here for a short time. My mom was so excited that he was coming, and I couldn't understand why. Not only did he have a lifetime of a horrible reputation that he arrived with, but he still had absolutely nothing to offer. He didn't seem to enjoy Mom's company, and he certainly didn't like us kids. We had no desire to be around him either. I mostly remember being tortured by his naps. It was impossible to keep from waking him up from his multiple daily naps, and we weren't even in the house that much anyway, preferring to be outside playing. We had to be extremely quiet out there too. He would yell at Mom when we woke him up, and she would yell at us. Luckily, we didn't see him again for another five years.

My grandmother Ida would come and visit sometimes while I was growing up too, and in spite of her own hateful reputation, I would look forward to her coming. I dreamed of finding some semblance of the beautiful grandmother/granddaughter relationships that my friends always talked about, but it never happened. Ida would make her rounds among her many children, visiting some longer than others. Our visits were always short because they weren't enjoyable. It was always the same. The family would be very excited and do everything we could to make her feel welcome, and we would beg her to take her hair down so we could all ooh and aah over it. It was her pride and joy, and it hung, thick and healthy, to her feet. She only wore it wrapped with large pins around her head and would take them out one by one and uncoil her hair as she went. It would take the better part of an hour to get all her hair free. From there, the visits were all downhill. She complained about everything and couldn't be pleased. She became very annoyed with us kids if we tried to engage with her, and we always seemed to be interrupting her from something. Often, it was her precious crossword and other puzzle books that were her constant companions, and I especially would try and sit next to her and help her solve the puzzles, which made her very irritable. Dad got so disgusted with her rude behavior during one visit when I was trying to help her that he suddenly left the house, then came back about fifteen minutes later with a handful of puzzle books. He gave them to me and told me they were all mine, and I didn't need to help Grandma with hers.

CHAPTER 35

"Saturday Night's Alright for Fighting"

(Elton John)

Aberdeen was a different kind of crazy and culture than we had in Hampton, but with the Hut and all the gang from there and our neighborhood, it was definitely another Mafia situation. Dad had a big reputation in Aberdeen as a good man, and he had many loyal friends and admirers. I think he loved to be a big fish in a small pond, and the Aberdeen environment was perfect for this. He also had a reputation as a fighter, as he did back when he met and got together with Mom, and this played out in the Hut. I heard so many stories told about his fights by Mom, family members, family friends, and acquaintances. Even the children of all these people knew the stories and talked about it among themselves.

Here's what Mom said about Dad and his fighting side: She never witnessed him starting any fights, but he never backed down either. He just always carried himself in an intimidating manner, with a look in his eyes that said, "Don't mess with me." So many dumb drunks would take the dare and come around and mess with him! He was very fast, and she never saw him lose a battle. She was just always amazed by the idiots who started crap with him. He *never* argued with other people. When someone would come up to him and try to start arguing, he'd have them hit and knocked on the floor before they even knew what hit them. In the beginning of their being together, the ferocity she saw in him used to scare her to death. He was so sweet and kind to Paula and her, yet brutal when he was in a fight. When he drank, he usually got angry easily, and that's the first problems they had in their relationship. She had never been around many drunks or drinking except when she was waitressing, and she saw that the more people drank, the worse their behavior became. She had no patience or tolerance with the drunk crowd but was subjected to them often because she worked graveyard shift a lot of the time. Dad didn't drink often back then. Heck, when you can't afford to eat, you certainly can't drink. But his old running buddies would come around, and they all drank, so Dad would too. Mom mostly stayed away from him when he was drunk because that was when he would argue with her. He held in a lot of hostility for years that all stemmed from his childhood, and it took a lot of years to put that all behind him.

One of Dad's legendary fights at the Hut occurred when he and Mom decided to go there with a friend named Don H., whom Ersel had picked up in Tennessee as a helper on the truck. Don had started dating an Aberdeen lady named Lil, and she was there as well. It was a Saturday afternoon, and when the foursome walked in, a big black man was dancing with a white woman, which was never done at the Hut, known to locals to be racist. They were shocked at the sight. It was a real redneck place with a strict clique of customers. GIs were not welcome to hang out in there either, but that didn't stop them coming in. The foursome settled at a table, and when Dad went to the bar to get more drinks, the black man came up to the table and tried to pull on Mom's arm, telling her to come and dance. Mom told him no three times, even after Don told him to get lost. When Dad returned, he asked what the guy had wanted at their table. Mom said nothing and tried to change the subject, but Don told him what happened, so Dad went up to the guy, who was now leaning against the jukebox, and said, "Dance with me, bitch!" The guy was so big that Dad, who was six feet, two inches, had to reach up to hit him. He landed an upper cut, causing the guy to start rolling around, to the left, across the jukebox, with Dad landing more blows all the while. Don then walked up and opened the outside door to the left of the jukebox, and the man continued rolling right out the door and onto the sidewalk.

During another fight in the Hut, Dad was playing pool when yet another black man put his quarter on the table to challenge for the right to the table. Dad was playing with Wendell, and Wendell said he couldn't have the table and shouldn't even be in there because black people weren't welcome. The man argued back against Wendell, and a fight ensued among several patrons, including Dad. At some point during the fight, Dad felt an irritation on the back of his right shoulder, so he turned around to see what it was and found some guy sawing on him with a steak knife. He knocked the crap out of the guy, but he wore the scar from the knife wound for the rest of his life. It was a source of amusement for him.

One of the most interesting fight stories from the Hut happened when John and Alice, Sam and Faye, and Dan were visiting and went out for a night there with Mom and Dad. Turned out, the bartender who had turned Dad out to get beaten by the five guys a few years earlier when we were living in Richmond showed up in the Hut. Dad didn't say a word, but Mom told John and Dan who the guy was. When he got up to leave, John and Dan followed him outside and hit him over the head with a beer bottle, then they started beating him until three soldiers jumped in to help him. Dad came out then, and he, John, and Dan each took on a soldier. Dan had his belt wrapped around his hand and hit one of the soldiers with his belt buckle, splitting his head open. The police showed up, and Mom convinced them that the whole thing was the bartender and soldiers' faults, so they let our guys go.

Along with Dad and the Smith boys, we three kids were fighters as well. We started having physical fights with one another at probably ages five, seven, and eight. We weren't encouraged to fight, but if we did, we had to follow Dad's strict fighting rules. He said, "If you're going to fight, you fight like men, not little sissies." We weren't allowed to pinch, scratch, bite, or pull hair. He taught us how to punch properly, and we sparred for fun with boxing gloves. We also fought among the three of us, especially Tommy and myself. It was a pretty fair fight, but I could best him just a little because I was two years older. We were tough and never backed down from a fight with one another, but if we picked at Paula enough to get her to fight, we were in trouble. She could easily whoop either of us and could even beat us both at the same time. The three of us, however, would have to band together to go against cousin Vickie, who was older and much bigger than all of us. We struggled to get the best of her unless our New York boy cousins were around and got involved. They could easily take her.

We kids fought with others sometimes as well, especially Tommy, being a boy, I guess. I had a girl in my fourth-grade class named Teresa who kept picking at me until one day, I told her at lunch that I was going to whoop her ass after school that day. Between the two of us and our small crowd of friends gathered around us, we decided that we would fight at a spot just outside of school grounds so we wouldn't get in trouble with the school authorities. We cautioned everyone to keep their mouths shut about the fight, but word spread among the students that afternoon. When the bell rang, Teresa and I made our way to our chosen spot with each of our gangs surrounding us along with quite a few other kids, anxious to see the fight. We each put our belongings on the ground and stepped into the rough circle formed by the other kids. I was so used to fighting at home that I wasn't even nervous. I walked right up to her and asked if she wanted the first swing. She landed a girl punch on my upper arm, and I returned with a boy punch to the right eye. She held her eye and started to whimper, so I asked if it was over. The other kids goaded her into continuing the fight, and she said we could keep going, so I punched her hard in the stomach. She doubled over and started full-on crying now, so I asked again if we were done. She and all the other kids said that we were, so I gathered my stuff and started walking home with my brother, sister, and some friends. The next day, Teresa came to school with a black eye. I worried that she would tell on me, so I found a chance to ask her if she had or intended to, and she said no, she wouldn't rat me out. To my surprise, a lot of the bloodthirsty kids pushing us to fight the day before were now treating me like I was a monster who beat up poor Teresa, even the boys. I didn't feel good about it, but I didn't feel bad either. She brought it on herself by constantly picking at me. Things soon went back to normal, minus her picking, and then she moved away a few months later, but I would see her again in a few years.

In spite of my confidence and ability with fighting, I made an ass out of myself the following year when I asked for, then backed down from, another fight. A very pretty new girl had moved to Swan Meadows, and she was taking away all the attention that we other girls were used to getting from the boys. We all complained about it, but me more loudly than anyone else, and I finally challenged the new girl to a fight. We arranged during school that day to meet at the baseball diamond at the front of the project across the street from the school. She and I and about a dozen other girls made our way to the spot after school. Paula was there, but she didn't agree that I should fight the new girl. She said she thought she was nice, and it wasn't her fault if the boys thought she was pretty. I ended up walking past the ball field to the back of our friend Tammy's house, then asking Tammy if I could come in her house. She let me in along with Paula, while all the other girls stayed out back behind Tammy's house, waiting for me to come out so the fight could start. I decided that I wasn't coming out, and I didn't want to fight. I'm really not sure why because I wasn't afraid. I think Paula and her logic had gotten to me because I had so much respect for her opinion. Anyway, I stayed in Tammy's house until everyone finally gave up on the fight and went home, and I looked like an ass.

CHAPTER 36

"I Can Help"

(Billy Swan)

Not everything that we did in this neighborhood was bad. Every summer that we were there, we attended Vacation Bible School, which we kids adored. I don't know what church it was sponsored by, but buses would come to our neighborhood and pick us up, and it seemed like we drove out into the country a bit. I continued my Bible story learning as well as learning new hymns, like "The B-I-B-L-E" and more. The social activities and games were fun as well, with Kool-Aid and cookies. I would like to thank whoever sponsored this VBS as well as all of them out there. I think that they're an important and effective way to expose children to Christianity. We did, however, have a very negative church experience when we were living here. Mom was always trying to find us a church to attend if we ever stayed anywhere long enough, and she did so here. I have no information about this church other than I'm sure it was Baptist, because we were, and I don't believe we knew anyone there or had any sort of introduction.

One Sunday, Mom, Alice, and we three kids got dressed up and got to church before the service started. We all had on typical appropriate Sunday's best wear, including Alice, who was a beautiful girl with dark, almond eyes, olive skin, and perfect teeth. She had long, curly hair, which she didn't always like in its natural state, and would iron it with a clothing iron at times. Today, however, she wore it in a large Afro hairstyle with big hoop earrings, as was the fashion of the time, and was wearing a little bit of mascara and lip color. The dress she wore was fashionable and completely appropriate, with no excess skin showing. We sat together in a pew, and we all felt the fire and brimstone that was burning in the patron's eyes and hearts directed toward us. We weren't greeted by anyone. I can't even remember a smile. When the sermon finally started, the pastor was visibly shaken. He seemed flustered, upset, angry, confused. He stammered and didn't know what to do with himself. He finally seemed to come to a conclusion within himself and said that he had decided to change the subject of his sermon today. He felt that the Lord had called upon him to speak about Jezebel, and the Jezebels of the world today. No surprise that every eye turned to Alice. Even as a child of about nine or ten, I understood all the lambasting that was being heaped upon Alice by this man, a man of God no less, along with his judgmental congregation. I can't remember if we stayed for the entire sermon, but I believe we did because it would have been rude to get up and leave in the middle of it.

Back in Swan Meadows, we kids were having the time of our lives, but our folks had come to believe that the neighborhood was a bad influence on us, and just a couple months into my fourth-grade year, Mom started searching for a better place for us to live. She found a townhouse in the Wakefield Manor Apartments in Bel Air about twelve miles northwest of Aberdeen. We kids were not happy. We were never happy when we had to move *again*, but it was especially painful this time because we all loved our friends, school, and neighborhood. My class bought me a going-away gift, a cute little denim purse, and everyone signed a "We'll miss you" card, which I still have.

Before we moved to Bel Air, Dan had gone on the truck as a helper with a furniture mover colleague of Dad's, also named Dan, so we'll call him Dan P. When they got back to town, Dan found out where we had moved to in Bel Air and came to live with us there. Meanwhile, we kids made the best of our new environs, as usual. There was a cool playground in the apartment complex, and I liked my school. We were learning about nutrition with the Mulligan Stew program, and I found it interesting and fun. I don't remember any particular friends there, which was especially lonely after having so many playmates in Swan Meadows. We got a treat when Mom's friend Carol came with her kids to stay with us for a few days. The reason for the stay, however, was due to a terrible accident.

One night after Carol had gotten her five young children to bed, she was working in her kitchen when a conversion van literally crashed through the living room wall and stopped in the middle of the room! The driver was a young woman who had been drinking, but I don't know the cause of the accident. By the grace of God, nobody was hurt, but they had a huge hole in their living room wall, so they needed somewhere to go while the damage was repaired. Carol called Mom right away, packed a few belongings for her and the kids, and Mom went and picked them up. Some of their property had also been destroyed, but the worst part was the shocking trauma of the incident itself. Carol was traumatized by the fact that she had just relocated one of her boys to his bed from the spot on the couch where he had fallen asleep; the couch that was now well underneath the van.

I can't say how long the family stayed with us, but I have a bittersweet memory of something that occurred while they were there. Paula and I were fighting over the attention of Tammy, as usual, and Paula was currently winning, leaving me with nobody to play with. I lamented my pain to my mom, who was surprisingly sympathetic, and attempted to cheer me up by taking me on her lap and singing a popular song at the time called "I Can Help." She changed the words to "I Can't Help" and added other silly lyrics along with tickling me and dancing with me in the chair. I felt so loved and special that Mom cared about my feelings and took the time to cheer me up. It's one of my fondest memories of Mom.

Another fond memory from this home was on Thanksgiving. The year was 1974. As I've stated, my folks didn't usually make much of holidays, but this year Mom went all out. I believe that all the older kids came for the weekend, but I remember John specifically. He had actually only lived in Maryland for a short time, and he and Alice had moved back to Hampton. They came back up to visit with us just for the Thanksgiving holiday. We all loved to have our whole family together. The mood was very festive, and Dad convinced Mom to put up a ping-pong table in the living room. We kids had fun being under the table more than anything, and we also enjoyed the tiny cordial glasses of wine that Mom set out for everyone, including us kids, which we thought was so grown-up and cool. Mom made a huge, wonderful dinner and didn't reveal until much later what had happened to the turkey that she served. She and Dad were alone in the kitchen trying to move the baked turkey from the baking pan to the platter when they lost their grip and dropped the turkey, which then slid across the kitchen floor! Being alone in the kitchen with a house full of hungry people, they made the decision to pick up the turkey, place it on the platter, and serve it up! Happily, that was the only drama we experienced during that holiday, and we didn't even know that it happened.

There was another dramatic moment when we lived here when Dad got mad at Mom for some reason. She had recently taken up painting on fabric with these special paint-filled pens, and she had all her supplies on the dining room table. I believe she was talking shit about something or someone, and he didn't like it, so he told her to shut up. When she kept talking, he started picking up her pens and throwing them across the room. He then said, "Shut up, Sherrill, or I'll bust your fucking colors!" By colors, he meant her paint pens. It was so ridiculous that finally, Mom couldn't help but laugh at what Dad was doing. It was an awesome example of using humor to diffuse an angry, tense situation. To this day, our family will yell at one another in mock anger, "I'm going to bust your (with or without the word *fucking*) colors!" Sadly, this method of diffusing anger and tension with humor wasn't a regular occurrence between my parents, especially at this point in time. Dan remembered Mom and Dad arguing on the phone for a long time when Dad was on the road here, running up $300 phone bills.

Dan and I were getting along really well while he stayed with us in Bel Air when he wasn't out on the road with Dan P. He shared his excitement with me about meeting Jo, a beautiful, smart, capable young woman with a good reputation, but who was only sixteen. We were actually related to her by marriage. I've mentioned my aunt Gaye, who was married to my dad's brother, Emmett. Well, Jo and Gaye were cousins on Jo's mother's side. Jo was best friends with Gaye's daughter Sharon, and Mom was on a bowling league with Sharon and Jo at the time. Dan said that one night, Sharon and Jo came to the house to visit Mom, and he was there. Sparks flew between Dan and Jo, and they started dating right away when Dan got her phone number from Sharon and invited her to a company party at Allied Van Lines, for whom Dan P. drove. Jo's parents said no to the party but said that Dan could come to their house if he wanted to see Jo. He went to their house and met her parents, and he was thrilled when they let Jo ride to Gaye's house with Dan to get his suit altered, so they got to be alone for a short time. From that point, Dan was at her house every day. Her family, as well as ours, were leery of Dan's wanton ways and didn't want him to break Jo's heart or treat her badly, but he was a perfect gentleman. He was crazy about Jo and talked about her constantly, especially when he came home from their dates.

I remember one night in particular when he was oozing love for her and dramatically flung himself to the floor, lying spread-eagled on his back, like he had been struck down. I laughed at his antics until we discovered that his earring was stuck to the carpet when he tried to get up and couldn't without resistance and pain. Dan was the first man I remember ever wearing an earring, and he made a big deal out of wearing it in the correct ear so he wouldn't be a "queer," although I never remember which ear it was supposed to be. I rescued him from the carpet, but the incident didn't dampen his mood. He was madly in love, and that's the first time I had ever witnessed such passion. It stayed with me always and taught me what being in love looked like. I knew that Jo was special because he had always been a ladies' man, and I had seen him with many of them, but this was different. They were always the ones crazy for him, and he just enjoyed what they had to offer. Dan was never the same after he met Jo. He had a calmer, happier demeanor, and although he was violent with others in the future, I can't remember him being angry with me after that. I couldn't wait for them to get married so I could finally be his flower girl.

One time, when Dan was off the road and staying with us, he proved that although he had calmed down a great deal, trouble still seemed to follow him if he wasn't the one looking for it first. Dad, Dan, and Dan P. were drinking beer one night, and Dan asked Dad if he could drive his pickup to go get more beer. Dad loved his truck and was very protective of it, especially when it came to Dan and his vehicular track record. He finally agreed as the store was just up the road, and Dan set off. He should have been back within ten to fifteen minutes tops but hadn't returned until forty-five minutes later, looking stricken. One look at Dan's face, and Dad began to say, "Not my truck, no, not my truck." Dan was clearly afraid of Dad's reaction and remorseful for whatever he had done. Apparently, he bought the beer, then stopped to get something out of Dan P.'s truck, which was parked in an empty lot near our apartments. The lot was dirt but was surrounded by tall weeds. The weeds disguised a twenty-foot-deep ravine. Somehow in the process of getting in and out of the parking lot, the truck ended up head-first in the ravine, so deep that you couldn't even see the truck when you drove past. Dan was uninjured, as was the truck, and he was able to climb his way out of the ravine, then slowly began the walk home once he realized there was no way of recovering the truck on his own. It was a short walk, but it took him a while to get up the courage to open the door and go in the house to deliver his news to my dad. Dan P. was able to pull the pickup out with his semi, and it only had a few minor scratches. Lucky Dan again!

CHAPTER 37

"White Line Fever"

(Merle Haggard)

According to Mom, we kids were not happy in Bel Air. I really can't remember how I felt, but it makes sense that we wanted to go back to our beloved Swan Meadows. If that's true, then this is one of the very few times that we were excited about moving. We rented a place at 49 Aberdeen Avenue about a quarter mile further up the road from number 7, which would have been much better for me. I decided to play the French horn in the school band and had to lug that big instrument home and back to school every day. Nothing about it interested me, so it didn't last long.

I was so happy to be back at Halls Cross Roads Elementary. It was a wonderful school, and I learned so much there. I can see now that some of the schoolkids from Swan Meadows must have been challenging for the staff, but I never felt any deficit in my environment. Paula and I sang in choir there, and I still remember all the songs that she and I both sang that year. One of mine was James Taylor's "You've Got a Friend," and one of Paula's was an interesting song called "Pollution," which gave me an early education about protecting our environment. It had been released in 1965 by Tom Lehrer, and whoever chose for the students to perform it at our school was successful in their teaching moment, at least for me. Another lesson I learned about protecting our environment along with every other kid in America came from the Woodsy Owl campaign TV commercials. "Give a hoot, don't pollute, your good outdoor manners show. Leave a trail that's nice and clean wherever you may go." They really did have good educational programs in the seventies, and they have stuck with me all my life. They were a perfect learning tool for me, however, because I have an uncanny knack for remembering jingles and TV series' theme songs.

Our aunt Bell and uncle Herb decided to leave New York and come to Aberdeen, maybe because of a job loss or something, and the family stayed with us for a very short time while waiting for housing in Swan Meadows. I wasn't concerned with why they were moving to Aberdeen, only ecstatic that my beloved cousins were going to be close to us! We had only spent that one day together back when I was six years old, but I had such a love for this family and was fascinated with them. My aunt Bell was the epitome of a mother figure in my opinion, and she came at a time when my own mother was especially distracted and neglectful. Bell was always in the kitchen, either cooking or sewing, and always with a cigarette in her mouth because she was too busy to hold it. It was impressive how long the ash would get on her cigarette before she tapped it in an ashtray. It never fell on its own. She had a husband and seven children to cook for, but her kitchen operated like she was a short-order cook. She would make a dinner for most of them but happily made special orders for anyone who desired. She was sweet and warm and funny, and it was impossible not to love her. I was indifferent to my uncle Herb for a while until he gave me reason not to like him.

My oldest Campbell cousin, nicknamed Rocky, still lived in Rochester, New York, and maintained his career with Eastman Kodak. I don't remember meeting him until after his family moved to Aberdeen, but my folks and all his family spoke so highly of him that I had much respect and admiration of him. When he did visit in Swan Meadows, he brought his beautiful bride with him, Mary, whom you couldn't help but love. After Rocky came four boys:

Buddy, Jimmy, Gary, and Danny. Buddy and Jimmy were older than us kids, but Gary was Paula's age, and Danny was mine. Then there were three girls: Debbie, Becky, and Denise. I loved the girls, but they were all younger than me and were well-behaved Mama's girls, so I spent a lot more time with the boys than I did the girls. They were so fun to hang out with, given all their crazy antics, but they got into some trouble immediately after moving to Swan Meadows.

Down at the far end of the neighborhood was a couple of basketball courts. I had spent very little time there, not being interested in playing myself, but my four boy cousins loved to play and spent a great deal of time there. The courts were mostly used by teenage, or a little younger, boys who were black. I don't remember any racial tension, although my cousins were about as racist as most of the people in my life at the time. They called black guys jigs and black girls bamas, which were terms I had never heard anywhere else. The problem was that my cousins had a nasty habit that the other ball players didn't appreciate. They chewed tobacco, and they spit the juice on the court, where you couldn't help but step in it and get it on the bottom of your shoes. I know there was some confrontation between the two groups, but I don't think they got into a physical fight. I believe the issue resolved itself when my cousins decided that they didn't want to hang out there anyway and found other things to do.

I had never been around tobacco chewers, and I thought everything my cousins did was cool, so I wanted to try it too. We had all been out running around one day when I tried it out. They gave me careful instructions and told me over and over again not to swallow the juice, but be sure to spit it out. I was sitting in my folks' kitchen afterward, not feeling well at all. My mom noticed me and asked what was wrong with me. I told her that I felt sick, like I might throw up. My cousins were there with us, and they told Mom that I must have swallowed my tobacco juice. Mom wasn't happy about me doing that, but I don't think I got into trouble. I think that just like when I had gotten drunk a few years earlier, she thought that I had already paid the price for my mistake. I never tried that stuff again. It could have been worse. Apparently, my grandpa Stanley also chewed tobacco and once found a bloody bandage with part of a finger in a bag of Beech-Nut tobacco. He switched to Red Man after that, which was also what my cousins chewed. It seemed like they were always doing something interesting. I remember them building cannons that shot tennis balls. They built them in their yard, then shot them off in the green space.

I have a hard time remembering a lot that happened from about the middle of fourth to the middle of fifth grade, but I do remember some activities from the summer. Mom and Dad had gotten the idea for Tommy to go on the truck with Dad, and his shipment schedule meant that it was going to be about a month until they returned home. I remember Paula and I being jealous and wanting to go as well, but Dad said he couldn't deal with all three of us at once and that we would get our turns in the future. Don went on the trip as well as a helper. He and Dad took a lot of home movies on that trip, where they spent a lot of time in the southwest. I can't speak for Tommy, but I would have cherished them if it had been me on the trip. There are shots of Tommy climbing on giant pieces of petrified redwoods along with a giant armadillo made of quartz. He can also be seen riding on a mechanical horse that was being transported in the back of a guy's pickup. My favorite is him playing in a pickup truck from the late 1920s that they came across on the side of the road somewhere. He's pretending to drive it, trying to turn the big steering wheel and shift gears. In another shot, there's a dairy truck overturned on the side of a road, with six to eight guys, including my brother and Don, sitting around drinking milk and orange juice from the piles of dairy products lying all over the ground. Apparently, they were waiting for a giant wrecker to come and right, then tow, the truck out of there. When Dad saw them and stopped to offer help, they offered him and his passengers their dairy products instead.

The CB culture was really popular at this time, which was the summer of 1975. Dad wouldn't let us play on his, however, because it wasn't a fad for him; it was part of his job. He would let us get in the cab of his truck and play, however, every time he was home. We loved his trucks for several reasons, not the least of which was because he let us keep all the change we found in there. It was like looking for treasure in all those nooks and crannies! We also loved it because it was such an integral part of his life and one we didn't get to participate in nearly enough for our liking. It was always taking him away from us. We were proud of our daddy being a trucker, and we knew from hearing countless stories of his driving abilities that he was a damn good one. Of course, we loved to use the arm signal on truckers when we were riding in the car to try and get them to honk their horns for us. Every trucker's kid knew about that, and most regular kids also knew back in those days. When we were living in Connecticut, Dad had gotten custom T-shirts made for us three kids. They were white with a brown silkscreen semi-truck across the front, and we each had our names inside the truck trailer. We can all three be seen wearing the shirts in a home movie taken in Connecticut right after we got them, and then I can be seen wearing mine again in at least two more home movies. I loved that shirt! I don't know where it ended up over the years, but it's okay because we can see it in the movies. Dad would also buy us trinkets from truck stops on his trips, and I still have some of them. Sadly, Paula lost most of her girlhood possessions in a fire on Dad's truck when he was moving her household goods from Virginia to Arkansas after she was married. It wasn't his fault, but I know Dad felt terrible about it.

That summer, Mom had started spending a lot of time with Lil, Don's girlfriend. The two of them went out a lot while their men were both on the road, and my sister and I got paid to babysit Lil's three little kids. It seemed like we kids were on our own a lot. One good thing that happened, however, was that my mom and Lil took all of us kids to Hershey Park, an amusement park in Hershey, Pennsylvania. My folks didn't usually do things like this with us, so it must have been Lil's influence. Of course, we did go to Buckroe Beach Amusement Park quite a bit when we were living in Hampton, but that was like part of our neighborhood and just didn't have the same excitement as Hershey Park. This park was new to us and much bigger than Buckroe Beach, and boy, did we have a blast! Tommy was upset when he heard that he had missed the trip, but I believe Paula and I would have gladly traded him for his alone time with Dad.

After Tommy was back home, the ladies decided to take us camping for the weekend, which we had never done before. They borrowed Wendell's camper and pulled it with Dad's pickup. It was Mom, Lil, and all of us kids again, but this time, we brought along Jeff and Eric, Wendell's two sons. We always loved spending time with them when they came to see their dad for a weekend. We drove to Elk Neck State Park, which was about twenty-five miles up and around the Chesapeake Bay in Northeast, Maryland. We were so excited and had a great time running around the park all day. At one point, Paula fell in the road and scraped up her knee. We were all tough, and the scrape wasn't a big deal, but Eric picked Paula up and carried her back to the camper to get some first aid. It was such a gallant act, and we all already knew that he had a crush on her, so it was very sweet. I remember having dinner that evening in the camper, but I don't believe we had gone to bed yet when Mom and Lil became very frightened by some people or noises outside the camper. There had been a rough-looking group of guys around the campground earlier in the day, and now the ladies were under the impression that they wanted to take advantage of two women with a bunch of children and cause us some sort of harm. I don't remember enough to know if it was a valid impression, but at any rate, they decided that we weren't safe, and we needed to leave. We kids were so disappointed that we had to leave. We had never slept in a camper before and were so looking forward to it.

We went to that park another time for a picnic with some of Dad's friends and their families that summer. Several scary things happened that day. First, one of the men had either found a snake at the park or brought it with him and, being well aware that my mom was horrified of snakes, thought it would be funny to surprise her with it. He walked up behind her and got her attention, then held the snake out to her. Everyone started laughing at the prank, but my mom began to have a panic attack because she had a serious phobia of snakes. She was trying to get away and was struggling to breathe at the same time. My dad quickly got to the guy with the snake and told him to remove himself and the snake from the area. After the guy took the snake away and returned to the group, Dad told him and everyone else in the group that they better never bring a snake around my mother again, or they would suffer the consequences.

Meanwhile, all of us kids had the run of the park as long as we stayed together. We had all brought inflated inner tubes to float the Elk River with, and it was time to begin. From what I recall, there was a large group of adults and kids on the river, and we floated together for some time when we reached a point where everyone got out of the river to walk back to where we had begun and float back again. Somehow, my brother and I didn't get out but kept floating down the river. The reason everyone got out where they had was because the rapids became faster and swifter at that point, and it wasn't safe for children any longer. It was probably not safe at any point because nobody was wearing a life jacket. Tommy and I were having a good time until we saw the mouth of the Chesapeake Bay up ahead and could see big ships in the near distance. We knew we better get out of the water before we ended up in the middle of the bay. We started trying to make our way to the edge of the river and tried grabbing on to the large, jagged rocks that we were passing, without any luck.

We were almost out of rocks and heading to the deep bay when Tommy managed to grab onto a rock and thankfully grab my arm as I was floating by. At this point, we had lost our tubes, which made it easier to maneuver in the water, and we managed to get to the shore. The problem was that we were on the other side of the river. We climbed up and out of the ravine and started heading back the direction we had come. We came across an old, dilapidated wooden trestle that stretched across the Elk River and were happy that we had found our way back across the water and to the picnic site. There were many boards missing on the trestle, and we had to navigate carefully to make it all the way across without falling through. It was several years later before I thought about the situation and realized just how dangerous it was. The trestle was probably 150 feet in the air, and if we had fallen, we would have landed on the jagged rocks that were in the river, surely causing serious harm, or worse. We made it through this situation safely, but there was another tragic situation of a different nature about to happen at home in a few months' time.

Looking back, I can see that it was coming, but I didn't know it at the time. Things finally culminated into Mom leaving us again for some young sailor named Danny. I know I met him at some point, but I can't remember the circumstances. As I mentioned earlier, Mom had become neglectful of us kids as her heart was clearly not in our home at the time. Dan had moved with us to 49 Aberdeen Avenue from Bel Air, so he was there when Mom left. Dad went on the road and left Dan with $20 to take care of him and us kids. He was there with us for six days before Dad kicked him out over the phone. Dan said he knew he was going to run out of money, so he and Charlie stole a bunch of food from Beanie's freezer that was in a shed in their backyard. Beanie found out it was Dan when she came over one morning, maybe to check on us kids, and I told her that we had a bunch of food in the freezer. She put two and two together and called the cops on Dan that same morning. When the cops knocked on our door a little while later, Dan went out a bedroom window, snuck over to a neighbor lady's house, and hung out a while, then went back home. Dad called that afternoon, and when Dan told him what had happened, Dad told Dan to leave, so he hitchhiked to Virginia.

He stayed with Patty and Keith and worked with Keith for a couple days, then hitchhiked back to see Jo in Edgewood, Maryland. He had gotten a ride to Richmond, Virginia, and was on Interstate 64, but when it came time for the road to split into North and South 95, Dan's ride was going south, and Dan needed to go north, so the driver pulled over and let Dan out. Unfortunately, a cop witnessed Dan walking on the Interstate before he could get on North 95, and he stopped him. He ended up getting arrested for warrants from Hampton because he hadn't followed the rules of the probation sentence that he got from stealing from Sarge. He hadn't been in the state of Virginia the whole time and hadn't been staying in touch with his parole officer, etc. They put him in jail on the Friday of Memorial Day weekend 1975, and he called Jo's dad and told him that he was in jail, and it looked like he was going to be there a long time with that seven-year suspended sentence hanging over his head. Jo's dad gave her a valium before he would tell her the news because he knew she would be devastated. Dan called her back later, and she told him that she was pregnant, which made them each feel even more horrible about the situation. The luck of Dan, however, shone upon him again. He stayed in jail until court on Tuesday, with Monday being a holiday, and when he met with the judge, he gave Dan a bus ticket to Baltimore, Maryland, and sent him on his way. Dan wasn't sure why; he thought just to get him out of the state of Virginia. The bus took him to Edgewood, and he walked to Jo's house, where she was shocked to see him after only a few days.

Meanwhile, Dad, Paula, Tommy, and myself were all devastated by Mom's leaving. Dad hadn't had time to line up another caretaker for us kids after he kicked Dan out, and he must have just worked local for a short time because he was there taking care of us by himself each day. I've never seen my dad so sad and lost. He would even cry with us kids, and that was very unusual. He did, however, decide that what was good for the gander was good for the goose this time, and he dated a gal named Betty. I met her one time. She was pretty and nice. Dad was trying to find someone to care for us kids so he could go back out on the road, and apparently, he had talked to Aunt Bell about it because, one evening, I was at their house, playing outside the living room window, when I overheard Bell and her husband, Herb, having a conversation. Bell asked Herb if he thought it would be okay for them to help out, and Herb started a long diatribe about how my dad was a drunk and my mom was a whore, and he didn't want anything to do with taking care of us kids. Although there might have been some truth to what he was saying, it was so painful for a ten-year-old girl to hear about her parents. I was shocked, hurt, ashamed, and humiliated to be talked about that way. I had never had a good feeling about Herb before, and now I had a good reason.

The timing of Mom's leaving was especially terrible for Paula and me because we had been sick with sore throats and fevers, and Mom had scheduled tonsillectomy surgery for both of us, as recommended by a doctor. Dad was determined to see us through the surgeries, and we had to take time off from school to get them done. I was very afraid of having surgery for the first time, and my only comfort was that my sister was with me. I felt embarrassed and violated when a nurse came in the night before our surgeries and gave us enemas without any explanation or preparation. Then I was traumatized the next morning when they gave me a drug to make me drowsy for the surgery. I hated the feeling of being drugged and not having control of myself. I still do. So I went under anesthesia feeling scared to death and woke up throwing up and struggling with trying to wake up. Then I was in pain. I really needed my mommy. Dad was there with us through the process, and he tried the best he could, but it wasn't the same as Mom. The nurses had promised us all the ice cream we could eat, but it was too painful to eat anything at first, even ice cream. I was having trouble with coughing up blood, and they didn't like the way I was recovering, so I had to stay in the hospital while Paula got to go home. That was devastating for me, and I felt horribly alone after she was gone. Luckily, I only spent one more night in there, and they let me go home the next day.

After our surgeries, Dan came back and stayed with us again for two weeks, and then he and Jo were married in Bel Air by the justice of the peace. Jo had found out that she could get married at age sixteen without her parents' permission as long as she had proof from a doctor that she was pregnant. Mom happened to be there when Dan came back, too late to help me through the traumatizing hospital experience, and he borrowed the $15 he needed to get married from her. He moved in with Jo and her parents, and sadly, Jo miscarried the baby she was carrying at three months. Shortly after, they got their own place to live very near to her parents, also in the Edgewood Projects. I was heartbroken when I found out that Dan and Jo were married by a justice of the peace, which was typical for our family, and they didn't have a formal wedding. After years of waiting to be a flower girl, my dream was dashed.

To make things worse, Mom left us again. Dad then called on my aunt Ruth for help. She rented the house at 69 Aberdeen Avenue, and Dad moved us out of our place and into hers. I have a few memories of her and my cousin Vickie, but we couldn't have been there long because we had moved back to Virginia by Christmas after Mom and Dad got back together. I can remember that we got a motel room our last night in town, and we kids stayed there while my folks partied at the Hut. They had been keeping a tropical fish tank for a few years now, and they put the tank in the trunk of the car to take with us to Virginia, full of water and fish. It was partially frozen, and the fish were dead by the time we arrived. I don't think they meant to leave it in the trunk all night when they could have brought it into the motel room but were probably too preoccupied and/or drunk to remember.

CHAPTER 38

"Right Back Where We Started From"

(Maxine Nightingale)

So here we were, back in the Holly Homes neighborhood in Hampton, Virginia, on a street called Bancroft Drive, which was two blocks over from Mojer. I enrolled in Captain John Smith Elementary again, this time in the fifth grade. I saw a few of the kids that were in my first-grade class, including Elaine, but I never really made friends with anyone here this time. Paula and I loved to roller-skate, and we went to the Plaza Roller Rink every weekend. They had lock-ins sometimes when we would spend the night at the rink, skating as long as we could, then usually passing out in the hours after midnight. Some of the older kids would make out under blankets until they got caught by the rink employees. Parents would come and pick up their kids any time after 6:00 a.m. The best part of living here was that we were reunited with the Smith kids. We spent a lot of time with John and Alice, and we had our precious Shannon in the family now. Shannon was the daughter of Sam and Faye, and she was the first of the Smith kids' offspring. She was a great kid, and we all adored her. She was only about ten months old when we moved back. We have a home movie of her in a walker on the sidewalk in front of our house.

All the houses in Holly Homes were the same, but someone had added a large recreation room onto the back of this house. John and David, one of the Mafia, came over on weekends and played guitar and sang, while Dad played the spoons. I remember them playing "Junior's Farm" by Paul McCartney and Wings, and "Can't You See" by the Marshall Tucker Band. I would give anything to have home movies of these performances, but there are none. We do have a movie of Dad and me dancing in the dining room here, which is pretty embarrassing. He only danced when he was drunk, and he wasn't a good dancer. He had one move that he called the hillbilly stomp. I would dance with Dad just to have that time with him, and I tried to emulate his dance step.

In the meantime, Dan had stayed in Edgewood for about six months after marrying Jo, then he decided to go down to Camp LeJeune to finally deal with his Marine Corps court-martial. He had been avoiding it for three years, but now that he was married, he didn't want it hanging over his head any longer. Plus, Sam had told him the FBI was coming to his house looking for him. Jo went with him, and they stayed in a little cabin there. The Marines told him that he would be discharged general under honorable, then honorable if he stayed straight for six months after he got out, like being on probation. They told him to go home and wait, so he and Jo went back to Edgewood to stay with her parents again. It was then discovered by the Marines that when Dan had enlisted, his recruiter had falsified his documents, omitting the grand theft auto felony that he had gotten on New Year's Eve. He should not have been allowed to enlist with that felony on his record. After this discovery, the Marine Corps decided to break their contract with Dan since it was their recruiter who had made the mistake. So he was free to walk away with nothing hanging over his head any longer. The unbelievable luck of Dan struck again!

They went back to Edgewood and stayed with Jo's parents again, then they decided to come down to Hampton for a family visit. They got to town and went to Sam's house first, but nobody came to the door. Then they came to our house, but it was dark and quiet, like nobody was there. Dan found his way into the house and noticed lots of candles everywhere. He figured out that the electricity was off and that we were gone. My folks might have been having some sort of financial problems, or they had just been really stubborn about paying the ridiculously high prices for electricity to the Virginia Electric and Power Company (VEPCO) because we had our electricity shut off for nonpayment. I remember Mom trying to cook on a little Coleman gas stove, but not much else about it. At some point, we went to stay with John and Alice at their place by Buckroe Beach because it got too cold to stay in the house.

Dan then went to where he knew John had been living on First Street by the beach and walked right into the house, only to find a strange guy. Dan told the guy he was looking for John, and the guy said John was living in the alley cottage behind this house now. Dan went there and finally found John, Alice, Mom, Dad, and us three kids. It was wonderful to have them back with us all in the same state again. We have an awesome home movie taken at this time at the Yorktown Battlefield with John, Alice, Sam, Faye, Dan, Jo, Mom, Dad, and David along with his girlfriend. We kids and Shannon are also in the movie. There had to be some partying done to celebrate everyone being together, and Dan remembered one particularly crazy story about him pulling Dad's tooth at our house one night when Dad was drunk enough not to feel it, and Dan was high on acid enough not to worry about trying it. Everyone but Patty was there, although she was still married to Keith and living in Hampton. I do know that Patty and Keith had a terrible relationship. He was abusive to her, even before they were married, and it's always been hard for me to imagine someone being so brutal with such a gentle creature as Patty. He was also rumored to be involved with dealing drugs. In spite of Patty not being there for the visit, we all had a wonderful time being together again, then Dan and Jo headed back to Edgewood to get ready for their upcoming baby.

We celebrated Christmas 1975 here, and my folks did a great job. Alice invited us kids over to her and John's place to make

Christmas cookies, and I don't believe we had ever done that before. Mom put up a tree, and we had lots of presents under it. I learned a valuable lesson from one of those presents. I had asked for a Jody and her general store and was dying to know if one of the gifts was it. I snuck out in the middle of the night, carefully peeled the tape back from the wrapping paper, and opened it up just enough to see that it was my desired gift. I put everything back in its place and was so happy with my knowledge until Christmas morning. When I opened my gift and had to pretend that I hadn't known what it was, I was so disappointed with myself for peeking and now lying about it in a sense and ruining the surprise for myself. I never peeked again after that and have never believed in peeking or snooping.

Although we had a generous Christmas, we were apparently still having problems with VEPCO because our power got shut off again. John had the knowledge to turn our power back on at the box outside our house, so he did so and left a note to VEPCO that said "The Lord Said Let There Be Light" and placed it inside the box. When VEPCO discovered that our power was back on, they came out and shut it off again, placing their own note inside the box that said, "The Lord Also Said Thou Shalt Not Steal." When John turned the power back on again, VEPCO came out and removed the electrical box from the property. That's probably when we moved out and relocated to an apartment in Newport News, where we three kids finished out the school year at Carver Elementary. At about the same time, Sam and Faye moved out of their trailer and into an apartment on Pembroke Avenue.

CHAPTER 39

"Black and White"

(Three Dog Night)

We moved into the Glen Gardens Apartments, and we had the coolest apartment in the complex because the windows on the side of the apartment faced the swimming pool. We couldn't have been any closer, and we couldn't have utilized that pool more. We went swimming in that pool every day of our summer vacation, and my brother would literally spend all day there, except when my mom forced him to come home and eat and take a break. I have wonderful memories of playing with Barbies out on our patio with my friend Carrie all morning long. Then we would eat lunch and stay at the pool all afternoon. It was so tempting to sneak out the windows and get in the pool after hours, but us kids never did. John, however, did do it one time, and he was our hero! It was all great fun, except for the time some girl overheard me talking to Paula and determined that I had called her a whore when she heard me say horror movie, and I apparently looked in her direction when I said it. I didn't even use the word *whore* at the time and definitely didn't use it to describe this girl. A little later, I dove off the diving board and swam down to the bottom of the eight-foot pool to touch, as was the custom, before shooting back up to the surface for a much-needed breath. When my head reached the surface of the pool, the girl who had misheard me was waiting and pushed me back down in the water, holding me there for a few more seconds. We kids often dunked one another, but I hadn't had a chance to catch my breath in way too long, and I struggled ferociously to come up and get some air. I was really shaken up and was happy that the lifeguard on duty had witnessed what happened and suspended the girl from the pool for the day without me having to be a tattletale.

I remember several of the lifeguards, most of whom were college kids on summer break. Our favorite was a guy named Steve, who looked and acted like he was one of the Mafia, with his long hair and laid-back hippie attitude. He drove a loud motorcycle, so we always knew when he was coming or going since the parking lot was in front of our apartment. One day, word spread through the apartment complex that Steve had been killed when he was hit by a car on his motorcycle, and everyone was invited by his family to attend the funeral. Many of the tenants attended, and I wanted to go, but Mom said I was too young. It was a sad and frightening blow to lose someone so suddenly who was so full of life, but unfortunately, there would be more of that to come.

In late spring, John, Alice, Sam, Faye, Shannon, Patty, and Keith decided to drive up to visit Dan and Jo in Maryland and go camping somewhere along the Bush River. After they arrived, Dan and John were catching up, and Dan told John a story that happened about a year ago when some guy named Wayne had ripped him off for $20. Dan had fought the guy at the time and ended up with a broken finger, causing him to lose his job. John's strong protective nature of his siblings soon had him saying that they were going to go after this guy, Wayne.

They gathered up three loads of cars, which included friend Charlie from Aberdeen, and headed to Edgewood Heights, where the guy lived. Patty and Alice were with them too, but Jo and Faye stayed behind with Shannon. They found the guy in the neighborhood near his house with a group of friends. They got out of the cars and started after the group. Dan got out with a tire thumper and went after the biggest of Wayne's friends and hit him with that. Mistakenly, he hit a woman on the back swing who happened to be in the group. John saw Wayne making a run for his house, with Dan chasing him, so he joined the chase. Just as Wayne got into his house and shut the door, John kicked it in, and he and Dan beat the crap out of the guy. Dan wasn't sure what else happened in the fight, but they then left Edgewood and took the back way to Aberdeen to an abandoned gas station to lay low. Descriptions of the cars had been called in, however, so the cops were out looking for them, and they found them. Each of the guys ended up going to jail for about two days and each paid a $200 fine. They also put in about $150 apiece for the lawyer who took care of them not having to appear in court, and the matter was put to rest.

I have fond memories of Shannon while we lived here. Sam and Faye would let us keep her overnight, and the whole family gave her attention and spoiled her rotten. She had turned one-year-old about the time we moved in. I was so proud when one day, Mom and Faye took us kids to Arby's for lunch, and I taught Shannon how to drink out of a straw. Tommy was playing on a pee-wee football team called the Mallory Midgets, and we have home movies of one of his games. Faye and Shannon were there with us, and Shannon was seen running around and playing with the cheerleaders' pom-poms on the movie. Mom got into trouble when Sam saw the movie and noticed that Shannon was chewing bubblegum, which he had forbidden.

Glen Gardens was the first place we lived where I experienced blatant racism. All my family was racist, but I never thought about it much. It was just the way things were, and we freely used the N-word. However, before I was even aware that I had this feeling, I believed that black people were generally more passionate and assertive, and I admired that about them, although my family was put off by that behavior. It wasn't a regular topic of discussion, but it was understood that as white people, we were set apart from and better than black people as well as anyone else of color. We were friendly with them at school and at work, but that was the extent of our interaction. We were basically indifferent unless there was a particular reason to bring up the subject, like the time Sam had a problem with the black kid at Spratly Junior High in Hampton, and it turned into a mini gang war between the black kid's family and friends and our Mafia. That experience was the first time I remember hearing the often repeated phrase among white people that "all black people stick together." This behavior was presented as a bad thing, although I was taught to always stick together with my own tribe, so it was confusing.

My mom worked at the same moving company as Dad as a packer. She talked about her coworker Bertha all the time and with great affection and admiration, and Bertha was black. There was also Rudy, Dad's friend Lawrence's son-in-law, back in Swan Meadows. He was black, and Mom and Dad had talked about what a great guy he was on several occasions, and he even married a white woman. I can only remember one black person ever coming to our home before we moved here, and it had been a positive experience. A black man named Roy who worked with my dad came a few times and had a beer with Dad when we lived on Mojer Drive. I talked to him and even sat on his lap and had a warm feeling about his visits, not seeing him or treating him any differently than any other man friend who came to the house. He brought me a ceramic robin one time, and it meant a great deal to me even though he had just found it somewhere and kept it to give me. I still thought it was special, and I gave him a kiss on the cheek as a thank-you. After Roy left, Dad pulled me aside and told me that I shouldn't kiss a black man, and I shouldn't sit on his lap anymore. If only he had been so protective of me with men because they were drunk rather than black, but I didn't think that at the time. I was just confused, but did as I was told.

We actually went to the home of a person of color once, but it was Dad's Asian coworker, Noda, and not a black person. We went as a family there to accept his dinner invitation. It was fascinating to look around during dinner and see our white family mixed together with Noda's Asian family in a home that was decorated with mostly Asian decor, while we ate traditional Asian food. We all loved the fried rice and egg rolls, which we ate from take-out restaurants often, but I don't think any of us liked the more exotic octopus and squid that they offered. We all displayed our manners, however, and tried at least a bite of everything, then ate as much as we could tolerate before politely begging off.

Glen Gardens was pretty integrated, and we kids had many black friends as well as white. We had a great time playing in the pool, on the playground, and just hanging around the neighborhood. We also went to Vacation Bible School for a week, which was held in the apartment's clubhouse. My eleventh birthday happened to coincide with a visit from my uncle Dean, who came out from California with his wife and daughter, who was a few years younger than me. I was too young to remember my uncle and aunt from when we lived in California, and I had never met my cousin before. We were all excited about their visit. My mom had planned a small party for me at the house with a few girlfriends. I was so happy that my girl cousin would be joining the group to celebrate my birthday. My girlfriends started arriving, and I was caught up in the excitement when I realized that my uncle, aunt, and cousin had gone out to the patio alone instead of staying in the house with everyone else. I went out to ask my cousin to come back in to the party—I wasn't so concerned with the adults—and I was told in a very stern way that she wouldn't be coming back to the party. I thought that maybe she had gotten into some sort of trouble and was being punished by being banished from the party. Soon after, Mom pulled me aside and said that she was going to join my uncle and his family on the patio because they wouldn't come back in the house as long as one of my girlfriends, who happened to be black, was at our home. I was shocked and bewildered. Mom asked me if I would send my friend home from the party, but I said no. After all, I knew her and liked her better than these relatives that I had been excited about but was now upset with that they were trying to ruin my party. Even at that age, I looked at them sitting outside, segregating themselves, and thought that they were ridiculous. They were throwing a fit about the color of a little girl's skin; a little girl who had done nothing wrong and couldn't possibly do them any harm.

A few months after my birthday incident, Paula got into a fight with a boy in the complex who tried to kiss her. The boy was black, which is what made my sister and the rest of my family so incensed about the incident. I really don't believe there would have been a problem if he had been white. She probably would have told the boy off, which she was very good at, and that would have been the end of it. In this case, however, she was furious and proceeded to ram the boy's head into a brick wall a few times before he got free from her. The family was very proud of her for defending herself against this black boy, and they told the story many times over the years. In my heart, I didn't understand why this boy trying to steal a kiss was any different than any other time that had happened to either my sister or myself. I did generally find black boys to be more outspoken about their attraction to me and really more assertive about everything, but it didn't disturb me or frighten me. If they offended me in some way, I dealt with it as I would if anyone offended me. My instincts never made me afraid of a black man, but there were countless occasions when I feared white men and for good reason. Although my parents warned us very sternly about our safety against strangers, I wish they had been more protective of me with people who were not strangers at all.

Mom told us all the stories in the headlines about children being harmed, which was probably smart in our case because we really weren't fearful and probably needed some shocking truths to convince us to be more cautious. We weren't allowed out after dark without adult supervision and were told to always practice safety in numbers. There was an incident that occurred shortly after we moved here that definitely put some fear in my heart. A girl who attended our elementary school, whom we didn't know, had gotten off her school bus and was walking home alone. Two older boys attacked her, beat her badly, and then set her body on fire. It was horrifying even to us dumb, immortal kids. It was with this story fresh in our minds that a terrifying occurrence happened in my own family.

Tommy was not nearly as cautious as Paula and me, and he wasn't good at following the rules about checking in and always letting Mom know where he was going to be. One late Saturday morning, Mom realized that she hadn't seen Tommy for a few hours. He wasn't at home and hadn't told her where he was going to be. She sent Paula and me out around the neighborhood looking for him.

When we came back without finding him, she sent us to knock on doors of his friends to see if he was indoors visiting someone. When we returned with no news, she began to worry. My dad had a big shipment that day, so he was at work, and it was just my mom, Paula, and me at home. We got in the car and drove around looking for my brother. The first place we went was the local 7-Eleven. It was the only place outside the complex we were allowed to go but only with specific permission and always with other kids. He wasn't there, and they didn't recall seeing him that day. We drove all over the apartment complex and within a few blocks of the complex but had no luck. By now, it was getting later in the afternoon, and my mom was frantic with worry.

After returning to the apartments and checking the complex one more time, she called the police. It was breaking a cardinal family rule, but we really needed help with something we couldn't do ourselves. Mom couldn't call Dad because he was at some shipper's house, and the office was closed on the weekends. The police came and questioned us, and shortly after, a whole group of people showed up to help search for my brother. They were a volunteer group who looked for missing children. They asked for pictures of my brother and set out on the search just as it was getting dark outside. Not long after they left, my dad finally came home from work, and as we three ladies tearfully ran out to meet him and tell him the horrible news, Tommy jumped out of the passenger seat of Dad's car. Turned out, he had asked Dad if he could go to work with him that morning when he was getting ready to leave. When Dad sent him back in the house to tell Mom that he was going with him, Tommy didn't do it; I don't remember why. He lied to Dad and told him that he did. My mother was mortified to tell the police and the volunteers about the false alarm, but it was overshadowed with the relief and joy that my brother was alive and well.

This incident was still fresh when I came home from a baseball game that I had attended with some friends one weekend, and my dad snatched me up by the arm without a word and literally sent me flying in the air with two whacks from the board of education. It hurt so badly that it took my breath away. I was in shock and pain and had no idea why I had been punished. Mom and Dad both proceeded to tell me how worried they had been and that I better never leave without telling anyone where I was going. After I calmed down, I explained to my parents that I had asked Paula to tell them where I was going. She declared to them that I had not. I tried to argue about it, but to no avail. Paula was the good kid, and I had already been punished, so the matter was over. I later asked Paula why she lied and said that I had not told her when I clearly had. She said she must have forgotten. That wasn't the last time she betrayed me, but it was the only time I was spanked by my dad that I was old enough to remember. I didn't soon forget it either. I just wish it had been for something I had actually done wrong. God knows there were plenty of opportunities!

CHAPTER 40

"Up Around the Bend"

(Creedence Clearwater Revival)

The first time I remember going to the Chickahominy River with the family was this same summer when I turned eleven. According to Dan, we would get there by taking Route 60 north a few miles outside of Williamsburg near the town of Toano and turn left down a winding road to a farmer's driveway on the right. Gary, one of the Mafia, had found out about the property when he went there with his realtor father, the same one who rented us the house on Mercury Boulevard. Gary talked to the farmer about letting him and his friends use his property there along the river and got his permission. From the driveway, we drove through a large cornfield to a cleared spot along the woods that ran along the river. You had to climb down the hill from the clearing up top to get to the water, which had a very tiny beachfront, and then the water soon dropped off to be really deep, so it wasn't the most pleasant swimming experience. We would bring lawn chairs to hang out in during the day, food to cook on the open fire, music, and alcohol. Mom, Dad, and we three kids always went home at dark, but the Smith kids and their friends spent the night sleeping really rough and partying all night.

It was very private, so everybody in the Mafia felt free to let their hair down. Dan remembered himself and some of the guys streaking around the campfire on more than one occasion.

The main attraction at the river was a very high rope swing tied up in a tree that was standing on the edge of a tall cliff overlooking the water. The boys would either stand on the cliff edge and take off on the rope from there, or when they were feeling even more adventurous, they would climb the tree, rope in hand, to get up even higher before flying out over the river on the rope. Then they either jumped or dove in. Dan remembered having to climb all the way up the tree to get the rope swing once and just jumped off the branch into the water, probably from the highest point ever. Another big accomplishment was to see how many times the rope would swing back after a jump, allowing the next guy to grab and go and so on. We had a home movie of Sam, John, and Sal doing this. Paula was on the same movie using the rope swing once. I never tried the rope swing myself. As brave as I was, I wasn't very confident in the water. The closest I got, as could be seen on the same movie, was to be in the water down below and hand the rope to someone on the next level if it didn't get swung back to them. I could be seen in the water looking very cold and handing the rope swing to Sam, who looked equally freezing. In addition to the movies, we had a few pictures as well. One of them was a shot of a heart carved in a tree by John, which said "Alice A + John S" inside. Above the heart was a self-portrait of John, depicting himself with long, straight hair and a very large nose. John did have a pretty large nose, but the one in this work of art was more caricature than reality. The tree also bore a peace sign and some other names and initials—some I know, and some I don't.

CHAPTER 41

"Don't Go Breaking My Heart"

(Elton John and Kiki Dee)

I started the sixth grade in Newport News in 1976, but shortly after, we moved to Williamsburg to live close to John. He had gotten a job at a tire shop there, and he and Alice found a roadside motel with about eight trailers out at the back. As usual, we kids were not happy about the move. It was embarrassing to be picked up by the school bus in front of a motel because everyone probably thought we lived there. Little did I know that we actually would live in a motel at some point in the future. There was a very sweet young mom named Martha that lived there with her husband and little baby. One night, we were alerted to a fire in their trailer, which we ended up watching burn to nothing but a shell before the fire department put out the fire. Nobody was hurt in the fire, but it was heartbreaking to see Martha and her little family watching their home and everything in it burn up. It was really difficult for my mom to witness the fire, given the history with my grandmother's death.

Dan and Jo came to live in Williamsburg too when Dan got a job with John at the tire shop. They stayed with John and Alice, but John and Alice left Williamsburg and moved out of the trailer just a few months later. They had to go back to Hampton to take care of Alice's baby brother. Her mother had the boy late in life and then was unable to care for him and had to be hospitalized, so John and Alice moved back in to her dad's house to care for the boy, whom I believe was about one year old. They were starting to make plans to adopt the boy and raise him as their own, given the circumstances and ages of Alice's parents. He was a beautiful, happy boy, and it was clear that John was completely in love with him. After about a month, Dan took Jo back to Edgewood to stay with her parents because she was getting pretty far along in her second pregnancy. He brought back a friend named Terry from Maryland when he came back. The two guys were only there a couple of weeks, but they did a lot of partying. One night, they stole a fifth of liquor and bought some packs of firecrackers, which they proceeded to light in the trailer. They were gone before Christmas, and Dan joined Jo and her parents. He paid me money to clean up the trailer after he moved out, but I couldn't get the burn marks and holes out of the carpet from the firecrackers. My only memory of Patty from this time was when she came over all excited about a way to cut your own hair, and she wanted to try it on me. I let her do it, and ended up with a bad haircut that luckily didn't take long to grow out and covered well with a ponytail.

The only thing close to where we lived, because it was a highway, not a neighborhood, was a little convenience store. The first time I ever tried to steal anything was from this store. I was with my brother, and we both stole candy. We were caught by the owner, who was a grumpy old man. He said he knew our parents, and he was going to tell them about the incident if we didn't tell them first. We knew it was always better to be honest with our parents, so we went home and confessed. My dad immediately took us back to the store and made us apologize to the owner and promise to never steal from him again. It was really embarrassing, and it kept me from stealing again for about a year. I'm grateful that I usually got caught whenever I tried to do anything wrong because if I had been more successful, I might have done more bad things, especially with the many particular opportunities I had around me as I grew older.

Speaking of stealing, I had a girl in school here in Williamsburg whom I thought was my friend, but she stole something from me. For Christmas, my aunt Faye bought me a bracelet from Avon. It was a sliver bangle that was open with two hooks on the ends to hold three different charms. I loved it and wore it to school after Christmas break. We girls were in the habit of wearing one another's jewelry, sweaters, etc. during the school day and then returning them at the end of the day before school let out. I let several girls wear my new bracelet, and they promptly returned it. When a girl named Judy asked me to wear my bracelet, I allowed her to, and I forgot to ask for it back at the end of the day. In fact, I forgot all about it for several weeks until another girl told me that she had stolen it from me and had the audacity to wear it to school with a silver ring on it instead of one of the charms. I was madder at myself than I was at her for not even remembering it. I watched out for her to wear the bracelet, and when she finally did, I told her that it looked like one I used to have but had lost. I asked if I could wear it for the day. She seemed reluctant but didn't really have a choice. At the end of the day, she asked for it back. I took the silver ring off and gave it to her, then explained that I knew she had stolen this bracelet from me, and she wasn't getting it back. I told her that it would be nice if she returned the charms that went with the bracelet now that I knew the truth, and surprisingly, she did.

I liked my school, Bruton Heights Elementary, along with my teacher, and I had a good friend there named Kathleen. I had a close call shortly after starting the year that could have been one of the most embarrassing moments of my life if anyone had witnessed it. I was wearing a maxi dress one day, as was the current fashion. When I had searched for clean underwear that morning, all I could find was a pair with the elastic broken at the waist. Mom had started becoming neglectful about things, like making sure we had appropriate underpants to wear, so I was on my own. I tried to tie a knot in the top of my underwear to keep them up, but it became untied while I was sitting at the lunch table. I planned to get up and take my tray to the garbage, then head to the ladies' room by myself, so my friends wouldn't know that I was trying to refix my underwear. I walked about halfway across the cafeteria when my underwear started slowly slipping down. I tried to stop it with the inside of my elbows shoved into my sides, but when I had to use my hands to start unloading my tray, my underwear flew straight down my legs and were lying at my feet on the floor. I stayed very calm, bent down, stepped out of and picked up my underwear, and quickly placed them in one of the available garbage cans in front of me. I then just as quickly and calmly piled some of the trash on top of the underwear and pushed it down into the can a bit. I walked out of the cafeteria to head for the restroom but stopped in the large doorway to turn around and see if anyone was looking at me. Nobody was, and nothing unusual appeared to have happened around the trash cans. I got away with it! Thank you, God!

There were other close calls at this school but of a completely different type. We had several bomb threats, which sent us students outside for hours in the frequent ice and snow while the whole school was searched and deemed safe from the bombs that they never found. That was a pretty miserable experience, but not as bad as when I broke my left wrist for the second time while I was doing the high jump in the gym during PE. When I was landing on my back after the jump, my wrist went down between the two thick mats that had been put together to break our fall. So it was my wrist that broke my fall. I got up off the mat, held my deformed wrist out in front of me with my right hand, and walked to the PE teacher to show her what I had done. All the kids were aghast at my injury as the teacher rushed me to her office and laid me on a bench. She alerted the front office, and they called my mom to come and get me. The teacher put an inflatable splint on my arm, which didn't seem to help as the pain was much worse than it had been the first time, and I fainted once while waiting for my mom to get there. She took me to the emergency room, where I fainted once more while waiting for the doctor. After X-rays determined the obvious, they numbed my arm and set the break by manipulating the bones with some kind of needles, at least that's how I remember it. It wasn't the simple snapping back into place and the pain going away like the first time. It's a horrible, pain-filled memory for me, and it was only made worse by beginning to throw up after the procedure and on the way home, probably as a reaction to the medications they gave me. Instead of taking me home, Mom took me to the motel in the front of our trailer park. She had become friends with the motel manager, a nice lady whose name I can't remember. The manager lived in an apartment adjacent to the motel office, and I fell asleep on her couch while she and Mom visited.

After that, it was the usual broken arm stuff, having to write and eat with my right hand and getting help carrying things. It was more serious this time though. I had to wear the cast for longer, and the doctor cautioned that if I broke that wrist again before adulthood, it might affect the growth of my arm, and it could be deformed. That scared me enough to stop my daredevil ways, and I've been cautious with my physical activities since that time. I did have an incident with my cast, however, but it wasn't because I was being a daredevil; it was because I itched! As was typical, my arm was itching very badly inside my cast one time, and I was relieving the itch by sticking a ballpoint pen down inside the cast. I didn't think it through, however, and was using the end with the cap on it, which slipped off. I tried retrieving the cap by continuing to stick the pen down there to capture it, which only pushed the cap down so far that the pen no longer reached it. I was freaking out about having the cap in there and got the idea to put a wire coat hanger down there to try and retrieve it, but it didn't work. I was afraid to tell Mom about it until my friends convinced me that the skin would grow over the cap and would have to be cut out of my arm. After I told her, we went back to my doctor, and he had to cut my cast down to below, instead of above, my elbow. The crisis was averted, and I had more freedom of movement now.

Jo gave birth to Jason two days before Dan's birthday in January 1977 while they were still living with her parents in Edgewood, and they were ecstatic with their new baby boy. All of us back in Hampton were happy about the baby, and we finally got to see him a few months later after the new little family had moved into their own cute apartment in Havre de Grace about a block from the bay on Bourbon Street. I remember visiting them there at least once, which Dan had started filling with handmade furniture and decorations.

Something else happened to my health here that would affect the rest of my life. That winter, I developed an ear infection, and I remember being in terrible pain but not seeing the doctor, and I apparently had a ruptured eardrum. From that point on, I've never been able to tolerate motion. It started with not being able to go on merry-go-rounds or roller coasters and being car-sick to getting sick on boats and airplanes to finally not being able to tolerate a swing, treadmill, or even one spin. In my forties, I started experiencing one inner ear condition after another, even leading to some hearing loss, and having chronic vertigo and dizziness. I have been diagnosed with cranial nerve 8 damage, which was probably a result of the damage sustained when I was twelve years old. I think that Mom didn't take me to the doctor because she didn't realize how serious it was, and she had become very distracted and somewhat neglectful, as she had before when she was dating the young sailor and ended up leaving Dad and us kids.

Sure enough, she had a man named Wayne come to the house one time and introduced him to us kids. He was balding and not very attractive, but dressed well, and he had a beautiful Lincoln Continental car that my mom was impressed with. He took us all to Colonial Williamsburg, but I can't remember exactly what we did while there. We didn't see or hear anything inappropriate between him and Mom, but I had enough experience now to know that my dad wouldn't have approved of this activity. It wasn't long before Mom left without any explanation or much indication of a problem other than the one visit with the guy named Wayne. She ended up calling us eventually and said she was in Florida with a man named Will. He lived out in the country and had a pack of dogs, and I don't remember any other details, including whether or not she met him in Williamsburg and went with him to Florida or if she traveled to Florida and met him there. It was shocking when she just left without a word, and we were traumatized again.

When Mom left, there was only one month of school left, so Dad, Sam, and Faye devised a plan for us kids to live with Sam and Faye in nearby Denbigh, and they were going to take care of us kids while Dad was on the road at least until school was out. God bless them, because I know it wasn't easy for them, and they were kind and gracious to us, especially Faye. They lived in an apartment with two bedrooms, one for them and one for three-year-old Shannon. They were young and sure didn't need three kids moving in. We were aged ten through thirteen at the time. Faye had to drive about twenty miles every morning with Shannon, Monday through Friday, to take us to school. Then she went back home for a few hours until it was time to come back, pick us up, then drive home again. What a sacrifice she made! Sam had always kept to himself and continued to do so while we stayed with them. He was very particular with their belongings and spent a lot of time cleaning the house and dusting things, especially his beloved onyx chess set. I mostly tried to leave him alone because that's what he seemed to want. Faye, however, couldn't have been more loving and caretaking of us three kids who were just unceremoniously dumped by our mom and not for the first time.

After a few weeks of this routine, Faye's younger brother Frank came over one morning and pressured Faye into letting us all go swimming instead of going to school that day. We kids were all for it, even Paula, and surprisingly, Faye said yes. We drove out to some kind of gravel pit or construction site or something that created a big, giant mudhole, and this was where we were going to swim. I have no idea why this was a good idea, especially when we had the ocean thirty minutes away. Anyway, we didn't have bathing suits on, just tops and shorts. Faye's brother and his teenage friends that came along stripped down and started skinny-dipping in the muddy water. This was not shocking to us kids as we had been streaking in the past with teenagers. My brother immediately stripped and started to swim, but my sister and I had gotten too old and self-conscious to skinny-dip, so we kept our clothes on and found a spot a little further away to start swimming. I don't think that Faye and Shannon even got in the water.

After everyone played for a little while, my brother was telling my sister and me that we should skinny-dip too, but we said no. I kind of wanted to join them but was shy, so I took my bottoms off in the muddy water where nobody could see anything but kept my top on. When my brother saw what I had done, he told me to get out of the water and be naked with everyone else. I kept saying no, so he came over and tried to get me out of the water. I sat down on the muddy bottom, and he grabbed one of my legs and tried to pull me out. I screamed and resisted until he finally gave up the fight. Little did he or anyone else know that the biggest reason I was screaming was because, as my behind was being dragged across the ground, it was being cut by what must have been a piece of glass or something similar that was embedded in the mud. The blood was immediately noticeable in the ugly brown water, and everyone started freaking out and running to me. I stayed in the water, not wanting to be seen naked, and when I looked at my behind, I saw a thin piece of flesh, about six inches long, hanging off but still attached to the bleeding wound I had just sustained.

I don't remember the details, but I somehow got out of the water, got my shorts on, and got in the car to go back to Sam and Faye's house. We probably didn't seek medical attention because Faye was not my parent, and I begged and pleaded not to go to the hospital. When we got back to the house, I wouldn't let anyone see my wound except my sister. She cleaned and dressed it and continued to care for me until it healed. I ended up with a deep gash about two inches long where I had full pressure on my bottom when the cutting started. The gash then became more of a cut about four inches long from lifting my bottom up until my brother let go of my leg. The gash ended up being an ugly, raised purple scar about one-fourth-inch wide that obviously should have had stitches. The rest of the cut was a long, thin white scar. I just thank God that I didn't end up with tetanus from whatever the culprit was or getting an infection. I'm sure Faye was thankful as well, being the kind caretaker that she was. Tommy and I put her through hell once when she took us with her to Dad's office to pick up his check one day. It seemed like it was just the three of us in the car, so maybe Paula was babysitting Shannon.

He and I started arguing on the way there and were still at it when Faye got out of the car to go in and get Dad's check. When she came back out to the car, she found us rolling around in the back seat beating the crap out of each other. She was frantic and didn't know what to do with us, but I recognized that her being upset was a good excuse to call a truce because Tommy was just about getting the best of me in the fight. Almost always before, I could beat him because I was two years older. Now, however, at ages twelve and ten, the boy was about to get the best of the girl. That was the last fistfight we ever had, but that didn't mean it was the end of our conflict.

There was one bright spot for me during this time. On the last day of school, we had a fifties day, where we dressed up like bobby-soxers, had a bubble-gum blowing competition, and a jitterbug dance contest. My friend Kathleen and I entered the dance contest, and thanks to my mom's lifelong expert lessons, we won! I was really disappointed when we didn't receive a trophy, ribbon, or certificate for winning the contest. It was probably silly to most people, but I never competed or won anything, unlike my brother and sister, so it really meant a lot to me. I do have a picture of me in my fifties outfit at the school that day, which is a rare and wonderful memento for me.

We kids ended up staying with Sam and Faye through the summer, and I had a lot of fun there. I had my twelfth birthday, and I got a new pair of roller skates. I went to the closest skating rink a few times but mostly used them in the parking lot of the apartments next to the house and taught myself to skate backward there. We had already met the teenagers across the street, Sally and David, after Sam and Faye moved in there, and now we got to spend a lot more time with them. They were brother and sister and were a few years older than Paula and me, but we all got along well. Paula and Sally were especially close, and David ended up being Paula's boyfriend. I met a boy named Ricky, who was David's age and went to school with him. We really liked each other, and he came over to see me a lot. He gave me my first real kiss during a romantic moment under a street light one night after asking for my permission. Sam and Faye had a great rock record collection, and it was a summer of Fleetwood Mac's *Rumors*, Boston's self-titled *Boston*, Pink Floyd's *Dark Side of the Moon*, Foreigner's self-titled *Foreigner*, Bob Seger's *Night Moves*, Heart's *Dreamboat Annie*, Aerosmith's *Toys in the Attic*, Ted Nugent's *Free-for-All*, Bad Company's *Straight Shooter* and self-titled *Bad Company*, and all five Lynyrd Skynyrd albums (*Street Survivors* hadn't been released yet). We teenagers (not quite for me) were also allowed to listen to records at a gal named Sherry's place. She lived in the apartments next door and was away for some time, so she paid Sally to feed her cat a pill for her diabetes every day. We would often stay there and listen to her music, my favorites of which were Steppenwolf's "Magic Carpet Ride" and Blue Oyster Cult's "Don't Fear the Reaper." I am so grateful for the rock and roll education I got that summer!

The last time I went out to Chickahominy was this summer. I can't remember who all was out there, but Sally definitely came with us. Someone had a canoe, and I took it down the river all by myself, without a life jacket, not being a very good swimmer, and known to have almost drowned once before. It was definitely one of those times when something really bad could have happened. This same visit to the river was also the first time that I tried hard liquor. It was tequila, which was a popular drink with the Mafia at the time. John drank the brand with a little red sombrero on the cap, and Paula collected the little sombreros for a while. They also liked to drink the kind with the worm in the bottom of the bottle and made a big deal out of who was going to eat it. Not me, thanks. At some point, Sally came up to me with a bottle of tequila in one hand and a plastic lemon in the other along with a shit-eating grin on her face. "Where did you get that?" I asked.

"Those guys over there said we could have it," Sally replied.

I looked over at the guys in question and recognized some faces, but none of them belonged to any family members, so the coast was clear. "Well, what do we do?" I asked.

Sally motioned me toward the woods and away from the party and then handed me the bottle and the plastic lemon. She took a saltshaker out of her pocket, the portable kind that you take camping with you, licked the back of her hand, and shook some salt on it. Then she grabbed the bottle of tequila and took a swig out of it, then grabbed the plastic lemon and squirted some of the juice into her mouth. She made an awful face and said, "Damn! That tastes like shit!"

So of course, I said, "Okay, okay, let me try it!"

We both had another shot and got a good buzz, but that was enough for us.

It was good times for me staying with Sam and Faye despite the circumstances, until something terrifying happened. Dan, Jo, and Jason had come back to Virginia with some happy news. When Jason turned six months old in Havre de Grace in July 1977, Jo told Dan that she was three months pregnant with another child. Mom had also come back from Florida, and she was staying with Dan and Jo in the apartment they were renting in Denbigh not far from Sam and Faye's place. Dad was home from the road, and I guess they were trying to reconcile, but it wasn't working out well. They were at Sam and Faye's house, and Sam and Dan were there too, so it must have been a weekend. Of course, everyone was drinking. I was in and out of the house, and there was tension between my parents each time I went in. Apparently, my dad threatened my mom with harm at one point, and it made Dan nervous enough that he left, went to his house, and got the rifle that he owned. He intended to bring it back to Sam's house to shoot my dad if he tried to hurt my mom or wouldn't let her go.

When he saw a cop sitting on the road by his apartments, he decided to pull in behind him and tell him what was happening. Dan told the cop he had a gun, and the officer asked where it was. It was in the front seat, so the cop advised him to put it in the trunk. While Dan was doing that, the cop left and was already there at Sam's house along with another cop car, by the time Dan got there. Dan parked in the apartments next door to Sam and Faye's. Just then, Mom and Dad walked out of the house and saw Dan and the cops, and Mom asked Dan, "What's this?"

He said, "They're here for you."

What neither Dan nor the cops knew, however, was that things had totally calmed down while Dan was gone. My folks were acting very happy together to the point that Mom had agreed to leave with Dad in his truck to go to the motel he was staying at while he was in town.

When they stepped outside Sam's door, however, an officer approached Dad in the front driveway and asked him for his identification. In no time, three more cop cars showed up, creating quite a scene in front of the house. Dad never wanted to comply with police officers and especially if he hadn't broken any laws, so he resisted the officer's request. Words were exchanged while more officers approached and began to surround my dad and the first officer on the scene, who was a handsome Hispanic man bearing a strong resemblance to an officer in a popular TV show at the time, so Dad immediately nicknamed him Ponch and only addressed him as such. They asked questions about my mom and where they were going. Mom said everything was fine, but they didn't seem to believe her, and Dad was becoming more and more belligerent with the officers. I'm not sure exactly what precipitated it, but the officers sprung on my dad, and it eventually took five officers to get him to the ground.

At this point, all of us who were in the house were alerted to what was happening outside, and we all came out. From the door, all we could see beyond Sam's car parked in the driveway was my dad's legs lying prone on the ground. We all screamed and yelled and ran around the car, and I expected my dad to be injured. Instead, he had the five officers on top of him, holding him down and trying to handcuff him. One of them had his knee in my dad's neck, and Dad was still resisting and spewing expletives and threats to the officers. We were asking or screaming for the officers to let him go, including Dan, and other officers on the scene were trying to subdue all of us. My brother began stomping on one of the officer's hats that was lying on the ground. I think the anguish of us kids got Dad to finally calm down and decide to comply. We kids were forced to go back in the house. They eventually took Dad to jail, and I don't remember any other details, like what the charges were or how long he was there. Later on, Paula and I had to go to court to testify about the incident. We waited outside the courtroom until they called my sister. When she came out, I was told that I wouldn't have to testify. Apparently, it was assumed that I would say the same thing that my sister had already said, so I never saw the inside of the courtroom. I don't think Dad was convicted of anything. At any rate, things ended up not working out between my parents again, and Mom wasn't in Virginia long before she returned to Florida.

CHAPTER 42

"Free Bird"

(Lynyrd Skynyrd)

Just before the 1977 school year started, Mom came back and reconciled with Dad, and they rented us a house back in Holly Homes in Hampton. This time it was at 803 Morris Street. It was the typical three-bedroom, one-bathroom tract home, but it had a fenced yard, a paved driveway, and a little garage in the back. There was also a pear tree in the backyard, and we ate lots of pears off that tree. Patty came around a lot when we lived here, usually with her new boyfriend, Dusty, who had patiently waited for her until she decided to divorce Keith. Years after Patty and Keith broke up, Keith and some girl ended up murdering a guy in a drug deal gone wrong, and they both went to prison, so it looks like she made a better choice.

Dan helped us move our stuff that we had been storing in Denbigh into the new house in a U-Haul truck that Mom had rented. He picked up the stuff and decided to stop near the new house to get a burger at the McDonald's located at Buckroe and Grimes. He got to the back right corner of the restaurant and came up short, tearing the whole roof off the corner along with a steel ladder that had been attached to the building that made a lot of commotion. Everyone in the vicinity went crazy, but Dan just got his hands on a hamburger and calmly ate it until the cops came. He knew that there had been no signage on the building, so it wasn't his fault. They let him go with no citations, and there wasn't even damage to the truck. Chalk up another one to Dan's luck!

John was also there a lot, and I remember Mom pretending she was mad at him one day for leaving his dirty fingerprints on the kitchen ceiling just to give her a hard time. He had come over after his construction job to pick up his favorite dessert, banana pudding, that she had made for him. She threatened not to give it to him unless he cleaned off the prints, but he got out of the house with the pudding and didn't clean them off. He only lived a few blocks away on Andrews Boulevard, and he loved to play basketball in the driveway at the hoop he put on the garage in the back. Other members of the Mafia came over and played with him quite frequently. Problem was, it was a one-lane driveway that was bordered by the neighbor's fence, so the ball was constantly going over the fence and into the neighbor's yard. The guys had no problem hopping the fence to retrieve the ball, except they had two big, gnarly dogs. They were always arguing about whose turn it was to get the ball and trying to come up with ways to distract the dogs while the unlucky player ran the gamut for the ball. It was hilarious. Nobody was ever bitten, but they were all chased!

The house backed up to a small forest about as big as two city blocks. On the other side of the forest and across the street sat Spratley Junior High. Sam and Patty had both attended this school at one time, and Paula and I were excited to be starting there. The one thing that gave us anxiety was the long-held tradition practiced on the first day of school called Smear Day. All the new seventh graders and any other new students to the school were besieged by the veterans of the school. They threw eggs and all sorts of other food items at the newbies, after which they were supposed to smear the products in to your clothes and hair. We had heard rumors back when Sam and Patty were there that they sprayed people's heads with Nair, and it made their hair fall out. I don't know if that ever actually happened, but the story terrified Paula and me. Mom had left again after only a few weeks, returning to her man in Florida, so Patty was staying with us and taking care of us. She and Dusty sat us girls down the day before school to give us the rundown. They told us to wear old, unwanted clothes instead of the new outfits we always wore on the first day of school. That way, we wouldn't care if they got ruined. They said to just try and play cool and not look like a frightened new kid, and maybe people wouldn't notice us. We made it through that first day without a smear as the tradition had mostly died off by the time we attended the school. When we arrived home triumphant in our cleanliness, Patty and Dusty attacked us with eggs, lipstick, and shaving cream. We thought it was so fun and knew that something like that would never have happened if Mom was living with us.

We were pretty happy at this new place. We had a peaceful home life with Patty, and we all got along well. She was really laid-back and was so sweet and fragile that we didn't want to hurt her by disobeying. Us kids liked Dusty too except when he was driving us somewhere in his souped-up Duster. He was a really fast and scary driver. He also had a motorcycle and really looked the part of a hippie biker with his long hair and goatee. I got the impression that the older kids didn't care for him being with Patty, but I didn't know why other than the fact that he was always dirty. Patty said she couldn't put her face against his without it breaking out from the oil and dirt and that his mother would wash his face and hands for him when he sat down at her table to eat. Paula and I had fun, active social lives here too. We made friends with a lot of neighborhood kids that we went to school with, and we spent time with them nearly every day. Paula's best friend was a girl named Barbara, who lived two houses away. Paula, Barbara, and I once choreographed a dance to the Eric Carmen song "She Did It." It was the first time I had done that, but it wouldn't be the last. It turned out that I really loved choreographing.

I tried something else for the first time here as well, skipping school. Us kids all walked through the woods to get to school and back and hung out there too. One afternoon while we out there, some of our friends were talking about skipping school the next day. Paula didn't seem tempted at all, but I was. The next morning, everyone who was going to skip hung back in the woods instead of crossing the street to go to school, and I was one of them. I think there was about eight of us, guys and girls. We walked to someone's house and spent the day there. I can't even remember what we did all day. When it was almost time for school to let out, we headed back to the woods and met up with our friends. Apparently, I liked it so much that I did it again the next day with some of the same kids. Again, we just hung out at someone's house all day. Mom was still living with us at the time, and when I got home from school the following week, she needed to talk to me. She knew I had skipped school two days in a row, and she said we were going to the principal's office the next morning to find out my punishment. When I asked how she found out, she said the school had called. It wasn't until many years later that my mom confessed that Paula had told on me. I was surprised and really disappointed. The school said that they were trying something new for punishment for skipping, in-school suspension. The next day, I had to report to a special classroom, where I spent the entire day in that room with a small group of kids who were also being punished, doing the work that our teachers had provided for us to do. We weren't allowed to talk. The windows were covered in brown paper, and we went to lunch in the cafeteria after all the other students were finished. We each had to sit at our own table. I did this for two days, and I hated it. The worst part, though, was that Mom also punished me by not letting me go to what was supposed to be my first concert—Peter Frampton. I don't think I've ever gotten over it. *Frampton Comes Alive* was my first album, and I knew every word to every song on the album. I was beyond disappointed.

Mom was also still living with us when Elvis died on August 16 of that year, 1977. She was really devastated when that happened. She had always been a huge fan and felt as if they were akin in some way because my dad had always been *her* Elvis. We all mourned his loss, but Mom took it especially hard. Mom was already gone back to Florida, however, by September 9. I believe it was a Saturday. Dad was in town and at the house when the phone rang, and I answered it. It was Alice asking for Dad. She said John had been in a motorcycle accident and was at the hospital. Dad spoke to her on the phone very briefly, hung up, and told me he was going to the hospital. I was worried but assumed that he probably got banged up pretty good and would be okay. I was thinking a broken leg maybe. I was also wondering how he had a motorcycle accident when he didn't own a motorcycle.

Dad came home a few hours later and looked stricken. Tommy and I were at the house, but Paula was at a movie theater with a friend. Dad sat us two down at the table and told us that John had died. What? I thought he would just have a broken leg or something! He was dead? No! That couldn't be! I pounded my fists on Dad's chest a few times and then broke down as he hugged me and my brother. We all cried and cried. Once we calmed down some, Dad asked me where Paula was, and I told him. He looked up the phone number for the theater in the yellow pages and called to have her paged. Paula was embarrassed and angry when she got on the phone at the theater, and Dad told her she had to come home right now. She argued with him and wanted to know why and probably thought it was some drama between Mom and Dad or something. She was so relentlessly argumentative that Dad finally blurted out to her, "You have to come home now because John is dead." Apparently, Paula fainted when he told her that, and she was helped to get home by her friend and her friend's parents. I was angry with Paula for being so obstinate and putting Dad in that position because I saw how it hurt him to tell her that, but I also understand her not wanting to hear what Dad might say. I think we three kids were starting to lose trust in our parents and what they might do to us next. Later, I realized that he shouldn't have called her at the theater and should have told her the news when she came home. Of course, people don't always make the best decisions at these times. Paula was always everyone's favorite of us three kids and especially John's. They had a very strong and special bond. We were all shocked and in pain, but she was absolutely devastated.

As I mentioned earlier, John and Alice lived five minutes from our house on Andrews Boulevard. Although the Holly Homes Subdivision was strictly residential, Andrews was the main thoroughfare through the neighborhood and was wider and busier than the other streets, with a grassy median dividing it down the center. John had a friend who had just purchased a new motorcycle, and the friend brought it by the house so John could check it out. John had been riding since he was a teenager and was considered a very good driver. When his friend arrived at the house with his girlfriend on the back of the bike, John and Alice came out front and checked out the bike. His friend suggested that John take it for a spin, and John agreed to just take it up and down their street. The speed limit was probably twenty-five, so there shouldn't have been any danger of hurting his friend's brand-new bike. With his friend and their two girlfriends watching from the front yard, John took off to the right and rode to the end of the median, then looped back around and passed the house. He took the following loop after that and headed back to the house all the while in sight of the others. Suddenly, a car entered Andrews Boulevard from a side street, running the stop sign and coming very close to hitting John on the bike. John swerved to the left to avoid the car, and the bike jumped up on the median. When the back tire hit the median, the force sent John flying off the bike to the left, through the air, and landing on the other side of the road. He landed on his head. And he wasn't wearing a helmet. Alice and his friends saw the whole thing. They ran to him and then ran into the house to call an ambulance. The oncoming car fled the scene and was never found. John was taken to the hospital, where he was pronounced dead on arrival from head trauma. Another horrible, tragic accident for the Smith family, and it was John! Not *John*! He had taken over for my grandmother after her death as the heart of the family, and they both died too young. Our family had an extraordinary share of death, but this one cut our family deeply.

The person who might have been the most devastated by the news was my mom. Dad had her phone number in Florida, and he called right away to tell her. She was probably the most broken person I've ever seen when she arrived home after catching the first flight out and Dad bringing her home from the airport. Whatever comfort we all needed for our loss was not going to come from Mom, but I couldn't resent her for it because she was in the worst shape of all of us. She cried nonstop or was practically catatonic for about a week. She barely made it through the funeral without literal support on either side of her. After that week, she was merely devastated. We all were. John had been one of those special lights in the world. He was only twenty-five years old and was the best of us, and now he was gone. He had been the proverbial heart of the family, and how do you live without a heart? He was the best son to my dad, the best brother to the remaining Smith kids, the best uncle to me and my siblings, the best boyfriend to Alice, and the best friend to the Mafia and so many more. He was really the best. His funeral was so large that after it became standing room only, people stood on the porch outside the funeral home with the doors open. Our family arrived in three limousines to the funeral home and then rode them again to the cemetery for the burial, where we waited about forty-five minutes for all the cars in his procession to arrive and for everyone to gather around the grave site. Everyone who knew John and many who did not but knew of him attended the funeral because he was just that kind of guy. The effects of his death on our family would linger on for a long time, and we would never be the same.

Mom displayed her grief over losing John, but Dad was more stoic. He did say shortly after John's death, however, that if John went to Hell, then he wanted to go there too. He said that John was the finest person he had ever met. The feeling was mutual. Not long before John died, he was at our house on Morris Street. Dad had just come home off the road, and John was there to greet him. Later, Mom, Dad, and John were all sitting at the dining table, talking. At some point, John told Mom that she could have married any other man to help raise the Smith kids, but she couldn't have found another man to love them like my dad did, and then he grabbed Dad's face in his hands and gave him a full-on kiss on the lips. They both cried and professed their love for each other. Alice called for John after a while and told him that he better be home in ten minutes. John said he didn't have a jet, so he guessed he wasn't going to make it. He then took us all out to dinner, then drank with Dad after we got back home and ended up spending the night. It was really out of character for John to defy Alice, but he wanted to spend time with Dad. Sal, from the Mafia, was another one who was devastated by John's death. He was either at the funeral home with John's body or with the family the entire time until John was buried. Dan said that John was truly liked and respected by everyone, and he was. I think of him every time I hear the Billy Joel song "Only the Good Die Young." Of course, we all remember the last time we saw or spoke to John. Dan said for him, it was at John's house, where he was working on his car and told Dan that they needed to get together and go fishing or something. Why did we have to keep having these horrible tragedies in our family? I believed for many years that we had some sort of black cloud or curse over us and it had some connection to my evil grandfather, Wade.

As if to add insult to injury, Lynyrd Skynyrd's plane crashed on October 20. Three members of the band and three other people lost their lives. Of course, our family didn't know any of these people personally, but we were all fans of the band and were still openly wounded from the loss of John.

CHAPTER 43

"I Wish"

(Stevie Wonder)

We moved to the next house before Christmas. It was in Newport News, in an old residential neighborhood right next to the shipyard. I loved this house. It had two stories, so I thought it was very luxurious. Paula and I had our own bedrooms here, which was unusual. I had gotten tired of sharing a room with her on Morris Street, so I talked Patty into letting me use the large pantry in the dining room as my bedroom. It had just enough space for my twin bed, and all my belongings had to go on the shelves. It felt wonderful to have my own space, and I prefer small spaces to large, so I was very happy. Mom was dubious about the setup when she returned after John died, but she let me keep it. She was done with the guy in Florida and was back to stay, at least for a while.

I went back to Carver Elementary when we lived here, and I loved it. I had a best friend at school named Laurie, and we thought it was so cool to wear crazy socks to school, trade each other one, then roll up our pants legs so everyone could see our matching mismatched socks. We played war ball in the auditorium, like dodgeball, using lots of the red playground balls but smaller. It was so fun. At Halloween, our class had an evening party at the school, which included a hayride, and I had the best time. At Christmas, we had a fundraiser, for what I don't remember, selling boxes of Krispy Kreme doughnuts. We took the orders in advance, and on the appointed day, our parents took us to the school to pick up our boxes of doughnuts that we'd sold. Then we had to go back around the neighborhood, deliver the doughnuts, and collect the money. I really enjoyed it, and I sold more than the average student. The school would show movies in the auditorium on the weekend, and I went to a few of them. They would play popular music while waiting for the movie to start, and once, they played "We Will Rock You" by Queen. I can't remember when or how the custom started, but all of us kids stomped our feet and clapped along to the music, and it was so cool!

The one bad thing that happened at this school was when I got into trouble and had to stay after school for a week of detention. This was highly unusual for me at the time. There was a boy named Steven who used to walk around the cafeteria at lunch and steal food from people's trays even though he had a tray of his own. This really annoyed me, so one day when he grabbed something off my tray, I happened to be opening a packet of mustard for my corn dog, and I impulsively squirted the mustard onto Steven's pants and yelled at him to stop. It didn't seem like a big deal at the time, but I got into big trouble. I got called to the principal's office the next day and was told that he had spoken to my mother about what I did. Apparently, Steven's mother called and complained that I had ruined Steven's pants with the mustard, and that he only had two pairs. I was shamed for my behavior, and nobody said a word about a kid stealing food from his classmate's day after day, like that was okay and I wasn't supposed to react to it. I was informed about my week of detention, and when I got home, Mom told me that I would be losing my $5 weekly allowance for two weeks to pay Steven's mother for his ruined pants. This was a good example of kids doing stuff like this all the time, but when I did it, I got into *big* trouble. So I never damaged anyone's clothing again, and Steven continued to steal our food.

At home, I had another best friend, Elizabeth, who was a year younger and lived in a big, beautiful colonial house one block over from me. I often went to her house after school because her parents weren't home yet, and she wasn't allowed to leave her house. We enjoyed making fried Lebanon bologna sandwiches and mugs of heated Tang. She had a rabbit hutch in the backyard, and I was so excited when her rabbits finally had babies until I went back a few days later and was told that the mother had eaten all her babies. That was so sad, disturbing, and disgusting to me. We used to enjoy going to the newly built Newmarket North Mall and hanging out. One of our parents would drop us off and pick us up a couple hours later. Elizabeth's favorite place was the Hickory Farms Store, where you could get free strawberry candies.

Paula had a friend right across the street named Kathy, and we didn't like each other much. Tommy had a friend whose name I don't remember, and I went with Tommy to his house once to see where he lived because it was a huge mansion from the turn of the century, the likes of which I've never seen before or since. The family was fixing the place up, so it wasn't pristine and had some construction going on, but it was still very impressive to me and nourished my love of domestic architecture. I developed another interest here also. Paula and I had started paying attention to teen idols like Shaun Cassidy, and we watched him on the *Hardy Boys* TV show, listened to his records like "Da Do Ron Ron," and bought magazines like *Tiger Beat* that featured stories about him and all the young heartthrobs. Paula got a crush on Leif Garrett, also a popular teen idol at the time, and she started collecting pictures of him from the magazines and keeping them in a photo album. I developed a crush on him soon after, and after a few months, Paula had already tired of him, so she sold me the photo album of his magazine pictures for $5. This began an obsession for me that lasted for years.

We had a couple of snow days home from school at this house, so one day, we played outside in the snow some, and then I went inside, but Paula and Tommy must have been somewhere else because I had Mom all to myself. She watched her soap operas every day when she wasn't working and would often watch an afternoon movie on the *Dialing for Dollars* program. I watched the movie with her that day called *Imitation of Life*. It was very interesting to me because it was about a light-skinned black girl who didn't like being black and could pass for white. I had never heard of such a thing, and I couldn't understand at the time why she wouldn't want to be black. Another day, I was home sick, and I watched another movie with Mom. It was *Penny Serenade*, about a couple who adopts a child, loses the child, and then adopts another. I love those movies to this day but less for the content than for the memory of getting to snuggle on the couch with Mom, eating snacks, and having her all to myself. I watched *Gone with the Wind* and *Cleopatra*, the one with Elizabeth Taylor, with Mom more than once when I was a little older, and it was a family tradition, which I still keep, to watch *The Ten Commandments* at Easter every year. I guess we both loved the beautiful, epic movies with the great cinematography.

Speaking of movies, I went to see *The Late Great Planet Earth* when we lived here, which was about the end of times, according to the Bible. It scared me to my core and sent me running to seek the Lord and Salvation that very night. I knelt by my bed and prayed for a long time and then accepted Christ as my Savior. Although it was fear that motivated me, I felt the Lord so strongly in my heart and remained a Christian until I started having doubts in my twenties, but my belief of God has never wavered.

I don't remember the Smith kids being around here much, but I do remember one very special occasion. Dan and Jo's second child, Wendy, was born in January 1978, but true to family form, not without some drama. When Jo went into labor, Dan was just about to get on the bus to leave for work at the shipyard as they didn't have a car at the time. So he told Jo that he was just going to pick up his check, then come back. He picked up his check but then ended up at our house getting drunk. Mom kept telling Dan he had to get to the hospital, and he kept wanting to drink. Sam was there, and eventually, Dan borrowed Sam's car, not to go to the hospital but to go have a drink from with some guy who was staying with us and helping Dad on the truck. On the way to the bar, Dan wrecked the car at a stoplight. Thankfully, nobody got hurt, and they walked away from the car to find a pay phone to call Mom to pick them up and finally get Dan to the hospital for the birth of his second child. Thankfully, a neighbor friend of Dan and Jo's had taken Jo to the hospital, and Jo's mom had come up about a week or two before to help out, so she was keeping Jason. Mom got Dan to the hospital, and they got there before Wendy was born, although Dan was a little drunk and a little beat up from the accident.

I do recollect having some family conflict about Alice keeping the car that John had when he died, which was a station wagon, but having been John's, it was sacred. I'm not sure exactly who the family wanted the car to go to, but apparently not Alice. As usual, we weren't here long, and I really wanted—needed—to stay in this house, this school, and this neighborhood. Living there restored my childhood in many ways; but the biggest, ugliest, most damaging bomb that either of my folks had ever built was on its way. And all the wishing in the world couldn't stop it. With a few months left in the school year, we moved to Virginia Beach, which was a first for us. We did, however, have a very clear reason for moving. Mom had found a job as a route salesperson for Krispy Kreme. Maybe she thought that getting a job besides housewife and mother would be good for her. Our plan was to relocate for the job, which was essentially a graveyard shift, and Alice would live with us and take care of us kids.

CHAPTER 44

"Night Fever"

(The Bee Gees)

Things started out great with this move to Virginia Beach in spite of the loss of my good friends Laurie and Elizabeth and how much I had loved my school, house, and neighborhood in Newport News. We made friends with lots of kids from the neighborhood right away. We had a skating rink, and Woolworth's close enough that we could walk to, and we were the first people I knew who subscribed to HBO. Mom slept all day for her overnight job, but we didn't notice much at first since we were still in school all day. She would get home before we left for school, and she brought home a box of doughnuts for breakfast every morning, so we kids loved that. We had always been big fans of Krispy Kreme because not only did they have doughnuts, but they also gave you a paper hat to wear and a hot doughnut to eat while watching the doughnuts make their way through the glazing process on the conveyer. We learned just how much quality meant to the company when Mom worked there. She had to deliver fresh doughnuts each day to grocery and convenience stores and pick up any doughnuts that hadn't sold the previous day. Those doughnuts went into a dumpster and could not be sold or given to employees because they were one day old!

We were all still trying to move on in our grief over the loss of John, and I learned about delayed grief on what was supposed to be the first day of school for us in Virginia Beach. I didn't feel particularly stressed about the process as I had plenty of experience in first day at a new school. Apparently, it was some pressure for me, however, because it pushed my grief over John's death to the surface that morning. Alice was taking us to school that morning, and I remember becoming very quiet and looking out the window, not moving or speaking for a long time. Alice asked me what was wrong, and I said rather loudly and emotionally, "John is dead!" Of course, this was upsetting to everyone in the car, and I felt guilty for not handling my emotions better. I didn't start school that day, but I don't remember a big deal being made of the incident, and I started promptly the next day.

Alice certainly had her problems processing her grief as well. She huffed a lot of paint out in John's car in the driveway and was once found walking down the street, extremely high, and wearing only a bra with no shirt. She obviously had her own struggles and wasn't really capable of taking care of us kids at the time, plus it was summer vacation, so Mom relieved her of her duties. I can't remember if she continued to stay with us or not or for how long. Mom made a big deal about how we kids would have to be more responsible for ourselves along with helping with housework and cooking, but we would get paid for our efforts. I can remember my sister making some dinners and both of us doing housework. Paula and I were sharing a room again, and we were both responsible for cleaning it once a week. We were equally messy, but Paula hated cleaning our room, and I didn't mind it so much. She learned that if she bugged me enough while we were cleaning, I would just tell her to get out and let me do all the work myself. She was a smart one.

In spite of the terrible experience Alice had at the Southern Baptist church we had attended in Maryland some time back, she was willing to try out a local church that Mom wanted to attend here in Virginia Beach. The two experiences couldn't have been more different. It was called the Rock Church, and it was the first megachurch I had ever heard of. Mom, Alice, and we kids showed up for a Sunday morning service and kept thinking we were in the wrong place because all we could find was a giant stadium rather than a church. It was well marked, however, and we parked in the huge lot, got into the "church," and were ushered to five seats. There were instructions read to the audience before the service began because the service was being televised, as always, and I'm sure they didn't want any embarrassing moments. This time, Alice was definitely anonymous along with everyone else rather than the star attraction of the house. We only attended that one time.

Since Paula had sold me her Leif Garrett photo album and apparently her obsession, I used all my earned allowance to buy as many teen magazines as I could afford and continued collecting his pictures. I also bought his records, listened to his music, and watched him on various television shows. I would cry and pull at my hair when I watched him, so overcome by obsession for him that I literally didn't know what to do with myself. I wouldn't let anybody speak while he was on television, and even Dad honored my request, and always let me watch any show that Leif was on. I joined his fan club, and I couldn't wait until he came to our area in concert so I could see him live. Tommy got mad at me once and threw my photo album, breaking it apart. So I threw his prized skateboard on the sidewalk and managed to break it too. We both considered it an equal insult.

Once school got out for the year, we had all the time in the world on our hands, so we spent a great deal of time hanging out with our group of friends around the neighborhood. I walked to the Woolworth's store by the house at least once a week to spend my allowance on new teen magazines, and a girlfriend who would go with me talked me into trying stealing again. We both did it a few weekends in a row, and I got away with taking a key chain, some lip gloss, and other stuff that I don't remember. We never got caught, but I decided not to do it anymore after those few times, and I never stole anything again. One of the high school girls named Shawn took us all to Princess Anne High School for their version of *The Gong Show*, which was very popular at the time. The students did a great job, and we had a good time. Some of our friends were already out of high school, including one named Wayne, and he and Paula were developing a crush on each other. When we weren't hanging out in the neighborhood, we were watching movies on HBO. We were the first people I know of to have the channel and the envy of the neighborhood kids. They came over to watch *Rocky* and *Slap Shot*, two of our favorites, which we watched over and over again. Although quite inappropriate for a twelve-year-old girl, *Slap Shot* remains one of my all-time favorite comedies, and I have shared it with my own daughter and grandson. The only other movie I remember watching at that time was *Equus*, which was a lofty drama way over my head, but there was a full frontal male nudity scene that I found fascinating and disgusting all at once.

The family had some good times and good news here. Dan, Jo, Jason, and baby Wendy came over for Easter, and we took some good-looking family photos. Faye announced that she was pregnant with her and Sam's planned second child, and we couldn't have been happier. Mom and Dad bought a used Volkswagen bus that I don't remember having for too long, but we loved it, and one of my best memories ever, which I happened to record on tape with my new tape recorder, took place in this van. We had a "pet" squirrel that lived in the backyard, and we could identify him because of the nick in his ear. We started feeding him peanuts in the shell on the back patio and eventually earned his trust enough that he would come in the house through the dining room and all the way down the hall of the house. Dad played catch with Tommy and me in the yard, and we loved having his attention until I missed a throw from him once and caught it with my nose instead. My nose bled and swelled but didn't appear to be broken, so they didn't take me to the hospital for it. About forty years later, I found out that I had a double-deviated septum, most likely from this injury and another time when I got hit right between the eyes with a hard-thrown Frisbee at the skating rink.

Paula decided this year that having a birthday right after Christmas really stunk, and she was going to start celebrating her half birthday, June 5, instead of her real birthday, January 5. That was the day before my birthday, but I loved my sister so much that

I didn't even mind sharing with her. Mom wanted to do something special for us girls because we had done such a good job handling the house in her absence. It was decided that she would rent the skating rink down the street for a birthday party for us—the whole skating rink for two hours! We could invite as many people as we wanted and Tommy too, and we could request any music that we wanted to play and have pizza and cake and presents. Wow! This was the coolest party I had ever heard of, and I couldn't believe it was *mine*!

I didn't hold onto old friendships as much as Paula did, so I only invited local kids. Paula, however, wanted to invite her friend Cathy from Newport News along with Sally and David, whom we were still close with as they were still across from Sam and Faye in Denbigh. We picked them up, and they attended the party, then spent the night. We had a blast! I was obsessed with my new tape recorder, and I played tapes and recorded TV shows and conversations all the time. The first time was the day after the party in the van when we were taking everyone back home. Mom, Dad, Faye, and Shannon were in the front bench seat. Tommy was on the double bed in the back of the van, and Paula, David, Sally, Cathy, Paula's current bestie Pam, and I were seated on the benches in the center of the van. We made fun of David for not having combed his hair that day, and Tommy complained of being hot, but Paula pointed out that he was wearing a sweatshirt during the summer. Faye asked if Shannon could come back with us, and we were always happy for her company. Shannon was only three at the time but was very well-spoken. She loudly busted out that she hoped Cathy wouldn't be coming back again, and we all laughed hysterically about how Cathy had been told by a three-year-old. I told Shannon I thought she might be a midget, and she replied, "*You* are a midget!" My daughter and I have continued to use this type of name-calling since then, "*You* are a (fill in the blank)." I still have this tape recording, having saved a digital version, and it is one of my most precious possessions.

Little did I know that this day would be the pinnacle of happiness for the remainder of my time living at home with my parents as things got pretty bad after that. I had just turned thirteen years old, and I wouldn't be happy again for a long, long time. We did have some more fun times in Virginia Beach that summer—going swimming, playing Putt-Putt, and walking around our neighborhood with our friends—except for the time a dog ran out of a yard into the street and promptly bit Paula on the butt! I somehow managed to escape a childhood dog bite, but I sure got my share of other injuries. Paula was becoming closer to Wayne, who smoked pot. Paula was more interested in pot than I was, and she tried it a few times but would become paranoid each time, once having to go to the emergency room for her anxiety. Wayne was pretty crazy about Paula, like all the guys were, but he was nine years older than her. My dad was nine years older than my mom, but Paula was only fourteen, and Wayne was twenty-three. She wanted to date him but was nervous about being alone with him, so she insisted that I accompany them on at least two of their dates, one to see *Saturday Night Fever* at the movie theater and one to see *Grease* at the drive-in. I think Paula was drawn to Wayne more than usual because things began to fall apart at home and within the family.

I don't know how it started, but Mom and David began an affair. At this point, Mom was almost thirty-three years old, and David was sixteen. He was also a close friend of Paula and mine, and Paula's ex-boyfriend. Wow. That takes a minute to sink in. I don't remember how they conducted their affair, like if he came to the house, if he even drove at the time. He was living at home with his parents and still in high school, so where did they *go*? I only found out recently from Dan that they would go to his and Jo's apartment. They might have also gone to Sam and Faye's house since it was conveniently across the street from David's. Even more devastating than Mom having this affair, however, was that Sam had also been having an affair, and what's worse, he had decided to leave Faye for the woman he had been seeing. This was shocking and painful news to the whole family, and it was breaking Faye apart.

Sam and Faye, despite getting married at ages fourteen and eighteen and not finishing high school, were some of the best our family had to offer. They were very responsible, and Sam started a long and lucrative career as a pipe fitter through the apprenticeship program at the Newport News Shipyard. They lived on their own in a decent apartment and even took in us kids when Mom and Dad separated earlier. They spent their money wisely. Sam went to work every day and gave it his best, and Faye made sure he came home to a clean house and dinner every night. They were also very responsible parents, who put a great deal of thought and effort into raising their child. These two young kids were the envy and pride of the family.

Apparently, however, things were not as idyllic as we all assumed. Sam had begun an affair with Darla, whom they had met through neighbor and mutual friend, Sherry, the gal whose records we teens would listen to while caring for her cat at her apartment while she was out of town. I can't remember if Faye discovered the affair or Sam confessed it, but he told Faye he wanted out of the marriage to be with Darla. Faye was obviously devastated, and Sam was guilt-ridden, so I remember there was a great deal of Sam going back and forth between his wife and lover during this time for him to please everyone and do the right thing.

One time, Faye went to Dan's house crying about how Sam had come home from Darla's and wanted Faye to feed him and do his laundry. Dan went to the house, where Sam was lying on the couch, snatched him up by the hair and dragged him outside, demanding for Sam to explain to him just what the hell he was doing. Sam wouldn't say anything; he got in his truck and left. Dan said that a few years ago, Sam told him for the first time what had happened with him and Faye. Everyone in the family knew that Faye was pretty strict with Sam, and apparently, she also began to withhold sex from him after she had Shannon, and he was really unhappy with that situation. When Sam met Darla, he talked to her all night long, which was remarkable because he had never been able to talk to anyone else that way. Then there was the sex that Darla offered freely. The incident between Dan and Sam caused them to not speak to each other for a long time as I recall. Everyone felt that this would never have occurred if John had been alive to bring the brothers together.

The family did everything we could to comfort Faye during this time, and she and Shannon spent a great deal of time at our house in Virginia Beach for the rest of the summer. It was especially tragic to see her grieve for the man who planned their second child together, and now that Faye was in the third trimester of her pregnancy, he was leaving her for someone else. We kids started school in the fall, but shortly after, the situations between Mom and Dad and Sam and Faye all came to a head. Obviously, it couldn't go on forever, and it was tearing everyone apart. One weekend, Dad was home from the road and had maybe just found out about Mom's affair but was furious nonetheless. They argued, and she ended up running out the front door, afraid that he was trying to put his hands on her. He was chasing her around the car parked in the driveway, and I must have believed that he would hurt her if he reached her because I broke one of the cardinal rules of our family. I ran down the street to the house where Wayne lived with his parents, which was where Paula had been spending most of her time, and I asked to use the phone to call the police on my dad.

I don't remember anything else about the incident except that my dad must not have gotten his hands on Mom, and things must have calmed down because they both talked to the cops when they arrived and nobody went to jail. I remember that everyone was mad at me for what I had done, except for Mom. Dad was angry that I betrayed him and the family by involving the police, and Paula was angry that I had involved Wayne's family even deeper into our ugly family business by coming to their home and using their phone. It was one of many times in my childhood when things seemed upside-down in my world. Wasn't my mom a victim of my dad's potential violence, and wasn't I a victim of two dysfunctional parents? Yet I seemed to be the one everyone was mad at for some reason. I was doing my best to cope with all this craziness, and so was Paula, but she had a crazy, radical idea to bring some peace and stability to her life.

CHAPTER 45

"Don't Stop"
(Fleetwood Mac)

As I mentioned earlier, Sam and Faye had gone to South Carolina to get married because he was eighteen and she was only fourteen. It did require her parents' permission, however. In the state of Virginia, they could have gotten married without her parents' permission if she had been pregnant. Our family was shocked beyond belief when Paula and Wayne decided to do the same thing. Paula approached my parents with an ultimatum: give her permission to marry Wayne in South Carolina, or she would get pregnant and marry him without their consent. Wow! This was Paula we're talking about. Paula was a straight A student who would sit at the table every afternoon and evening studying, if necessary, to keep her grades perfect. She was also full of common sense, wisdom, and maturity. She didn't do stupid, impulsive things, like Tommy and I did. She never got into trouble. She was damn near perfect. This just couldn't be happening. It's so ironic that Dad was always teasing Paula and me that if we weren't married by the time we were twelve years old, he would put us in an old folks' home. I'm sure he never dreamed that his joke would come true, just off by only two years.

But it was happening. Mom and Dad gave in to Paula's demand, and they went to South Carolina for the simple wedding. Tommy and I didn't go. Paula and Wayne continued to live with Wayne's parents for a long time, and Paula dropped out of school, although I don't know exactly why. She had only completed the eighth grade, and I don't know if she even got a GED. Now it was time for us to move again but this time without Paula and without Dad. Mom and Dad were splitting up again, and Sam was not coming back to Faye, so the two women got a place together in the Aqueduct Apartments. Dad said Tommy and I could stay with Mom this time, but I would have been happy to be anywhere else. Mom was seeing David, and he was there all the time. It couldn't have been more awkward. Shannon, Tommy, and I shared a bedroom. Shortly after, beautiful John Thomas was born. The only thing I liked about my life at this time was spending time with Shannon and John. Paula and Wayne came over to visit once, but it wasn't a positive experience because she and I got into a fistfight about a shirt that she said I stole from her. I don't recall if I had the shirt or not, but if I did, it wasn't a deliberate theft. Wayne admonished Paula so badly about acting like a child instead of a grown, married woman that I ended up feeling sorry for her instead of myself. Sally and I got closer during this time now that Paula was an old married lady. We decided to become blood sisters, so we each pricked our fingers with a needle and put them together to mix our blood. I still have that needle. Ricky, the boy who asked me for the streetlight kiss, stopped by the apartment with a friend one time, but Dad chased him off. Dad was there talking to Mom, and when my friends came in, he told them to "get the fuck out of here." When I yelled, "Dad! Why?" he said, "They're friends of the 'punk', right?" That was his nickname for David.

I said, "No, they're friends of *mine*, not David's!"

Then Dad said, "Oh, okay, then they can stay."

Of course, by now it was too late. The guys had already gotten the heck out of there after what my dad said to them. I grabbed a jacket and walked outside, looking for them, but there was no sign. I never got to see Ricky again, and I really hated Dad for ruining the one tiny sliver of joy I had had in months.

I got bussed to Carver Intermediate School, and it literally took ninety minutes to get to the school. That's three hours on the bus every Monday through Friday. I couldn't have cared less what color the kids were at my school. This was ridiculous. At this point, I had been smoking cigarettes off and on for a year or more. Now I was probably smoking a pack a day, and I actually smoked on the school bus. We smokers sat in the back of the bus and kept the windows down and smoked all we wanted. The bus drivers, who were different every day, couldn't care less what we did. When I was at school, I hated it. I didn't make any friends, and I had a really bad attitude. With everything that was happening in my life at the moment, making any effort in school felt impossible. So I had a lot of days that I just didn't go. I would get ready and walk to the bus stop, but many times, I would start walking back home when we kids saw the bus coming. Mom obviously didn't care enough to do anything about it. This went on for a few months when Dad finally put his foot down and declared that we kids couldn't stay with Mom any longer. Fine with me.

He took Tommy and me to stay with good friends Ersel and Shirley back in Aberdeen, Maryland. He had to be on the road all the time, like usual, so we didn't see much of him. I think Tommy and I were relatively happy being there. They had a two-story house on Rigdon Road, located just outside Swan Meadows in a nice neighborhood. I liked the house, and I liked staying with them because they treated me like a princess. Shirley had lost a daughter years before, named Mary, and she still grieved for her, especially since she had four boys and no other daughters. Thus, she and Ersel treated me like the daughter they never had and gave me some much-needed attention and affection, for which I am eternally grateful. I think Tommy liked it there too because Ersel and Shirley's son, John, was the same age and they were good friends. For me, it was a welcome respite from being around Mom and David and hating my life in Denbigh, and it was great to be back among old friends.

Pardon my sarcasm, but we couldn't have us kids getting any joy in life, so we moved again after a month. Apparently, Dad and the lady he was dating at the time decided that Tommy and I should move in with her and her two children at her home in Havre de Grace. This was the first and last time that we lived with Dad and a girlfriend. Marsha was a beautiful, if a little full-figured, lady who always looked perfect, smelled great, and spoke eloquently. Mom compared her to Elizabeth Taylor, and I can agree with that. She was a really nice lady, and her little girl of about six years old was very sweet. I probably wouldn't have minded living with just the two of them, but her son, whom I think was Tommy's age of twelve, was a miserable jerk. He was spoiled, overweight, and sullen and didn't try to hide the fact that he hated Tommy and me being there.

For our part, we really wanted to be back at Ersel and Shirley's, but of course, we didn't get a say in the matter. I can't really remember the details, but I know that we were so desperately unhappy being there that we started to plan to run away. It wasn't so bad when Dad was there, but he was gone out on the road most of the time, as usual. One day when Dad was in town, he let me go to school late because I wanted to watch Leif Garrett on *Good Morning America*. I knew he was going to be on the show because I perused the TV Guide every week, looking for anything interesting to watch, and especially any Leif Garrett appearances. I kept that habit until I became a mother years later and my life didn't revolve around television and trying to escape boredom. Unfortunately, the TV Guide had been wrong because I watched the entire two or three hours of the show, and Garrett never appeared. I was so disappointed, but it meant a lot to me that Dad allowed me that indulgence. It was the only bright spot of that particular domicile.

Lucky for us, it was time to move again. Just as Tommy and I hadn't known that Dad was seeing Marsha, we didn't know that he was seeing Mom back in Virginia and trying to patch things up with her. They had decided to get back together, so Dad brought Mom to Havre de Grace, and they rented a crappy motel room on Route 40 for us to live in. It had a double bed for them in the main room and two singles for Tom and me in a kind of alcove, but there was no privacy from each other, and Mom and Dad were rekindling their relationship, if you know what I mean. Tommy didn't seem to be bothered by the noises coming from the other part of the room, but it was very disturbing for me.

We continued to attend the same schools in Havre de Grace that we had started at Marsha's house, and I was mortified for anyone to find out that we now lived in a motel room. Luckily, it was close enough to walk, so nobody had to see us getting off the bus. School was pretty good, and I even linked up with an old enemy from fourth-grade Halls Cross Roads in Aberdeen, who now became a friend. It was Teresa, whom I had a fistfight with one day after school with a large audience, and won the fight by a good punch in the stomach after I gave her a black eye. I think we both felt stupid about our fight from years before and would never consider such a thing at this age.

At Christmastime, I was in a school performance with a bunch of other girls. We were required to wear a black leotard with black tights, and we stapled silver garland in loops to the waistband of the tights, so it looked like a skirt, but you could still see through the garland when we moved. It wasn't a problem to expose a bit of the black tights underneath, not for everyone else anyway, but it was for me. I was excited about the performance because it was a dance routine to a couple different Christmas carols, and I loved to dance, especially with choreography. It was also a good atmosphere with our teacher and all of us participants. It was fun! I had a black leotard in my wardrobe, but I needed the black tights, so I told my folks about it. They told me that they didn't have the money to buy them, and Mom said she would ask friends to try and find me some to borrow. I was so worried until I came home one day and Mom said she had some for me. When I held them up, we discovered a large hole cut out of the crotch and down the inner thigh! I was so upset at the prospect of wearing them, but Mom said it wasn't a big deal. I tried to explain to her that the tights would be exposed when I moved, and people would be able to see the large hole! She said it wasn't a big deal, and they were the only pair I was going to get, so I had to make the best of it. Of course, I was mortified. Looking back, I don't know why I didn't just not go to the performance and claim illness when I got back to school. My folks didn't plan on going to support me, and I probably wouldn't have been too missed, but I went.

When I arrived at the school and met up with my classmates and teacher, we were told to take off our coats and pants or skirts to reveal our black leotard and tights underneath. It was time to staple the garland on and get ready for the show. I tried my best to keep my legs together while my classmate stapled the garland to the waistband of my tights and did my best to manipulate the garland to be denser in the front and back rather than the sides. I felt a little more comfortable making my way to the stage, but when the time came to start dancing, I realized that I could not keep my legs together any longer and had to take my chances. I made it through the mortifying performance, and didn't notice any funny looks from the audience or my classmates, but I was really traumatized by the experience. I couldn't believe that my folks would put me in such a position and that we really didn't have the money to even buy a pair of tights.

Mom and Dad's enthusiasm for Christmas and gift giving had always been a little hit or miss, but this year was the worst. I guess we really didn't have any money because Tommy and I were informed that there wouldn't be any gifts. Not only that, but there wouldn't be dinner, visitors, or any type of celebration that year in our motel room. I was so excited when I found out that we were invited to Ersel and Shirley's for Christmas dinner, where Shirley made my favorite creamed peas and chocolate pie. Then like guardian angels, they gave Tommy and me both a gift. I got a nice watch that meant the world to me. It was almost a Christmas without one gift, and they saved the holiday for me.

After Christmas, Tommy and I were on vacation from school, and the folks left us alone in the motel all the time. I'm assuming that they were at the Hut. We never got along well, and being stuck in a room together constantly was miserable for both of us. One time, the folks left us alone there, and I didn't have any cigarettes. At fourteen, I had been smoking at least half a pack a day for two years. I was seriously addicted, and being without a cigarette for hours and not knowing when I would get one was pure torture. I finally decided to puff on a cigar that Dad had but didn't even have a lighter or matches, so I had to light it on the electric stove. It was not at all satisfying. Life at that motel was nothing but dismal, but there was one bright spot. Jeff and Eric were in town seeing their dad and ran into Mom and Dad at the Hut. They told the guys that Tommy and I were at the motel, and they came over for a visit. It was so nice to see their old, friendly faces.

CHAPTER 46

"I Was Made for Dancin'"

(Leif Garrett)

Thankfully, we weren't at the motel long before we moved to a house back in Swan Meadows, this time on Swan Street. I don't remember much about this place, except that I got caught smoking once. I had started hanging out with a gal named Carol, and she was at my house one day, where we were stretched out on my twin beds in my room. I was smoking a cigarette with the window open when Mom opened my door and caught me red-handed. She asked what in the world I thought I was doing, and I said I was holding the cigarette for Carol, who had permission to smoke. She asked, "Oh, it's Carol's, huh?" I said yes at the same time I looked over to see that Carol had fallen asleep. Mom and I both had to smile at my stupidity, but I still got grounded.

Carol was faster than I was, like most of my girlfriends, and she introduced me to a few things I had never done before. One night, I was sleeping over at her house, and she said we were going to sneak out, which I had never attempted. We left the house after her folks went to bed and went to some older dude's house. I felt a little uneasy in his company but not frightened. We smoked cigarettes and talked, and then he gave Carol some pills. She encouraged me to take one with her, but I had never taken pills before and wasn't keen on the idea. She and the guy assured me that it would just pep me up for a while and wasn't anything to be afraid of, so I took it. It wasn't long before I started feeling antsy and energetic and couldn't stop talking. It wasn't a bad feeling, but I never liked the way drugs took over my body, so I didn't care for it. Carol and I went back to her house and stayed awake all night. I never took speed again.

On Superbowl Sunday 1979, we went over to Ersel and Shirley's to watch the game along with more of Dad and Ersel's friends. My least favorite of Dad's friends was a disgusting-looking and disgusting-acting man named Bob. He had been leering at me since I was a small child and gave me the big creeps, and he was there that day. I was trying to stay in the kitchen and dining room while the men were watching the game in the living room, but I had to go upstairs to use the restroom. When I came back down, Dad called me over for a hug, and then I settled next to some other folks standing against the wall to watch the game for a minute. I didn't notice that Bob then left the living room to go upstairs and, when he came back down, walked out of his way to come over and start talking to me, playing with my hair and rubbing my shoulder and basically making me sick. When I ignored him, he returned to the spot on the opposite wall that he had left and continued to watch the game. The next thing that I saw was my dad leave his seat and walk over to Bob, and without so much as a word, he punched Bob in the face so hard that his head went into the wall and left a large hole. Then Dad returned to his seat and took a drink of his beer. Everyone was shocked and silent for a moment until Ersel asked Dad, "Tom, what the hell did you do that for?"

Dad said, "He walked across the room to put his hands on my daughter, and that shit don't flush." Bob was trying to recover himself and was apologizing profusely to Dad, but Dad told him, "You better get the hell away from me before I hit you again." Bob made a hasty retreat, and the crowd turned their attention back to the game. I went to the kitchen and stayed there, and Dad later gave Ersel some money to fix the hole in his wall. While I appreciated Dad coming to my defense from the slimeball, I resented the fact that he always subjected me to the slimeball in the first place.

I had another unpleasant happening when Paula and Wayne came to visit us. I was happy to see both of them, and apparently, I got too friendly with Wayne for Paula's liking, and I was accused of flirting with him. I believe I had smacked him on the butt at some point while we were kidding around. I felt comfortable with Wayne, and he was always teasing me. Now that he was my brother-in-law, I felt even closer, and I guess I thought smacking him on the butt was okay. I would have done that with Tommy and all my uncles. I remember feeling really hurt by Paula's accusation because my intentions were really innocent.

I don't know why, but I think it was just a couple months later that we moved to another house across the street, which only had two bedrooms, so Tommy and I had to share again. I was so upset about this along with the fact that we didn't have living furniture any longer, so the only room that felt normal and comfortable was the kitchen. I'm assuming that we had money troubles again or still. I can't think of why we could afford a three-bedroom house for a while and then not. The whole financial picture during that period in Maryland didn't make sense to me.

I finished the eighth grade and spent all summer hanging out with Donna, a gal who lived next door to Aunt Bell and wasn't as fast as Carol. She was innocent, sweet, and funny. Our favorite activity was choreographing dances to songs on her portable cassette player in her front yard. I had done that once with mine and Paula's friend Barbara back on Morris Street in Hampton, and I loved it. I bought a Leif Garrett cassette at one of the shops next to Sid's Grocery across the street from Swan Meadows. It contained his hit song "I Was Made for Dancing." That was our favorite song, and we must have driven the neighbors crazy listening to it over and over again, but gosh, it was great fun!

I had another person that I spent time with in the evenings named Mark. He was a few years older than me, and he worked all day at a crab shack. I would have innocent girl fun with Donna all day and try to be a grown-up in a relationship with a boy at night. I turned fourteen that summer, and it was a time in my life where I was torn between being a little girl and a woman. Mark and I just sat outside talking or walked around the neighborhood, but I never even kissed him. The relationship ended abruptly when he came over from work one evening without showering, and he stunk like crabs. I was completely repulsed, and I lost that loving feeling immediately.

I met a much older guy, whose name and how we met I don't even remember. He drove a cool car. I thought he was hot, and he smelled really good. Scent is still very important to me. He would drive around the Projects in his car and stop and talk to me while I was hanging out and about. Then he asked me out on a date. I told him that I had to ask my parents' permission, and unbelievably, they said yes. I told him so next time I saw him, and he said he would pick me up for a movie the following Saturday night. I was so nervous and excited for that date and still couldn't believe my parents were letting me go. Dad was home when the time came, and I asked him to keep an eye out for a "hunk" while I was primping in the bathroom. A few minutes later, he said, "Sis, your hunk is here."

I came out and ran to the door, looking for his cool car, but didn't see anyone. I asked, "Where is he, Dad?" and he said, "It's that pile of dog shit lying out there in the yard. Isn't that your hunk?"

I was amused and offended all at once, and right at that moment, he pulled up. He didn't get out of his car, and Dad didn't even insist on meeting him, so I walked out to the car, opened the passenger door, and got in.

I was pretty nervous on our drive to the theater, where we were supposed to see the *Amityville Horror*. We drove around for longer than we should have, and then the hunk told me we didn't need to see the movie, that we were just going to drive around, talk, and listen to music. He asked if I was okay with that, and I felt like I had to say yes. We ended up on a dirt road in the middle of nowhere, which he said was a back way to take me home. I was getting really anxious, and then he stopped the car and started to kiss me. I was okay with that, but then he got really handsy, and I was not okay with that. I told him to stop, but he didn't and just became more aggressive.

When he started to try and take my clothes off, I got angry and yelled at him and pushed him off me. I told him to take me home *now*! He was saying, "Okay, okay, you don't have to get so mad. It's cool, etc." I didn't talk to him all the way home, and he kept trying to apologize. He took me home, and I got out of the car without saying a word. The house was dark. Tommy was gone to a friend's house for the night, and my folks were asleep. I lay in bed for a long time, thinking about what happened and how it could have been much worse. I was still shocked that I was even allowed to go on a date with this guy, and I felt very vulnerable and unprotected. Nobody was even waiting up for me when I got home. Parental responsibility definitely fluctuated with my folks, based on what they were going through personally, and they were actually going through a lot.

My mom was diagnosed with precancerous lesions and was told that she needed to have a hysterectomy, at which time they would see if there was any active cancer. She was in the hospital for a few weeks, and my dad was completely lost. I guess he was afraid to face the possibility that Mom had cancer, and he thought she might die. He stayed at the Hut all the time and didn't want to visit Mom in the hospital, although Tommy and I did. Sam and Faye came up to see Mom, and we got to go with them to see her. Shannon was with them, and they were a welcome blessing in the dismal life we were living at the moment. Mom had her surgery, and they didn't find any cancer. She had a long recovery from the hysterectomy and was out of commission for a month. Dad was very attentive and helpful to her at this point, and before the summer was over, Mom was back to normal. They took us school shopping for clothes and supplies, and I was excited to start the ninth grade with my best friend, Donna, and kids that I knew. Then the folks told us we were moving to Washington State before school started, and the bottom dropped out from under me. Sam and Dan were both living in Tacoma now, which I assume was why we were moving there.

We went down to see Paula and Wayne to say goodbye before we left for the West Coast, and I was the epitome of an uncooperative and sullen teenager. I was so pissed off about moving again and still hurt and offended by Paula's accusation, and I didn't want to be there. Dad tried to take some family pictures while we were there, and I had my head down in every picture. He called me out on my behavior, but I didn't care, and it didn't change. My attitude only brightened when I saw Leif Garrett's tour schedule in one of my teen magazines and saw that he was playing at the Washington State Fair in Puyallup shortly after we were due to arrive there, so I was finally going to see him in concert! A couple days before we were set to leave, my maternal grandfather's girlfriend called and said he was very sick and needed help. She didn't think he had long to live. We had been hearing that for a lot of years now, but Mom became very upset. She wanted to visit him in Porterville, California, before we headed north to Washington.

CHAPTER 47

"Little Dreamer"

(Van Halen)

When we got to California, we stayed a few days at my grandfather's girlfriend's place while he was in the hospital. At this point, they had been together for about ten years, and the Smith kids had met her, but we had never met her before. She was a schoolteacher, and she was very sweet. I don't know how or why she tolerated my grandfather, who was now well enough that he was getting out of the hospital, but he needed a caretaker. My mother wanted to do the job. I never understood why she would want to care for someone who had been so cruel to her, but she did. So just like that, our plans changed, and we were staying in Porterville instead of going to Washington State. My one shred of joy, seeing Leif Garrett in concert, wasn't going to happen now.

Dad went on the road. Mom stayed with my grandfather in his apartment, and Tommy and I stayed with my aunt Rosie, her husband, Frank, and their five children. Rosie is the aunt who had been married to my mother's late brother, Don. The four oldest children still at home belonged to Don, and Rosie and Frank also had a daughter of their own. We settled adequately enough at Rosie's house, where we were treated well. It was fun getting to know my cousins, and they had a pomegranate orchard near their house. I was in awe of all the beloved fruit available, and it hurt my heart to see my cousins throwing the fruit at one another to get busted on the ground. Such a tragedy to waste them. My oldest cousin by my uncle Don was Debbie. She had gotten married and was living with her husband and their beautiful baby boy. I enjoyed visiting with Debbie and the baby until her husband started hitting on me. I was uncomfortable and made excuses not to visit after that.

Mom would bring Tommy and me to visit with her at Wade's house when we weren't in school. He made it very clear that he didn't want us there and resented when my mother offered us a soda or some chocolate. He had cases of soda stacked in the kitchen, some so old that the bottles had exploded and oozed in a big mess. There were lots of messes in his neglected apartment, and Mom worked hard to clean and throw things out, like the boxes and boxes of chocolate that had gotten so old it had turned chalky white and was inedible. Apparently, Wilma brought more of the soda and chocolate every time she visited so much that Wade couldn't consume it all. He still didn't want to share it with anyone though. I always told Mom that I didn't want anything. I wouldn't take anything from that hateful old man if I was dying of thirst or hunger.

I think we were only at Rosie's for a week or two before we got an apartment. I was very unhappy about the fact that it was only two bedrooms, so Tommy and I were sharing again. We started our school year, and I went into high school as a ninth grader. I made fast friends with a cute little gal named Dawn, who was with me in choir. She introduced me to some California food that I hadn't been familiar with, like avocados, which I didn't like then but I love now. The funniest discovery was one day when we went to Taco Bell for lunch as we had an open campus. The only Mexican food I knew was hard tacos, so that's what I ordered. While we were eating, I noticed a girl at another table eating something with her hands, and she was accidentally eating her napkin along with it! When I pointed this out to Dawn, she informed me that the girl was eating a burrito, not her napkin. Boy, did I feel dumb.

Outside of school, I spent time with Rodney, who was the son of my uncle Dean's wife's sister. It sounds complicated, but it was family. Rodney and I took an instant liking to each other but ended up having a love-hate relationship. He was my age but went to the other high school in town. I got mad at him one time, and I'm not sure how I even got my hands on his gold chain, but I flushed it down the toilet. He couldn't believe I had actually done it, and I wish I hadn't, but I did. I gave him my silver chain to try and make up for it.

We had a neighbor named Vida, who was a single mom of twin babies, and I got to know her and loved playing with the babies. She was separated from her husband, and her family came to visit all the time. She had a teenage brother that I thought was cute. He invited me to the birthday party he was having at his mom's house in the nearby town of Visalia, where he lived. I wanted to go, but I knew my parents wouldn't allow it. The neighbor lady said we could tell them we were all going to a movie and out to eat, and then I was spending the night at her apartment. They said it was okay, so Vida, the babies, and I headed over to Visalia. We arrived at a large two-story house where there were already a lot of people of all ages and more to come. I was greeted warmly by everyone, and they all offered me something to drink, and I tried it all.

I had some wine, beer, and different liquors, and I was feeling no pain when Stan, the birthday boy, decided to give each of the ladies at the party a hickey. I mean, he just ran up on us, sucked the heck out of our necks, and ran away. I was drunk enough not to care at the moment. Not long after, I found myself in the bathroom, which turned out to be the only one in the house. I locked the door and began getting sick in the toilet, then passed out on the floor. I awoke to people knocking on the door and demanding that I open it. I didn't move from my spot on the floor, and I heard them trying to figure out who was in there. They finally figured out it was the girl who came with Vida, but Vida wasn't there. Vida and Stan's mom started talking to me through the door and convinced me to open the door just for her. I let her in, and she washed my face with a cold cloth and suggested I go upstairs and get in a bed since I wasn't getting sick any longer. A big, strong guy came in and scooped me out of the floor and carried me upstairs to a bed, where I slept.

I was awakened by Stan, who said that Vida was ready to go home. I got myself together enough to get downstairs and out to the car. Vida's estranged husband was going to drive us back home, and there was some serious tension between him and Vida. They put me in the back seat, holding on to a twin on each side. They started a heated discussion as soon as we got on the road, which escalated into physical violence. He kept backhanding her and grabbing her by the hair, then shaking her back and forth like a rag doll, with the car following his motions back and forth all over the road. She was screaming, and the babies started screaming, but I didn't make a sound. I was just praying for God to watch over me and those babies and not let us die in a car accident. I was never so relieved to arrive at a destination. Thankfully, Vida's husband took off in her car after we all got out safely. I helped her get the babies in her apartment and couldn't wait to go home. Mom woke up when I came in. Apparently, she knew that I had been through hell when she took one look at me. She told me to go to bed, and we talked about it the next day. I told her I had learned my lesson about drinking, and I pretty much had. She didn't allow me to hang out with Vida and her family any longer, but I was okay with that too. It didn't matter anyway because we were moving again.

CHAPTER 48

"Refugee"

(Tom Petty and the Heartbreakers)

I guess my mom decided that taking care of her father wasn't her calling after all because we were heading to Washington State after just a few months. We arrived in Tacoma and stayed with our old friend Dolly until we could get a house. I think it was about six weeks. I loved Dolly, and she was very kind to us. She had given birth to three children since the last time we had seen her almost ten years prior: two girls and a boy. Tommy and I enrolled in school in Spanaway, which happened to be on a year-round school schedule. Mom put Tommy and me on different tracks, and mine happened to have just gotten out for break, so I didn't go to school for about three weeks. During that time, I caught the flu for the first time that I can remember, and it was terrible. I had a high fever and was somewhat delirious at one point. When I finally started school, I liked it okay, but we found a house in Lakewood, so I was changing schools again.

We moved to a house on Occident Street, and Tommy and I enrolled at Lochburn Junior High School. When I had started school in California, I had algebra for the first time, and I was doing well at it. When we moved to Washington, my algebra teacher in Spanaway actually used the same book I had been using in California, and I picked right up where I left off. Once I got to Lakewood, however, there was only one algebra teacher, and his classes were way ahead of where I had been in the other two schools. I was completely lost. I might have been able to catch up with the rest of the class if my teacher had given me some extra help. Instead, he put me in a desk in the corner of the room by myself and gave me different work to do, but it was still too advanced for me. This teacher had no patience with trying to help me or any other student. He would lose his temper if students answered questions incorrectly or couldn't understand what he wanted from them. He threw an eraser across the room once and then took off his shoe and threw it in another of his classes. I soon gave up and requested to be transferred to a basic math class, where I finished out the school year.

Sam and Dan lived next door to each other in some apartments on Ninety-Sixth Street, not far from the house we rented on Occident Street. We had no furniture when we arrived, so apparently, Dan stole a two-bedroom furnished apartment full of furniture from a vacant unit in their complex and put it all in our house. I remember thinking how ugly it all was and feeling wrong for having stolen furniture in our house. Dolly gave me a daybed for my room, which I also thought was ugly, but at least it was honest.

Sam had been the first to go to Washington this time, while we were still in Maryland. He had finally decided that things were over with him and Faye, and he and Darla had gotten married. He had gotten on a bus to go accept a job at the Bremerton Shipyard, and Darla followed along with their newborn baby girl, Jessica. Dan, Jo, Jason, and Wendy followed soon after. I hadn't been around Jason and Wendy much, and they were very energetic and even wild sometimes. They were difficult for me to handle, but I babysat all three of the kids when asked, and I always loved my baby cousins.

At some point, Sam and Darla moved to Gig Harbor on the Olympic Peninsula, which was closer to the shipyard in Bremerton where Sam worked. It was after Sam had moved out that Dad and Dan had another incident with a gun here, but this time, shots were fired. According to Dan, Mom and Dad were at his house drinking while Jo and the kids were back in Maryland visiting her parents. Mom and Dad were arguing, and Dad popped Mom in the mouth, so things got ugly and tense. Then Dad said something to Dan about his "goofy wife," meaning Jo. Dan said they knew Dad really loved Jo and wasn't really insulting her, just talking shit to Dan, but Dan was pissed. He got up and got his rifle, pointed it at Dad, and told him to get out of his house. Dad told Dan that he didn't have the balls to shoot him, so Dan fired. He shot the chair leg out from under Dad. Dad told Dan he was crazy, and he and Mom walked out.

Unbeknownst to Dan, the bullet had traveled though the wall after it hit the chair leg, into the neighbor's apartment, and a piece of it went into a woman's leg. She came out of her apartment and showed my parents what happened. Dad knocked on Dan's door, and Dan answered with the rifle pointed at Dad, but Dad informed him that he had shot the woman next door. An ambulance came for the woman, and police also arrived. They charged Dan with discharging a weapon in the city limits, and he was fined $25, even though he was a convicted felon who wasn't even allowed to own a weapon. Dan's crazy magic luck struck again. As for Dan and Dad, they made up, and Dan said he thought Dad had a newfound respect for him after he actually fired a weapon at him.

Dad was working as a long-distance furniture mover as usual, and Mom got a job waitressing at a restaurant in Tacoma. The restaurant was owned by a close friend of Dolly's. After Mom started working at the restaurant, I soon got a job babysitting for her and her husband. They had a lovely, beautiful girl, and two rambunctious boys, but not so much that I couldn't handle them. The whole family was wild in a different way than I had ever experienced. First was their home, where I would watch the children and sometimes, spend the night. They had a large, somewhat rural home, but it had no kitchen. It was in the process of remodel, I suppose, so the kitchen consisted of a side table with a hot plate and a refrigerator with nothing but milk and once, a large raw fish. They owned a restaurant, so they either brought the children there to eat or took the food home for them. They had three bathrooms in the house, but none of them had a door on them. I have no idea why. Being a fifteen-year-old girl, I was mortified to use a restroom with no door and the possibility of anyone seeing me use the bathroom. I would wait as long as I could, then try to get the children deeply involved in some activity so I could quietly sneak away and quickly use the bathroom, anxious and praying that they wouldn't find me. The little girl was very creative, and the boys could be as well. Once, they decided to unfurl an industrial roll of paper used to create bags of sugar and take turns tracing their bodies on the paper with crayons. Their bodies, however, were naked. I wasn't comfortable with anyone other than a very small child being naked and tried to encourage the boys to keep their clothes on, but they weren't the only nudists in the family, as I would find out later.

Patty came out from Virginia to be with the rest of the family, and she brought the cutest, tiniest, little imp with her also—her daughter, Jamie. Patty had married Dusty, and they had this precious baby together, but their marriage was over, so she came to stay with us until she could get on her feet and take care of herself and Jamie. The two of them shared a room with me, and I didn't mind it a bit. I loved getting to be with Patty again, and Jamie was irresistible. Patty got a job as a cocktail waitress in the bar at the restaurant where Mom worked. She soon got her own little apartment, but Jamie stayed with us often while Patty was working, and when she wasn't at our house, she was at Dan and Jo's. Jamie was so smart and sweet and brought joy to all of us. Patty had strict rules about Jamie's care, but Mom and Dad didn't always follow them. One memorable time, Patty came to pick Jamie up after she had stayed with us for a few days, and she was changing her diaper on the couch before taking her home. She suddenly yelled "Tom and Sherrill!" She got everyone's attention, and we all came running to the couch to see what was wrong. Patty then said something like, "I can't believe you would do this. You promised!" While we were all asking what she meant, she showed us what was in Jamie's diaper. I'll spare the details, but the important thing is that there was a Reese's Pieces candy in there, and Mom and Dad had promised not to give Jamie any candy. The evidence was clear, and they were busted. Just like when Sam saw Shannon chewing gum on the home movie years before.

Patty started dating the restaurant owner's brother, whom she had met at the restaurant. He was a handsome divorcee with three young boys, long hair, and very strong opinions on everything. He came to the house with Patty a great deal, picking up and dropping off Jamie mostly. I liked him instantly even though he said a few things that put me off, like the fact that he didn't like girl children. This was surprising, not only because he was dating a woman with a girl child, but he was also a child development instructor at a local vocational-technical school, who ran a day care as part of the child development program, presumably so they had children to practice on. Although he was somewhat indifferent to Jamie, he certainly didn't mistreat her in any way, and I think he became more attached to her with time. He became attached to Patty enough that she moved into the big craftsman-style house on Fifty-Sixth Street that he rented with a roommate. I visited Patty and Jamie there and attended the great parties that her boyfriend would host. He was always playing Led Zeppelin on the stereo, whom I had recently fallen in love with after buying their latest album, *In through the Out Door*, and then going out and buying their older ones. Sadly, the group disbanded not long after I finally found them due to the death of their drummer, John Bonham. Patty's boyfriend and his friends also played Dungeons and Dragons with great enthusiasm, which was the first time I'd ever heard of the game. Their family was interesting to me. They were like a tribe with their own customs and language, much like the old Mojer Mafia that I grew up with. Several of them worked at the restaurant or were there eating very often, so that's mostly where I saw them. The youngest son in the family was a couple years older than me, and he also worked at the restaurant. I developed a crush on him, but he never considered me as anything more than a friend and probably a young and dumb one at that, although we did hang out and have fun together at his brother's parties, and he invited me and others from the restaurant to go sailing a couple of times, which I had never done before. We went out on a big catamaran, and it was an awesome experience. I had some motion sickness, but not enough to ruin my fun.

That summer, after school got out and I turned fifteen, I had a couple more new experiences, courtesy of my aunt Darla. She seemed to take an interest in me and took me under her wing. She got us tickets to a concert at the Seattle Center's Memorial Stadium. I had always loved music, and it was one of the most important things in my life at that time, so I was thrilled to be going to my first concert even if it wasn't Peter Frampton or Leif Garrett. It was actually Black Sabbath (sans Ozzy Osbourne), Blue Oyster Cult, and Molly Hatchett. We had a good time at the show and didn't realize until after we were home that Sam and Dan had snuck into the concert and tried to find us, without success. The next event was my first plane ride. Darla and baby Jessica were going to Sacramento for two weeks to visit her parents and her brother, and she invited me along. Everyone was very sweet to me during the visit, although Darla's brother was a little too sweet to me even though he was married and had a young son and was much older than me. I finally expressed my discomfort to Darla and then to Sam on the phone, and he was made to back off.

We went on a day trip to Lake Tahoe during the vacation and spent time at the Harrah's Casino. I wasn't old enough to gamble but hung around the cheap slot machines and played them a few times when I thought nobody was looking. I talked to a nice old lady a little bit, and she pointed out actor George Kennedy, from the *Airport* movies, and encouraged me to ask him for an autograph. I noticed that other people were approaching him to sign their paper money, but I didn't have much to spare out of my spending money, so the nice lady gave me a scrap piece of paper along with a pen from her purse. I was so nervous, but finally got the courage to approach him and ask for his autograph. He grabbed the paper and pen without even looking at me, signed his name on the paper, and handed them back to me without a word. I thanked him and walked away still starstruck but gave it a lot of thought afterward. I couldn't imagine being so rude to someone who cared about you enough to ask for your autograph. It wasn't until years later that I realized how awful it must have been to have people bothering you for such things when you were just trying to live your life every day. I decided then that I would never want to be a celebrity or be famous for any reason. The fame would never be worth the lack of privacy to me.

I had a lot of time on my hands there on vacation in Sacramento, so I watched the movie *Hair* on HBO over and over again. I loved the movie, which was filled with intriguing characters and great music. I was shocked and thrilled at the same time that it contained a song with the words *sodomy*, *fellatio*, and *cunnilingus* in it. I was just learning about what words like that meant, courtesy of Sam and Darla's *Penthouse Forum* magazines, which I read at bedtime when I spent weekends at their house in Gig Harbor. I was becoming more curious about sex, but the stories I read and the movies and TV shows I watched didn't match up with my real life whatsoever. My curiosity was tainted by being just as curious about why sex made people do things they shouldn't do. I thought of all the times I had had inappropriate experiences with men in my life and how they had hurt me. Some of them I've written about here, and some I haven't. Some weren't that serious, and some were devastating and hurt me to this day. I didn't get to have innocence when it came to sex because several people had taken that away from me. I had immature crushes on boys and dreamed of romantic love, but I also knew the darker side of what can happen between a male and a female. When I was attacked and almost raped by someone close to me during this time, it pushed me over the edge, and I decided to find out for myself what this sex crap was all about. I was going to do it on my terms, however, and under my control. Being out of control and vulnerable sexually was something that would be difficult for me for a long time, thanks to all my abusers.

After I returned from my vacation, I went back to babysitting for the restaurant owner. One of the times I spent the night, I was greeted in the morning by her husband, who didn't have one stitch of clothes on. He was completely comfortable and innocent in his nudity and didn't make one tiny inappropriate look or advance toward me, but I was mortified and didn't want to be in that house any longer. I ended up spending the night at their home one more time, however, because I had a plan to execute, and it had to happen at their house. The restaurant owner's husband had his nephew from out of town spending the summer with the family, and he was my age. We hung out together with the restaurant group, but I couldn't have cared less about the guy. He was, however, perfect for me to test out my new sexual curiosity on since I wasn't attracted to him at all, and he was weak and easy for me to manipulate. Of course, I really had a crush on the restaurant owner's youngest brother and was attracted to him, but I didn't have the courage to let him know how I felt, and he was way too important to me to have sex with.

The next time I had to babysit and spend the night and the children had all gone to bed in their rooms downstairs, I asked the nephew to join me in one of the bunk beds in a room upstairs. I told him that I wanted to have sex with him, but it took all night to get the job done. I was a mess of indecision, telling him to try, then telling him no. Finally, with my shirt on and my naked lower body under the covers, he managed a small degree of penetration in spite of my legs being firmly closed. There was no romance in sight, and probably only a very horny teen boy could have been enticed by this situation. With very little movement involved, he quickly rolled off me. When I asked what was wrong, he said, "Nothing. I'm finished." Okay, then. I felt a mess between my legs and had to think for more than a minute before I even realized what it was. I told him to leave and go to his room, after which I went to the restroom to clean up. I put my clothes back on and laid in bed awake until the parents came home near dawn. I asked the father for my ride home and never spent the night in that house again. My mission had been accomplished.

It wasn't until later that day that it occurred to me that I could be pregnant, and I was filled with fear every waking second until I got my period again. It would have been miraculous for a pregnancy to occur, given that I don't think any sperm actually came close to my vagina. I actually found out later when I had sex again that I was technically still a virgin, and that my hymen was still intact. It was enough to satisfy my curiosity, however, and I was done with the idea for a while. I relate so much to the movie *Little Darlings* with its depiction of naive innocence and disappointing reality in the sex lives of teenage girls.

When school started that year, an arsonist was on the loose in Tacoma. I didn't pay much attention to the news, but everyone was talking about this situation with fear. On the morning of February 23, the fear was realized when we arrived at school that morning to learn that one of our grandstands had been burned down the night before. The campus had already been outgrown, and many of the classes were in portable buildings. Plans were in the works for a new campus to be built next door, but it would take a few years to finish. Just after class started that morning, we were still reeling from the news when we were told to evacuate. The fire alarm didn't go off, but apparently, there was a fire, and we had to get out. One of the teams, clubs, or groups at the school was having a paper drive fundraiser at the time, and all the paper was being stored on the stage located in the gym/auditorium. A disgruntled student set that paper on fire, and the school was burning.

By the time the fire was put out, the gym/auditorium, band rooms, and a few classrooms had been destroyed. We were sent home that day, wondering how we were going to possibly continue attending this campus. We were kept out of school for a few more days while the administration figured out what to do, and our parents were told to file claims with their homeowner's insurance for musical instruments, sports equipment, or any other items that were lost in the fire. I lost my gym clothes that were in my PE locker, but I only cared that I had lost the T-shirt I won on the KNBQ radio station. I loved participating in contests on the radio, especially trivia contests, which I was very good at. At school, they decided to have music and business classes off campus, and PE classes would be held somewhere on campus. Everyone rallied and got on with the school year with the awesome school spirit that they had at this school. It really was a great school with good kids and so many opportunities for involvement, but it was too late for me to take any interest. I had long given up on being involved at school, only to be disappointed when it was time to move again.

I was taking driver's education in school, and I got my learner's permit. Mom and Dad took me driving in their Cadillac, which was the longest car I'd ever seen besides a station wagon. They traded that in for a van, and I didn't like driving it as much, but I was a pretty good driver.

Unusually, we ended up staying in this house for my entire school year at Clover Park High School, which had only happened one other time for me—in the first grade. I really enjoyed a PE class I had that year, which was modern dance, where we got to do my favorite thing—choreograph dances! We worked in different groups for a few different productions. We got to choose a current popular song once, so my friend Colleen and I made up a dance to Devo's "Whip It." Another time, we had to choose an instrumental song, and I came up with the song "A Walk in the Black Forest" from a Herb Alpert album that my parents had. I had a drama class that I liked, although I discovered that I didn't want to act but liked being involved in theater production. I had been living my double life for several years now, one person at school and one at home, and never should the two meet. I had a lot of friends at school from just about every social group, but never involved them in my homelife.

Our family had several visitors from around the country while we lived here. Paula was pregnant with her first child, and she flew out to visit for about a week. When the time came for her baby to be born, Mom flew back to Virginia Beach to be with her. She had a beautiful boy named Wayne Jr. My cousin Vickie came to visit for a short time and shared my room. She had gotten married in the past year, and it hadn't worked out, so I think she was kind of searching for herself. Unlike the time I spent with her in the past, I really enjoyed her company now. She introduced me to the *Rocky Horror Picture Show*, and we went to a midnight showing at a small, older theater out in Parkland. It was a blast! We took rice, toast, newspaper, and a squirt gun with us and used those items in the audience participation duties. I couldn't believe that so many people had dressed up like the characters in the movie and then acted out the entire movie down in front of the screen. I had never seen anything like it, and it was one of the best events I ever attended. Vickie had the soundtrack album, and we listened to it all the time. She ended up giving it to me when she left, and it was a prize possession of mine, which I still have. She was really into the Urban Cowboy scene at the time, and we listened to that soundtrack a lot as well. I was so glad that we had that time together and that it was a wonderful and much different experience than we'd ever had.

My uncle Dean came to visit from California for just a few days when Dan picked him up and brought him down to see everyone, and it was the first time that all the Smith siblings had been together in one place in a long time, maybe back in Glen Gardens, when Dean insulted me and displayed his racist views at my birthday party, and John was still alive. The family made a big deal out of everyone spending time together on this visit, but I spent the minimum time I could and with a sullen attitude. They were never all together in one place again.

We also had an old family friend from Aberdeen, Maryland, come to visit us too. His name was Charlie, and he and Dan had become friends back when we lived in Swan Meadows. We all loved Charlie, but he and Dan were especially close. He was a really sweet guy who probably went along with other people's ideas too easily, so he made a great sidekick. Sadly, he had recently been through a horrible tragedy in his life and was trying hard to grieve his losses and recover his life. He had married a gal back when we still lived in Swan Meadows, and they had a little girl. I can remember stopping by his house to visit once, and Charlie was opening a can of spaghetti to feed the little girl for dinner. Her mother was nowhere in sight, and apparently, that was typical. The word in the neighborhood was that she was always out running around with other men, treated Charlie badly, and neglected the little girl. After we moved out west, they had another little girl together, then their mother left Charlie for a soldier from the Proving Ground, taking the girls with her. She and the girls were living in a motel with the soldier when they both apparently snapped and horribly abused the two girls. The details are so gruesome that I don't want to repeat them, but the baby was killed and the older girl was seriously injured but survived. Charlie tried his best to get custody of the girl after this occurred but wasn't able to for reasons that I don't know. He had finally given up on his pursuit, and that's when he came out to stay with Dan for a while. It was one of the worst incidents I've ever heard of, and I couldn't believe it happened to someone that we knew. We all tried to love on Charlie as much as we could, but I had to step back when he started telling me he was in love with me and wanted me to marry him and go back to Maryland with him, where we could get his daughter back and raise her together. I was shocked and confused that he could think such a thing was possible when I was just trying to offer him friendship and compassion. I was very naive about how people perceived my actions.

My dad's brother Ellis was actually already living in Washington State before we got there this time around, having moved from Phoenix, Arizona. Like my parents many years before, he had brought his family to the state looking for a change, and they lived with my aunt Helen in Puyallup until they got on their feet. Things didn't end well for them at Helen's either, but that's not my story to tell. I remember that we used to spend time with Ellis, his wife, June, and one of my cousins, and I always enjoyed their company but I barely remember meeting my two other cousins. I don't think I missed much.

CHAPTER 49

"I Wanna Be Sedated"

(The Ramones)

When I started to develop a painful, hard lump on my right Achilles tendon near the bottom of my foot, Mom took me to the doctor, and they determined that I had a ganglion cyst. It had gotten big enough to make it difficult and painful for me to wear shoes and to walk around, and they said it would continue to grow and must be removed surgically. After my experience with surgery five years previously, I was not happy about the prospect of doing it again, but I didn't have a choice. I spent a couple days in the hospital, and didn't have any complications. Dolly brought me some flowers, and it meant so much to me. I had to undergo physical therapy after the surgery to stretch out my tendon and be able to walk again properly. I absolutely hated it and complained about it profusely. What was even worse for me was that I had to wear the Dr. Scholl's sandals that had been popular years previously, but not any longer. They were ideal to help build up the muscles in my feet and legs to support my recovery. Not only were the shoes not popular any longer, but it was still wintertime when I had to wear them, which made me very cold and I stuck out like a sore thumb. To top it all off, when the doctor found out that I got a ride to and from school from my mom instead of walking, he insisted that I had to walk from now on. I felt as if the doctor and physical therapist were conspiring to make my life miserable and cause me humiliation. If it hadn't been so frustrating and embarrassing, it would have been comical each time one of my sandals went flying off my foot when my muscles couldn't hold it on any longer. Thankfully, that improved as my muscles strengthened.

The restaurant owner also had a little convenience store with a deli in a somewhat rural location in Tacoma not far from the restaurant. She was looking for someone to run the place, and my parents decided to take the job, although neither of them had any experience in that area. It was a chance for Dad to be home from the road, so we all liked that idea. They both worked at the store full-time, and I worked there with them part-time. It was fun for me, and I enjoyed being a cashier. I didn't enjoy making the sandwiches so much, but I loved eating them! We had fresh bread, deli meats and cheeses, and a cool steamer to put the sandwiches in after they were made that warmed and softened them perfectly. My folks weren't there long, and I don't know why they left the jobs.

Dad went back on the road, and Mom went back to waitressing at the same restaurant. I wanted to work and earn money, so she would have me come in and help her bus tables during busy times, like Sunday afternoons and special occasions, like Mother's Day or Easter. I really liked it and ended up also getting paid under the table by the restaurant owner to work as a dishwasher sometimes. I liked that too, so when she offered me an official job, I said yes. When it came time to get my first check for the hours that I worked rather than being handed cash after my shifts, I didn't receive one. When I finally got up the courage to ask the owner about my check, she said she didn't know what I was talking about. I was confused but reminded her that she had hired me to wash dishes, and then I went to the kitchen to get my time card with my hours and gave it to her. She was really annoyed and pissed off with me and grumbled things under her breath about freeloaders. I was beginning to get upset when she said she would write me a check and stormed off to her office. My head was swimming with confusion, and my feelings were really hurt by the way she was treating me, but I was also getting angry with her because she was treating me unfairly. She offered the work; I did the work. I wasn't a freeloader; I deserved to get paid. She came back out and gruffly handed me a check for some $80, which was correct for the hours I'd worked. I thanked her, then walked out and never worked for her again. With my very first real paycheck, I bought myself a new raincoat and scarf and I can't remember what else.

There was an incident one night at the restaurant that was disturbing and ultimately humiliating for me. It was some sort of private celebration for the employees and their families along with many members of the owner's family, maybe for Christmas. The adults were all gathered in the bar, while we younger attendees—adolescents, teens, and young adults—were hanging out in the dining room. This part of the restaurant was the nicest, with leather booths and nice wood tables and chairs. There were white tablecloths on all the tables along with glassware and utensils, including steak knives rolled in linen napkins. There were also bowls of individually wrapped crackers, bottles of ketchup, and, of course, salt and pepper on each of the tables. I think some of the older people in the group were somehow stealing alcohol from the bar to drink, and most of the group were sneaking into the kitchen and huffing the gas from whipped cream cans. I didn't participate in either activity, but my brother was part of the huffing group. From what I recall, we were just sitting around in the booths in the dining room when suddenly, some of the group started tearing up the place. They were running around the dining room, grabbing ketchup bottles, and dumping the contents all over the place—on the tables, chairs, booths, and carpet. Then they started crushing the packages of crackers, opening them, and throwing them around the room. Someone had brought some of the cans of whipped cream from the kitchen and were now spraying the contents on top of everything else. The mess would have been bad enough, but some of the boys unfolded the napkins containing the utensils, took out the steak knives, and were throwing them at the leather booths, trying to get them to stick. When that didn't work out as well as they liked, they started cutting into the leather, making long gashes with the knives.

Shortly after that happened, we all apparently decided to flee the scene of the crime even though we hadn't all committed it, and we went out to the large hallway between the dining room, kitchen, and bar. The restrooms were also located along this hallway as well as a side door to the building that employees and patrons used to access the bar more directly than coming in the front door and going through the dining room. What interested us in the hall, however, was the arcade games located there. The only one I knew how to play was *Asteroids*, which I didn't particularly enjoy, but it was better than destroying the premises. I noticed that at some point, the owner and some of the other adults made their way through the hallway from the bar and into the dining room. They had apparently gotten wind of what had happened in there and went to check it out. They came back through the hallway and went back into the bar. A few minutes later, my mom and dad came out of the bar and headed straight for my brother and me with very angry looks on their faces. They had heard from the owner and the others who checked out the dining room that we kids had destroyed the place, and my parents were pissed. They didn't bother to ask whether or not we had participated. Instead, my dad grabbed Tommy and me both, one with each hand, and started marching us toward the exit. When my brother protested and tried to ask what was going on, he got a big slap in the face from my dad, who continued to march us out the door and into the van sitting in the parking lot. I was crazy embarrassed that my dad had gotten physical with my brother with his slap in front of all of the owner's family, my coworkers, and the peers whom I had been in the dining room. None of my peers were being scolded by their parents or any other authority, and they had shocked looks on their faces as my dad squeezed mine and my brother's arms and directed us outside. I already knew that I wouldn't be going back to work for that woman because of the disrespectful and unfair way she had treated me, but my dad's humiliation of me was even worse than the restaurant owner's.

Dad had another ugly display of anger while we lived here, much worse than what happened at the restaurant. Tommy had a friend nicknamed Cuda, who lived down the street from us and happened to be black. Unlike me, Tommy would have his friends over to our house often, and Cuda was known and liked by everyone in our family. One time, he was spending the night at our house, as he had done before, and Dad came home drunk rather late that night and acted like he didn't know Cuda and certainly didn't want him at our house. When he saw Cuda, he yelled to my brother, "What's this n—— doing in our house?" Tom, Mom, and I all tried to calm Dad down and remind him that this was Tom's friend and he was welcome in our home. Dad was so drunk that he couldn't think straight. He told Tommy to "get that n—— out of here." We all believed it was best for Cuda to go home before Dad's behavior got any worse, and when Tommy asked Dad if he could walk him home, Dad said yes. Problem was, Cuda's parents had gone out of town for the night when they knew their son was spending the night with a friend, so there was nobody home, and Cuda was locked out. He told Tommy that he would wait on the porch until his parents came home and he would be okay. Not knowing what else they could do, Tommy left him there and came home. The next day, Dad didn't remember what he had done, and when we told him all about it, he felt really bad. He wanted to apologize to Cuda and tell him that he was always welcome in our home, but understandably, after what Dad had done to their son, Cuda's parents wouldn't allow him back to our house. See, Tommy? This is why I don't have friends over.

I liked my school here, but it didn't keep me from skipping and sometimes spending the day riding the city bus with a girlfriend, usually going to the Tacoma mall to hang out. One time, we came back to campus early to attend a class that we had a test in, and when we were walking back on the school grounds, we were spotted by a truant officer, who thought we must be students from another school trying to sneak onto this campus. My friend went straight to class, but I wanted to smoke a cigarette before I joined her and did so in one of the ladies' rooms. I smoked in the stall, fanning away the smoke, and when I came out, a lady truant officer was waiting to take me to the principal's office, where my friend was waiting. I was so proud of myself that the officer was in the ladies' room while I was smoking, and she didn't even know it! She escorted me to the principal's office, where he discovered that my friend and I weren't from another school but were sneaking back onto our own campus. He snickered a little about that since everybody else got caught sneaking off the campus, not on. My mom was called, and we had a meeting with the principal the next day, where my mom requested that I be put in in-school suspension, as I was the last time I got caught skipping school. The principal said that they didn't have such a thing there, but he arranged for me to sit in a desk outside his office for a day. I saw a boy go into his office because he was in some kind of trouble, and that boy ended up being the one who set our school on fire. Near the end of the school year, I didn't even have to skip anymore when I didn't feel like going or staying there. I could just tell Mom that I didn't feel like going in the morning or call her from school and ask if I could come home. We seemed to have both lost interest in my education. As long as I maintained As and Bs on my report card for Dad, nothing else seemed to matter.

My biggest passions at this time were smoking cigarettes and listening to my record collection. I liked the Ramones, and I watched them in the movie *Rock and Roll High School* over and over again when it played on HBO. My favorite artists at the time, though, were Tom Petty, Billy Squier, Led Zeppelin, AC/DC, and The Police. I have loved the Beatles since I was a small child, so I was devastated when John Lennon was shot and killed outside his Dakota apartment building in New York City on December 8, 1980. John Bonham, drummer for Led Zeppelin, had died just a few months earlier, so just like when my uncle John died, I was waiting for the third death to happen. Sure enough, it would come, along with a fourth, that summer.

CHAPTER 50

"Watching the Wheels"

(John Lennon)

I made it through the tenth grade, and summer vacation had begun. We decided as a family that the four of us would go on the truck together because Dad had shipments for back east, so we had a chance to see some family and friends. I was turning sixteen, so I had a little party at the restaurant with a few of my friends. It was pretty quick and low-key because we were getting in the semi and leaving as soon as the party was over. We said goodbye to Patty and Jamie there at the restaurant and hit the road. Putting Tommy and myself in the four-by-seven sleeper of the cab in an eighteen-wheeler for twelve hours a day was probably one of the most irritating experiences my parents had ever had. Tommy and I hated each other, and after he almost bested me in the back seat of Faye's car several years ago, we no longer had physical fights, but we were masters at verbal slaughters. I was especially irritated with my brother's presence and was constantly complaining of "Tommy is touching me" or "Tommy is looking at me" or "Tommy is breathing on me." You get the picture. I'm sure it would have been even worse if Dad hadn't been right there to cut down on the nonsense.

True to form, Dad was all business on his truck unless he was visiting someone who hosted a drinking party. That was his only pleasure during his travels. He didn't stay at nice places, eat good food, or see any sights. The only fun we had on the way to Virginia was one or two nights at a motel that had a pool. Of course, we didn't get off the road until dark, so that wasn't nearly as fun as swimming in the sunshine. The only other moments of entertainment came from Tommy's mortal embarrassments in public. The poor kid was about six weeks from his fourteenth birthday and was the epitome of awkward. Once, in a truck stop in Barstow, California, he knocked over the pitcher of ice water that was left on our table right into his lap. He turned fifty shades of red and proceeded to run out of the restaurant to make for the truck. We all understood, and we felt bad for him, but we laughed hysterically after he ran away. We brought him his meal in a bag after we were finished. Another time, in another restaurant, he was trying to get ketchup from a bottle by pounding on the bottom of the bottle. We've all been there. There was not a drop coming out of the bottle until suddenly, his meal was flooded with ketchup all over his plate. I don't think he ran out that time, but I'm sure he had to get a replacement meal. Nobody likes ketchup that much. The funniest incident took place in San Antonio, Texas. We were loading a shipment at a high-ranking military officer's home, and Tommy was at the age where he really wanted to prove himself physically. It was time to take a baby grand piano from the house to the truck, and Tommy insisted that he could carry one leg of the piano without a problem. Everyone was gathered around to watch the biggest piece of furniture be taken away when my dad, a helper, and Tommy each lifted their leg in the air. But when Tommy brought the leg close to his body to rest on his abdomen, the piano leg slipped right down the front of his pants and down his pants leg, leaving him trapped and in need of rescue. Nobody could stop themselves laughing, including Tommy. It was hilarious!

We made our way back to Hampton, Virginia, and got to spend a short time with Faye, Shannon, and John. I hadn't seen them in almost three years by that time, so it was wonderful to be with them again. Faye had gotten married to a guy, whom I liked right away, and we shared a love of music. We went to the Buckroe Beach Amusement Park and had fun with the kids. That would be the last time I went to the park before it closed down in 1985. We also got together with Chris, one of the Mafia latecomers, who had been close to John. Dan described him as one of the younger boys in the gang, who didn't hang around the house like most of the other guys. He was so easygoing and pleasant that everyone loved him. He would always put a hammock up at Chickahominy, and Dan would flip him out of it all the time because he just laughed and never got mad about it. He was unemployed at this time, living at home with his dad, and they were not getting along. He was ready for a change. He begged Dad to let him get on the truck with us and go out to Washington, where he could visit with Dan and Sam, then go back to Hampton. He had gone on short trips with Dad before. He was a good worker, and he knew what to expect. Dad was obviously reluctant and couldn't believe that Chris was willing to put himself in mine and Tommy's four-by-seven space for three thousand miles. Chris was desperate and willing, and we all loved his company, so we took him with us. His presence kept Tommy and me from fighting, so it really was a blessing. He was fun and very chill, and you couldn't help but love him.

After we picked Chris up in Virginia, we headed to Murfreesboro, Arkansas, to see Paula. She and Wayne had relocated there shortly after little Wayne's birth and were living with Wayne's elderly grandfather and taking care of him. Murfreesboro is located in Southwest Arkansas right in the middle of Hot Springs to the northeast and Texarkana to the southwest, with each town a little over fifty miles away. It had a population of 1,500 at the time. Having always grown up in the city or suburbs but nowhere near the country, it was a new world for my brother and myself. We couldn't believe how small the town was, with two gas stations and a few restaurants but surprisingly two grocery stores. There were no stoplights, but there was one blinking light. There was no entertainment whatsoever. There had once been a movie theater there, but no longer. There was, however, a drive-in theater thirteen miles away in the town of Nashville, which also had a Walmart. The closest bowling alley was forty miles away in the town of Hope, where future president of the United States Bill Clinton was born. The nearest malls were in Texarkana or Hot Springs.

The primary industry in Murfreesboro was a Weyerhauser plant, but it would shut down in 1982, making the employment market even tougher. They also had a chicken processing plant, hatchery, and gypsum mine. A lot of folks found work in these industries, but some commuted to similar employers in the vicinity. Very few, however, traveled as far as Hot Springs or Texarkana for work. The town had once been the site of a German POW camp during World War II and currently had a few interesting attractions. There was the Ka-Do-Ha Indian Village, where you could, among other things, literally walk a few steps up a mound with the top and insides dug out and look down into the mound to see the ancient bones of Caddo Indians where they were buried, and their graves were now desecrated. What is really unique about this town is that the Crater of Diamonds State Park is located there. It contains the only active diamond mine in all of North America and is open to the public. What this means is that they periodically plow up huge fields of dirt on the property, and people pay a small fee to take the pan and shovel provided and walk out into the field and start digging for diamonds. You keep any diamonds that you find, and they are found on a regular basis, with the largest one being 40.23 carats, found in 1924. The park brings some tourists to Murfreesboro, but the town does not cater to them.

The night we arrived there, we visited with Paula and Wayne until pretty late, and they and the folks were ready to call it a night, but it was too early for Chris, Tom, and myself, so we went out walking, looking for something to see or do. It was such a strange behavior for Tom and me to be on the streets after midnight, having grown up being told to never practice this particular act. It was an amazingly free feeling of security and wholesomeness, which we would soon ruin. The convenience/gas stores were the last places open in town, and they closed at midnight. Chris had been smoking weed, and he really had the munchies, but there was no place to buy them. We found the only school in town, where grades K-12 all attended together. We spotted two vending machines under the covered outdoor area that contained picnic tables for the students to eat outdoors if they wished; one had soda and the other snacks. Jackpot! Unfortunately, the area was fenced off, gated, and locked. The guys decided that they could climb the fence to access the machines, while I kept watch at the gate. I can't remember if they had or used any change in the machines, but they soon began rocking, pushing, and pulling on them to get the contents out. They were making a ton of noise, especially when there was literally not another sound for miles, except the dogs that started barking in response to the noise. I was trying to quietly get their attention and tell them to get the heck out of there and was becoming more and more frantic and afraid. They finally had enough and ran back to the gate, throwing drinks and snacks over the top for me to try and catch. We ran away from the area and made our way back to Paula's house, where we quietly enjoyed our loot on her back porch.

The next day, we spent time on the square in town, which contained a few shops. One was antiques, and another was Hawkins Variety Store, which was like a five-and-dime with the awesome advertising slogan, "We have most everything if you will help us find it." There really wasn't anything else to do in the town if you didn't want to go to the Crater of Diamonds or hang out at beautiful Lake Greeson. I think we only spent the one night, maybe two, and were back on the road again, heading west. Chris was really fun and funny for all of us. Even Dad couldn't help but laugh and lighten up. One evening, we were staying at a hotel, with Tommy and me sharing a room with Chris, as usual. Chris got it in his head that he was going to shave his full, conservative-looking beard into a Fu Manchu. He wanted Tommy and me to help him because he said he'd never done it before—as if Tommy or I had! I don't recall who did what work on the beard, but it came out looking very nice, and it was so much fun getting it done! The fun we were having, however, wasn't meant to last.

CHAPTER 51

"You Are My Sunshine"

(Jimmie Davis)

I don't remember where we were at on the road, but we arrived at a shipper's office, and there was a message there for Dad from his home office that he was supposed to call Dan. When he did, Dan told him that Jamie, precious little Jamie, who was just days away from her second birthday, had drowned in the restaurant owner's swimming pool. She was gone, and they were getting ready for the funeral. Of course, we were all devastated by this news, crying and mourning for this baby girl that we loved so much. We were also angry that someone had neglected this child, and that was the only way this could happen. We decided as a family that we wouldn't rush back for the funeral. We didn't want to be there.

Patty, Jamie, and Patty's boyfriend had moved from their place on Fifty-Sixth Street, bought a travel trailer, and set it up on the restaurant owner's property in Parkland. I don't think they had been there long because I never visited them until after Jamie was gone. There was an above-ground swimming pool in the yard, which was there when I used to babysit, and I heard stories about the boys jumping from the roof into the pool. Neither Mom, Dad, nor I were there when Jamie drowned, so this is the story according to Dan. He said that Jo would go there to clean the restaurant owner's house and take her kids with her. They would play in the yard, and the restaurant owner was supposed to watch them while Jo was cleaning. Dan told the restaurant owner not to let his kids go near the pool, and she told him he was being overprotective. About a week later, Jamie drowned. The first time Dan saw the restaurant owner after the accident, they locked eyes, and then the restaurant owner hung her head.

When the incident occurred, there were two adults outside, one of the restaurant owner's brothers and a lady, supposedly watching the kids while Patty was cleaning her trailer. These adults weren't paying any attention to Jamie and one of the restaurant owner's nephews around Jamie's age, who were throwing toys into the pool from the deck. Apparently, Jamie fell in the pool, and the restaurant owner's nephew was trying to tell people that Jamie was in the water. Eventually, she was found and someone tried to revive her, but it was too late. Patty and her boyfriend went to Dan's house that night and told him that Jamie had drowned. Dan grabbed her up and hugged her, and they cried together. Her death hit Dan worse than any other he experienced. Dan took a week off work to be there for Patty.

Dusty, Jamie's father, and his parents came out for the funeral. They gathered at the restaurant owner's house and drank $90 bottles of champagne, and everyone was happy. I guess they were celebrating Jamie's life with a wake. Dan drove home drunk and slept in his car. They were all hungover the next day when Dan, Dusty, Patty's boyfriend, and Sam dug Jamie's grave to save Patty some money. The graveyard was a short walk down at the end of the road where the restaurant owner's property was located. Dan didn't remember the funeral, but he did remember going to the funeral home with Patty beforehand. Dan didn't blame anyone for Jamie's death, not Patty or the restaurant owner or the family members who were supposed to be watching the kids the day she died. He thought that God was going to take whomever He wants when He wants.

Meanwhile, our family kept traveling west and ended up in Red Bluff, California, at my uncle Dean's house. We visited with him for a day, and Mom decided that she and I should take a bus home from there, while the guys would continue on in the truck with the business of delivering and picking up shipments. The guys left, and the plan was for Mom and me to spend one more night at Dean's house and get on the bus the next morning. That night, Mom and Dean were talking, and I cannot remember any details, but it began to get heated between them, and it ended with Dean condemning my mom with the most venomous wrath I had ever witnessed. I don't remember what the reason or content was; I can only remember that Dean was a master of a wicked tongue and the ability to slice and stab with his words, and I felt so bad for my mom. Nobody deserved to be talked to the way he did her. She cried and pleaded for him to stop, but I believe it went on for about two hours before he finally stopped. I was so shocked and afraid that I didn't say a word. Later, I wished that I had come to her defense, but I wasn't able to at the time. I learned right then that I hated my uncle Dean, and unlike the lack of boundaries in the rest of my family, I would never forgive him for his actions. I also learned where I myself had gotten this wicked tongue from. It was a Smith family trait.

We still spent the night at Dean's house, and we left on the bus the next morning. Mom was a wreck after learning of Jamie's death and being berated by Dean. I tried to comfort her on the ride home. It was really painful walking into our house after we arrived and finding Jamie's things all over the house. She had toys, spare clothes, toddler dishes in the kitchen, her toothbrush, and bathtub toys in the bathroom. Mom and I cried and cried to find these items. One of my most precious possessions is a recording of Jamie with Mom, Dad, Tommy, and myself, which I have gotten digitized. On the recording, we are all in Mom and Dad's bedroom, gathered together on their king-size bed, playing with Jamie. She wasn't even two years old, but she had the ability to sing songs and recite nursery rhymes. She was definitely gifted in that way. We were laughing at her trying to recite things from our requests while she had the hiccups. She was complying with our wishes but was also preoccupied with her favorite toy, a string of pop beads. She loved to pull them apart but couldn't get them popped back together, so she would hold them up and ask us to "fikkis," which meant to fix it and put them back together. I kept some of those pop beads to remember her by, along with a long leaf from the weeping willow tree that was planted at her grave. There are other items too, like a photo of her at my birthday party the day we left Washington to go on the truck and the last time we saw her alive. Patty was never the same after losing Jamie. I've never seen anyone so broken from grief, not even Mom when John died. The loss of a child is an unspeakable tragedy.

CHAPTER 52

"Lonely Is the Night"

(Billy Squier)

We hadn't had much time to recover from Jamie's death when the guys got home to Tacoma from the road. It felt good to have the family all together since the tragedy, and it was a rare treat to have a Mafia member come all the way across the country to visit. We all enjoyed Chris's company, but after a few days, it was time for him and Dad to hit the road again. It was the weekend, and Dan, Chris, and Sam were at our house to party one more time before the guys left. It was July 31, 1980, Tommy's fourteenth birthday. It was getting late when Dad went to bed and passed out, dead drunk. Mom went to bed shortly after. Dan had taken Chris up to Mount Rainier during his visit, and Chris wanted to go back and spend the night this time. They left the house to head for the mountain, and they took Tommy with them. Nobody remembered how or from whom Tommy got permission to go with the guys, but Dan said they did have permission to take him with he and Chris. They stopped by Dan's house and were going to get Jason to take with them too, but Jo Anne said no. Dan and Chris had both been drinking alcohol and doing cocaine all day and night, and now they stopped at a 7-Eleven and got another case of beer that they were drinking on the way along with smoking weed.

They headed up the mountain, and Dan was driving okay in spite of his drinking and smoking weed. Tommy said he hadn't been scared of Dan's driving, and they were all laughing and having a good time. Dan was driving in both lanes because they were going around curves, and he would have been able to see any car lights coming. Tommy said Chris got scared when a car was coming, and Dan was moving over to his own lane when Chris grabbed the steering wheel and jerked it over to the right, making the car go off the road and down over the cliff. The car flew sideways through the air with the passenger side down, and the top of the car hit a tree and wrapped around it backward, bumper to bumper, with the hood and the trunk touching in a U shape. Dan woke up in the car with his legs pinned along with the car seat between the steering wheel, and it was down on the floor board. His upper body was on top of Chris in the passenger floor board. He looked at his legs and knew they were really bad. There were two humps in the steering wheel where his legs had been.

Back at the house, the only people still awake were me, Sam, and this disgusting friend of Dad's named Fred, who had been hitting on me all night, and it had gotten much worse after Dad passed out. I had liked Fred at first, and I even went to his house with a friend whom I was skipping school with one day, where we hung out for an hour or so. He kept my secret about skipping from my dad, and I thought he was a cool guy. Then he started with the hitting on me and acting like a disgusting pig, and I couldn't believe my dad would tolerate his behavior, but he did. I was just expected to fend for myself in these matters. That night at the house, I let him know how I felt about his behavior. He finally asked Sam to drive him home, just about five minutes away, and I couldn't have been more relieved. It was eerily quiet in the house after a full day and night of raucous partying, and then the phone rang. I answered it, and it was Tommy. He said that they were in Enumclaw on Mount Rainier and that they had had a car accident. He said he wasn't sure if Dan and Chris were still alive. I woke Mom up, filled her in, got her on the phone, and started getting ready to leave the house. I was gathering purses, sweaters, keys, etc. when Sam walked in the door, and Mom was just getting off the phone with Tommy.

We did our best to wake Dad, but it wasn't happening, so we left him a note, and Mom, Sam, and I got in his car to head to Enumclaw. What should have been a forty-five-minute drive was taking a lot longer because we couldn't find our way out of town. We must have all been so upset and flustered that we weren't thinking straight, and we couldn't find State Highway 512 to take us to the mountain. We were all quite familiar with it because we took it to visit Uncle Ellis and Aunt June in Puyallup on a regular basis. We finally found the highway, then continued to make our way up the mountain toward Enumclaw without further problems. We had been on the dark, winding road for what seemed like forever when we finally saw that we were coming in to Enumclaw. By the time we arrived, it had been about two hours since Tommy called. We had been discussing whether or not we could find the accident location since it was out in the middle of nowhere. That wouldn't be a problem.

The scene went from almost complete darkness and barely any signs of humanity to about twenty vehicles taking up both sides of the road and lighting up the night with tons of lights—yellow, red, and blue. There were different types of police cars, regular cars, and fire department vehicles. We knew we must have found our accident, and we knew it was going to be really bad. Sam pulled over on the side of the road, and we all three ran into the traffic, looking for our people or some indication of where they were. Then we saw three ambulances lined up on the road, with people inside and out, tending to the patients inside. There was a bunch of other people all over the place, and they must have known we were family when we ran up on the scene. Basically, ignoring whatever they had to say, the three of us split up. Mom went to Tommy, Sam went to Dan, and I went to Chris.

We couldn't get very close to Dan or Chris but saw very quickly that Tommy looked unharmed and said he was okay, except his ankle was a little sore. They made him sit on the bed in the back of the ambulance and wrapped him in a blanket. Once we all knew he was okay, we three just went back and forth between Dan and Chris to find out how they were. We were told by a firefighter that they had just gotten them out of the car when we arrived after two hours of peeling the car open like a sardine can to get to them. They were trying to stabilize them to take them to the hospital. Dan was pretty quiet and was covered in blood, His legs looked too flat, and his chest was huge. They said he was critical, and we thought we were going to lose him.

Chris, on the other hand, had transformed from a mild-mannered, chill dude to angry, thrashing, cursing man. He was also covered in blood and was fighting against the EMTs who were trying to help him. Mom stayed with Dan, and Sam and I tried to talk to Chris, calm him down, and tell him to accept the help he needed, but he didn't hear us. It seemed to take forever for them to stabilize the guys to take them to the nearest hospital, Good Samaritan in Puyallup, where Tommy had been born. While we were waiting at the scene, smoking cigarettes, and walking around, some "nice" creep with alcohol on his breath pulled me aside and tried to give me a bottle of water and a blanket and "comfort" me. Does a pervert have no shame? I was polite to him for a moment until I figured out what was happening, then made an escape, telling him my family needed me. I think it was always hard for me to believe that people were that bad or inappropriate at first, but my "spidey" sense would finally emerge.

We were finally told that Dan, Chris, and Tommy were being transported to the hospital. Mom was going to ride with Tommy, whom they insisted ride in an ambulance. Sam got directions to the hospital, and we said we would be right behind them. We walked back down the hill to his car and noticed the trailer house with the big light out in the yard, where Tommy must have gone for help. He had told us the story while we were waiting. He had been in the back seat of the car when it suddenly veered to the right, off the road, and started down a deep ravine where it crashed into some trees and got stuck there. He wasn't wearing a seat belt, and upon impact with the trees, he went flying toward the back window, which popped out of place, and was thrown a few feet from the car onto the soft ground.

He was pretty sure that he was knocked unconscious but wasn't sure for how long. When he awoke, he sat up and looked at the car, which was wedged off the ground between two trees, and he couldn't hear any noise coming from the car, so he thought Dan and Chris might be dead. He knew that they needed help but couldn't get to them, so he started to climb up the ravine back to the road. When he reached the road, he couldn't see lights anywhere but remembered that they had just passed a trailer house that had a big, bright light in their front yard, so he started down the mountain.

When he reached the house, it was dark and very late, but he knocked on the front door. An older lady turned on the porch light, opened the door a crack, and Tommy asked if he could use their phone. She was apparently frightened of him and told him that they didn't have a phone. She shut and locked the door and turned off the light. Tommy started back toward the road, not knowing where else to go or what to do next since this was the only sign of civilization they had seen in a while. He decided that they might not have a phone, but they had a couple of cars parked out front, so they could take him to a phone, so he went back to the front door and knocked again.

This time, the porch light came on, and a younger woman opened the door. Tommy told her that he had been in a car accident up the road, and he was afraid his family members might be dead and needed help. He asked if she could take him to a phone or someplace for help. She said that she had a phone he could use and invited him in. He called the police and got help started on the way and then called our house. After he was off the phone, the younger lady explained that her mother was spending the night with her and was very frightened when he knocked on the door in the middle of the night, and that's why she told him that they didn't have a phone. He waited at the trailer with them until they heard the sirens coming to help.

When Sam and I saw the trailer house belonging to the lady who had helped Tom, we decided that we should go and thank her for her help. It made perfect sense to us at the time, even though we were supposed to be following the ambulances containing our family members to the hospital, where we prayed they would survive. We discussed it later, and we agreed that we must have been trying to avoid what we felt sure was going to be another death in our family. When we got to the trailer and explained who we were, we were greeted warmly and invited in for coffee and breakfast pastries or something. We stayed and chatted with the ladies until we realized the sun was coming up, and it seemed to finally dawn on each of us that we had someplace else to be. We thanked the ladies and got on the way to the hospital.

When we got to the emergency room, we found Mom in the hall, and she said that Chris didn't make it. Just then, they opened the door to one of the rooms and wheeled out a body covered with a sheet. I was wondering if it was Chris when they ran over a cord cover on the floor and jostled the bed, causing an arm to swing out to the side of the bed. I recognized Chris's lacerated arm, and I started to freak out, but Mom said that Dan was in critical condition, and they needed to move Chris out of that room because it was better equipped to help Dan. Dan was conscious and still looked horrible when I saw him being taken into that room, and I thought he had knocked his front teeth out, but it turned out to just be blood. He remembered being in the ambulance and being unable to breathe, and then he remembered being in the emergency room and Jo told him that Chris was dead. Even though he was conscious, he said he didn't remember anything else for about the next five days. When he was finally coherent, Mom told him that he was legally under arrest for involuntary manslaughter but told him not to worry that they had hired him a lawyer, and they told everyone that Chris was driving the car, which would have made the accident Chris's fault. It felt wrong to me that Chris had just died, and the family was so quick to pin a lie on him; however, the thinking, especially for Mom, was that Chris was dead, so he wouldn't care. And this could protect Dan. We all wanted to protect Dan, and I'm sure Chris would want to as well. Protect the family!

A few days after the accident, some of us went out to the junkyard where they had towed the car to get any belongings that were left in there. It was shocking to see the condition of the car and the blood that was in there. As we were going through the car, I found the key ring that Chris had always carried. It had what looked like a house key on it, but it was really a roach clip. I still have it, along with a picture of him that we took in front of the truck during our trip. It was classic Chris with his too-short shorts, a button-down uniform shirt that was completely unbuttoned, and the sleeves cut off. His pretty strawberry-blond hair was styled perfectly, and he was holding a beer. I had loaned Dan two of my Led Zeppelin albums, and they were still on the rear deck in the back seat where he had put them. They looked like they were unharmed, but when I picked them up, a bunch of broken pieces fell out of one. The other one was in perfect condition. Dan also had Don's tools in the car and was able to recover most of them, thankfully, because they had been passed from Don to Dean to John to Dan, and Dan still had many of them. He gave some of them to one of Don's sons, and he gave Don's belt buckle to one of his daughters. When we left the junkyard, we were on our way back home in the van. It was Mom, Dad, Tommy, my uncle Ellis, me, and that disgusting friend of my dad's, Fred. A conversation started about the legal trouble that Dan was in from having the accident, and Fred was asserting his opinion about what we should do. I guess my temper snapped from the trauma of the accident and the fact that I didn't like Fred already and the way he always leered at me, and now he was inserting himself into a very serious and private family matter. I went off on him. I can't remember everything I said, but I didn't hold anything back. I told him that this was none of his business and he needed to shut his mouth, that he was a piece-of-crap pervert who was always trying to creep on me, and was doing it when Dad was asleep and the accident happened. At some point, Fred asked Dad if he was going to let me talk to him that way, and Dad said yes and that he better keep his hands and his eyes off me. I continued with my criticism until finally, Fred became so uncomfortable that when we were stopped at a red light, he got out of the van and started walking. These types of passionate displays were normal for our family, but I think my poor Uncle Ellis was completely shocked at this behavior.

We may have been discussing potential legal problems for him, but Dan sure didn't need to worry about anything other than his physical recovery. Jo said Dan was in a room that looked like a workshop full of tools, and that's where they inserted pins in his legs with ropes and pullies in traction. Dan thought they were going to cut off his legs with all the drills and tools they had. He was very lucky not to have lost his legs. Jo had told the doctors that they had insurance so they would work on him, but they didn't know if they did or not. They didn't realize that his insurance had just gone into effect the Friday before the accident Saturday morning. There's that Dan luck. He had a fractured skull that they were concerned would kill him. He also had five broken ribs, had ripped the right side of his face off, and his left hand was broken. He says his legs, however, were his only source of pain. He was in the hospital for three weeks, with the first one in intensive care. When he left the hospital, he didn't have his legs in a cast because of the rods they had inserted, which he had for two years. He had to walk with a walker. They had removed the stitches in his face, but he had glass coming out of his ear for a couple of years and was still picking glass out of his arm for years after that.

Chris' father was really pushing for Dan to be charged with vehicular homicide for the death of Chris. He had hired an attorney in the state of Washington, so as I stated earlier, Dan had a lawyer as well. It had been determined through forensics that Dan was driving the car, and when Mom and Dad found out that Tommy would be made to testify on the stand that Dan was driving the car rather than Chris, they decided that we needed to move to Murfreesboro to get Tom out of the state of Washington and away from the law, and it was also a chance to be close to Paula and baby Wayne Jr. We packed up and left within a week of them getting the information about Tommy being made to testify. When we left, Dan was still in the hospital, and Jo and the kids were relying heavily on the help of June and Ellis.

Once Dan was released from the hospital, he was still living in the house on Ninety-Sixth Street and was drawing state benefits. He didn't have any legal problems from the wreck hanging over his head because of Tommy's statement about Chris grabbing the steering wheel. During the two and a half years he had been in Washington, he felt guilty about having the kids so far away from their grandparents and Jo from her parents. He told Jo's father that he had a little money saved up to put a down payment on a place back in Virginia if he could find them one. Her father had dealt with a man who was very good about helping people find property and financing it for them. Dan bought five acres of land and moved his family back there to start a new life. They lived in a tent for three months until it was almost time for Jason to start school. Dan wanted a house for the family, so he made a trade for this property on another lot of 1.65 acres with a house on it. The house had a twelve-by-twelve living room, one bedroom, a twelve-by-seventeen kitchen, and a small bathroom. He eventually added on another bedroom and laundry room.

The first time Dad went to see Dan in Virginia, he was coming into town in his eighteen-wheeler, and saw an upside-down log truck that was still running with the wheels still rolling. He knew Dan was driving a log truck for a living, but there wasn't anyone in the truck at the time, so he didn't stop. It had, indeed, been Dan's truck, and he wrecked it due to some fault in the brakes. He was stuck inside the truck after the wreck and ended up hurting himself more than from the accident just trying to get out of the truck. He was finally able to bust through a window by kicking it with his feet and got out of the truck. A nice couple came upon him and told him they would take him to the hospital and get him help. He said that he wasn't that injured and asked if they would take him home instead. They agreed, and while they were driving through the town, Dan saw Dad at an intersection and tried to holler at him, but Dad had the windows up and didn't hear him. Dad made it to Dan's house before Dan did and told Jo about the wrecked truck. She said it sounded like Dan's truck, and they both hoped that he was okay. They didn't have to wait long to find out when the nice couple brought him home right after, and they found out he had sustained minimal injuries. Still lucky, I guess. He insisted that Dad take movies of him doing cartwheels, running, and jumping, so he could show all the family how well he was doing; and it was a joyful sight for all of us, for sure.

CHAPTER 53

"Arkansas" (Chris Stapleton)

My daughter once said that you needed a passport to visit Murfreesboro, Arkansas, and she couldn't have been more correct. I had lived in several states and even more towns, but this tiny town in Arkansas was not like anything I've ever experienced. We found a little three-bedroom, one-bath house on Second Street in town. It was only a few blocks from the school. As I mentioned earlier, it was the *only* one for every student, kindergarten through twelfth grade, in the town of Murfreesboro. The culture shock of moving to this place along with the trauma and grief of the car accident and the deaths of Jamie and Chris had me very unsettled. There was literally nothing for me to do in this place except watch TV and walk over to Paula's house just a couple blocks away to visit with her and her son. I don't know if she made a suggestion one day because she was trying to be helpful or she was trying to get rid of me, but she said I should walk a few blocks down her street to the Junior Mart store. She said there was a nice high school girl named Tina that worked there, and I should make friends with her so I would already have a friend when school started a few weeks later.

I took her suggestion in spite of the fact that nobody seemed to walk anywhere in that town, and ended up making friends with Tina, who was very nice, extremely helpful to me in my new life in the country, and is a friend to this day.

When I started school, the first thing I noticed was that I was overdressed. Unlike the kids here, who wore jeans to school every day I only wore jeans to school occasionally but only with a button-down shirt or sweater and nice shoes or dress boots. Most of the time, I wore dress slacks, and I usually wore a dress once a week. I only wore T-shirts after school or on the weekends. I never wore tennis shoes at school, except in PE, and I didn't own a pair of cowboy boots. I believe that every single person in this town had at least one pair of cowboy boots. So in many ways, the style was much more casual, but then they also had a rule that the boys had to have their shirts tucked in at all times. The preppy movement was very popular for teens at the time in my last school, so the boys wore button-down shirts, untucked, with a pair of Levi's 501 jeans and slip-on loafers. The boys here wouldn't be caught dead in a pair of slip-on loafers unless maybe they wore slippers at the house. An untucked shirt might get a schoolboy some attention from a teacher or administrator, but more serious offenses would get him a paddling. Out of all the schools I had been to across the country, this was the first that allowed corporal punishment, and it happened all the time. The boys seemed to have fun taunting the teachers into ordering them out into the hallway, where they got a few whacks with a wooden paddle, but having to go to the principal's office for a paddling from the man himself was no joke.

I was used to everyone speaking with a Southern accent, having spent most of my life in Virginia, but I wasn't used to everyone being so very polite. It was an adjustment coming from the West, where they just weren't as polite and friendly to one another, to the deep South, where everyone acknowledges you, opens the door for you, and addresses you as sir or ma'am. I was raised to be very well-spoken, using proper grammar, and having a pretty large vocabulary, and also to be respectful to adults, but we kids were never required to address anyone with a ma'am or sir. I ended up adopting that habit for the rest of my life. When meeting all these new people in town, I also discovered that everyone was related to everyone. I would mention that I met someone else, and the person I was with would say something like, "Yes, he's my second cousin on my daddy's side." Sometimes, they would even be double cousins, related on both their mother and father's sides.

The school was small, but adequate. It had a cafeteria, but most of my friends ate at the picnic tables provided outside under a covered area. The food was very ordinary with no options, but there were those snack machines… The three age groups at the school were separated from one another even though most of the school was under one roof. There was a beautiful new gym, like the ones I was used to, and an old gym with lots of character, which I preferred. They actually had a smoking area at this school, but only a few people that I wouldn't want to hang out with used it. Most of the friends I made were smokers, but we didn't do it at school. It seemed like a lot more kids drove to school here than in the city where I'd come from, where most kids rode the bus or got a ride from their parents. They had school buses here, but I guess there was more necessity to have your own vehicle when you lived in the country with no city buses or taxis, so most of my friends drove their own cars. There were a lot of pickup trucks in the student parking lot and many with rifles in their gun racks mounted onto the back windows. That wasn't a sight I was used to, but all the boys here and some of the girls were hunters or at least knew how to use a long gun. On the first day of deer season in November, most of the boys weren't in school, and apparently, some schools in the area called that day a holiday and closed the school for everyone. Hunting was something that I had no exposure to, and I had the typical ignorant city attitude that it was cruel to shoot Bambi, and I would prefer the nice, pretty meat in the grocery store.

I learned in school almost immediately that every student was expected to participate in extracurricular activities, with some considered more important than others. I had given up on these activities long ago, having gotten discouraged from putting my heart and interest into things and especially people, then leaving shortly after. At this school, however, as I mentioned earlier, there was no anonymity. Although football was popular at my last school, it was more akin to a religion here. Every boy was expected to play if he could and support the team if he could not by being a team manager, water boy, etc. The bare minimum was to show up to every home game and try your best to make it to the away games. This expected support was the same for the girls. There were only a few spots available to be a cheerleader, but every other girl was expected to be a member of the pep club and go to every game because you could ride the bus to away games as a member of the club.

There were other requirements as well, as I soon learned, when I was persuaded to join. Mom had to take me to a special shop in Nashville to get custom shirts. Our team was the Rattlers, and our colors were red, black, and white. Thus, one shirt was red with white trim, which was to be worn to school on every game-day Friday. The other was red with black trim, to be worn to every game that evening. We also had a pin that we wore on our shirts above our right breasts that said "Rattler Fan." Each week, we were provided with a different ribbon to attach to our pins for that specific game and opponent. The only one I can remember said "Gash the Gators." Finally, we were given red and white paper pom-poms on a stick as an accessory to the repartee between us club members in the stands and the cheerleaders on the floor at the pep rallies and the field at the games. It felt good to be a part of something, and it was good, old-fashioned fun. The varsity football team were local heroes and took up most of the space in the town newspaper, but even I made the paper with a photo of me cheering at a game. My brother would get a great deal of attention in the paper, but that was my one shot.

I was also expected to join the Future Homemakers of America, as was every high school girl. Conversely, every high school boy had to join the Future Farmers of America. The first activity that I remember participating in for the FHA was the initiation of the new members, which were all the girls now in the tenth grade and any new students, no matter what grade. When I found out what was entailed in this initiation, I flat-out refused to participate on the side of the initiates and threatened to quit if I couldn't be considered a matriculated member. My wish was granted. The initiation ceremony consisted of all members meeting in the auditorium one evening, dressed up in skirts or dresses, as was required for such events. Different people spoke about the honor and importance of the initiation, and it was all very formal. Then the initiates were dismissed to the ladies' room to change into their grubby clothes for the remainder of the initiation. The initiates were blindfolded and led by the upperclasswomen to the picnic tables outside, which were set up with a series of nasty things that the initiates had to experience. The only one I remember is a potty chair containing a Baby Ruth bar floating in water. The girls were told to reach in the water, grab whatever they found, and take a bite out of it. Then their blindfolds were removed just enough to peek at what they had just eaten and where it was located. I'm sure I don't have to tell you what it resembled.

Some of us older girls were becoming bored with this activity, so I snuck away with a girl named Teresa to the ladies' room. There, we found individual piles of clothing all over the large floor, where the girls had discarded them for their grubby outfits. I noticed that most of the piles had a pair of pantyhose on the top, and I got the idea to take all of them, tie them together, and stretch them across the stage in the auditorium, where we would all gather again after the dirty stuff was over and the girls had changed back into their nice clothes. Teresa helped me, and I was very pleased with myself and my efforts. After all, we were playing tricks on the initiates, right? The reaction to my stunt, however, wasn't the funny one that I expected. When the staff and all the girls walked in the auditorium and saw the pantyhose, they were just quiet and looking at one another, like they were trying to understand what was happening and why. I don't remember much after that, except that the next day, Teresa told me she wanted to confess what we had done. Confess? Why? There was no way that anyone knew it was us. We got away with it! She wouldn't let me talk her out of it, so I went with her to the Home Economics teacher who was in charge of the FHA, and we confessed. She said that everyone was upset because we had, in essence, destroyed all the girls' pantyhose since they had no way of knowing which belonged to whom, and nobody wanted to wear someone else's, so they were all thrown away. We were given a stern lecture, but we didn't receive any punishment. I felt guilty afterward and started considering saving my allowance to give each of the girls the money to replace their pantyhose, but I soon abandoned the idea.

In addition to those two clubs, I was also a member of the library club, which happened automatically because I worked in there for one period each day. I found a biography about the Beatles, which I checked out immediately. I loved it so much that I didn't want to give it back, so I told the school that I had lost it and paid for the value of the book. It wasn't like me to steal anything, but I rationalized that I had paid for the book. There weren't many choices of which classes to take at this school, understandably for its size. At Clover Park, I had a plan in place to be a secretary, my chosen profession. I had taken the first years of typing, shorthand, and business machines and planned to continue them the following year, then I would attend Clover Park Vocational School in my senior year to learn whatever else I needed for the profession. The only career plan option available here was that you could take off afternoons to work at a job in your senior year. I was able to continue my typing here, but my favorite class was history. The teacher talked about history differently than I had ever heard it before. He talked to us like adults being told the real story rather than being made to memorize dates and names and such. He simply lectured the class Monday through Thursday, while we students took notes. He preferred that we write them word for word. Each Friday, we were tested on the material. I discovered how important it was in my learning to write down the information. Most times, I didn't even have to look at it again; just the act of writing made me remember the material. My least favorite class was PE. We started each daily class with running, which I absolutely hated and still do. Then I can't really remember what we did specifically, but it certainly wasn't getting to choreograph dances to songs of our choice, as I had loved in Tacoma. I'm pretty sure they didn't consider dance as exercise here.

There were fifty-four students in my eleventh-grade class, and most of the kids had lived in Murfreesboro their entire lives and known one another since kindergarten. They had a kinship with one another that I'd never experienced with my classmates anywhere.

Even though there were kids who most people didn't want to hang out with or were different from most of the others, there were no outcasts, and I never saw or heard of any bullying. There was a sense of acceptance that I loved and seemed to be a throwback to times when most people lived in small villages and depended upon one another. There was no anonymity, like you could have in the city. You didn't have to like or spend time with everyone, but you were all a part of a small group that needed to stick together for your survival. I had plenty of experience at being the new kid in town, but this was on a whole new level. It was rare for new people to move to this town, and my family drew curiosity from everyone. We were literally the talk of the town for a short time as the weekly newspaper published tidbits about someone visiting friends or relatives here in town. As they say, everybody knew everybody else's business, but I learned that there were a lot of secrets kept in this town as well.

At lunch and other times away from the adults and general school population, my new friend group would make snide comments about how one of the guys was sleeping with one of the elementary schoolteachers at the school. I was absolutely shocked by this. I couldn't imagine a teacher and student having a sexual relationship, not only because of the age difference but also because of the level of esteem I held for teachers. I had been to a lot schools in several different states, but I had never seen or heard of this happening anywhere else. I knew that this was obviously a big secret, and I didn't tell anyone about it, but I couldn't help but express my shock and disgust at this behavior, and sometimes a little loudly. I received a bit of a warning from the guy who was sleeping with the teacher to keep my voice and my opinion quiet. Little did I know at the time that my own brother would end up having a sexual relationship with another of the teachers at that school, one whose son was a good friend of his.

That teacher was just one of many of my brother's romantic or sexual conquests in that town. As soon as we started school, I had many girls coming up to me and asking if Tom was my brother. When I answered yes, they became overly friendly with me, asking me questions about Tom and inviting themselves over to our house.

It was so obvious what they were doing that it was ridiculous. Let me just say that the biological desire to propagate our species was very strong in this town, I assume because it was such a small gene pool, and a decent new face in town was hot property. So Tom got a lot of attention in Murfreesboro from the ladies.

Tom was also a good football player, although he was still only junior varsity at the time. The stereotypes I'd heard about football being like religion in the South were very true. Everyone in town seemed to know about his skill on the field, and him being featured in the newspaper almost weekly made it feel like he was a celebrity.

CHAPTER 54

"Wild Eyed Southern Boys"

(.38 Special)

The time I spent outside of school was a learning experience as well. There was nothing for young people to do in Murfreesboro, so a lot of the high school kids spent time riding around uptown, especially on the weekends. They would park in a lot big enough for others to join and talk to one another. Of course, this was a typical activity for high schoolers everywhere. There was a Dairy Dip restaurant that we would stop by, and they had a Pac-Man game machine in there. A few years later, the Pizza Shack restaurant opened, and they had a separate game room with pool tables and pinball and game machines, which gave kids a tiny bit more to do. There was a big boulder sitting next to the highway on the road to Nashville, just outside of town, and it was tradition for the high school kids to spray-paint it. Most of the painting was football related, with player's numbers and Rattler colors. Years later, the town used a machine to pick up that boulder and move it way out into the woods, where nobody could see it and the kids couldn't paint it any longer. Another thing the kids would do, in secret, was soap the fountain. The fountain was located on the town square, and people would pour dish soap or who knew what other kind of soaps into the fountain in the middle of the night on the weekend. People who were out early on Saturday or Sunday morning would be greeted with a giant mound of bubbles on the road. Sadly, they put a stop to that too by filling the fountain with rocks instead of water. They said the soap wasn't good for the fountain waterworks or something like that. There was a drive-in movie theater in nearby Nashville, and we kids were known to watch the movies over and over again just to have something to do.

I spent almost all my free time with Tina, and she introduced me to an older crowd, by roughly ten years. There were only a few high school boys who hung out with them, and Tina and I were the only girls who were around consistently. This crowd reminded me of the Mojer Mafia. They had their own culture, language, and unique activities and I was fascinated by them. One particular conversation I had with a member of this group really illustrates the difference between myself and these country folks. We compared different words and the definitions for them. For example, a "coke" to me was one particular type of carbonated beverage or soda, as I called it. But to this guy, *coke* was the word for soda and could be any type. So you could ask someone to get you a coke at the store, and they would probably ask what kind. The fact that I called a group of people "you guys" and they used the word *y'all* was an instant giveaway that I wasn't from around there.

One unexpected difference that I ran into was the local pay phones. I was out riding around with Tina one night when my curfew was coming up, so I wanted to call my mom and ask if I could stay out later. I asked Tina if she could find a phone booth, so she pulled up at the one located on the square in front of the courthouse. I got out with my wallet, searching for a quarter while I walked up to the booth, but soon discovered that the phone didn't take quarters at all. Instead, it only took dimes. I put the quarter back in my wallet, found a dime and put it in the machine, and dialed my home number. My mom answered the phone, and I started talking to her, but apparently, she couldn't hear me. I tried again with the same result, then walked back to Tina's truck and told her at the driver's side window what was happening. She asked if I put the dime in after I dialed the number, and I replied that I put the dime in before I dialed the number, like you're supposed to. She said that I wasn't doing it right, that I needed to dial the number and, once someone answered the phone, put the dime in the phone then. This sounded ridiculous to me, but it hadn't worked the way I had done it before, so I gave it a try, and it worked. I told Mom what had happened, and she wasn't familiar with a pay phone operating that way either, but she did give me permission to stay out later. So many of the things I experienced in this small town really perpetuated the stereotype of country folks that you hear about, but I'm so grateful that I lived here and experienced it for myself, or I would never really understand what they sang about in all the country songs, and I would have missed out on so much life experience, for better or worse. It was fun, beautiful, ugly, stupid, etc., just like every other place I ever lived.

I had my learner's permit, so I would drive my folks' van sometimes. One time, I drove it out to a friend's house in an area the locals called Boto, which was about six miles from town, out past the Diamond Mine. About five more miles past this gal's house was the birthplace of country music star Glen Campbell, officially in Delight, Arkansas, and would one day be the location of his grave as well. Anyway, I hung out at my friend's house for a couple of hours and, after it had gotten dark, decided I better go home. I backed the van down her driveway, but when it came time to back around to the right to get out on the highway, I cut the van too close and ended up in the ditch between the highway and her yard. I tried to correct my error but just managed to go further in the ditch until the van almost tilted onto its side. I knew I needed help at that point, so I very carefully got out of the van and walked back up to my friend's house to use her phone to call my dad. I explained to him what happened, and he said he would be there ASAP. When he got there, he got in the van and drove it carefully back to the side of the road, where I got in it and followed him home. I was so embarrassed by my ineptitude but grateful that Dad rescued me and that we hadn't had to get a tow truck to haul the van out of the ditch.

The older group that I was hanging out with would ride around uptown too, but they also had parties, big and small, out in the woods. Having a party at a house would attract more attention, but there were some held still. They had to avoid the cops, so the secret word would get out at the last minute where the party would be. They were held at places like the right left or the left right, indicating which way to turn on the different dirt roads in the woods surrounding the town. Of course, there were many right-left or left-right combinations possible, but the insiders knew which roads these referred to. They would gather in a spot and build a fire, then back their cars or trucks around the fire to make seating if you liked. It was cold outside at that time of year, so the fire was essential. I wasn't fond of going home smelling like wood smoke, but it was better than when someone would burn a tire, and I would have that smell on me along with a black residue in my nose and sometimes on my clothes or shoes. If it was a big party on the weekend, there might be a keg of beer. For smaller parties during the week, there was much less alcohol. It wasn't easy to come by even though most of these guys were old enough to buy it, because Murfreesboro is located in a dry county. That means, roughly, that the sale of alcohol or possession of too much alcohol is against the law. The closest legal places to buy alcohol were Hot Springs and Texarkana, but there were bootleggers on the way to those towns that would save you about twenty miles if you knew where to go and didn't mind paying more than you would in the city.

I wasn't much of a drinker, so I didn't care whether the county was wet or dry, but I did like to smoke a very small amount of weed. I never bought it for myself, except for a $1 joint in Porterville a few times. I had money but didn't care enough to even buy it. There was always someone around offering it to me, especially when I only wanted a couple of tokes and I was done. One of the guys in the older crowd was particularly known for being the go-to weed guy, and we had a conversation once about pot brownies. I told him that I liked them because I loved brownies, and I didn't really like the taste of weed, so the brownies made that easier to deal with. He said that he was going to make some and bring them to the party the following weekend, so I was looking forward to it. This particular party was at a local family's deer camp, which was a rough log cabin with gravel floors and was virtually empty except for the woodstove located in the center. I preferred it to the outdoors, however, being the city girl that I was. That night, when the weed guy proudly produced his pot brownies, I was surprised to see leaves and stems sticking out of them and was appalled when I took a bite out of one and got a mouthful of those leaves and stems along with seeds and even dirt! I was too intimidated not to finish my brownie and managed to gag it down.

About an hour later, my stomach started feeling really sick, and I had to ask the group that I had ridden with to take me home back in town. They weren't thrilled to leave the party, but they didn't give me a hard time either. It took about twenty minutes to get to my house, where I thanked them and quickly got in the house. I had to go through my folks' bedroom, where my mom was sleeping, to get into the bathroom, so I woke her up when I started vomiting in the toilet. She came in and asked what had happened, and I explained. Once again, I didn't get into trouble for what I had done because I was already paying a heavy price for it. I was sick all night and into the next day until all the wretched brownies had left my system. You see, the brownies that I was used to eating were restaurant quality, literally. The leaves were dried and ground so finely before they were added to the batter that you couldn't even taste the marijuana, and there was certainly no sign of stems, seeds, or dirt! Why in the world did I eat that disgusting thing? Such a stupid girl.

It was only a few months before we moved to another house in Murfreesboro. Even in this small town with very limited housing options, my folks could find a way to move us around. This house was directly across the street from where my sister lived with her husband's grandfather. It looked like a big, traditional farmhouse-style home but only had a living room, kitchen, three bedrooms, and one bath inside. The floorplan was strange, and you had to go through the kitchen to get to the living room. The entire house was surrounded by porches, and each bedroom had an exterior door with access to the porch, so it would have been a great house for sneaking out, but I never needed to do that.

Tina and I spent most of our time with the older crowd, and she dated one of them for a short time. His name was Donnie, and he was divorcing his wife, so Tina had to keep a lookout for his ex, who was thought by many to be mentally ill. Tina wanted to break it off with this guy, and I remember he sent her a dozen roses once to try and keep her in the relationship, but it didn't work. I know he must have been around and at the parties, but I really don't remember him at that time. I dated another of the guys a few times, but he only wanted one thing, as they say, and I wasn't willing to give it, so that didn't go anywhere. Thank goodness I never got together with him, or with the guy I soon developed a huge crush on, because one was going to murder the other about 15 years later. Tina started dating a guy from nearby Nashville, and I went on a double date with her and a friend of his once. I really enjoyed this guy's company because he was a musician, so we talked about music the whole time. We drove around Lake Greeson for a while and talked about the Beatles and what an amazing songwriting team Lennon and McCartney had been and so on. The guy said his favorite album of theirs was the White Album and asked if I was familiar with it. I told him that I didn't know it that well, and then he parked the car and started to tell me about how the album contained a song with the most profound lyrics that the band had ever written. He talked it up so well that I was totally amped to hear it. He started the song, and all four of us were really quiet, waiting to hear the song and its profound lyrics, and then we hear, "Why don't we do it in the road?" It was a brilliant moment for us two Beatles fans, and we both laughed like crazy. We drove around the lake more until we hit a skunk and had to stop the car abruptly and get the hell away from it. The smell was so strong that I thought I might be sick. I hated having to get back in the car and ride all the way to Nashville to get Tina's truck. In spite of the skunk, I really enjoyed my double date's company, and I would have gone out with him again, but he never asked. I wasn't bothered by his lack of attention, however, because I was developing a serious crush on someone else by this time.

I can't explain the connection between me and this young man, but it was very powerful. I wasn't physically attracted to him, and he was so shy and quiet around me that it was hard to be attracted to his personality, but I was attracted nonetheless. He was one of the high school guys who partied with the older crowd, so I spent time around him in school and out. I wanted him to ask me out, and he finally did, although it was very casual. He stopped by my house one day, where I was outside mowing the lawn. I shut down the mower and walked over to his driver's side window, where he asked me if I wanted to go with him to the party that Saturday night. He had his best running buddy with him. I said yes, and he told me a time that he would pick me up. When he picked me up on Saturday, I made it easy for him and came out to the car to meet him so he didn't have to knock on the door. When he opened the car door for me to get in, I saw that his running buddy was in the back seat, apparently riding with us to the party. So it was even more casual than I thought. When we got to the party, we found seats around the fire on a tailgate, with me in the center and my companions on either side. As hard as I tried, I couldn't get my date to open up to me and show me any interest, so I ended up spending more time talking to his running buddy and having a good time with him. By the time we left the party, the running buddy and I were secretly holding hands next to the interior passenger door, with me in the front seat and him sitting behind me.

After that, my crush didn't ask me out again, apparently because even though he liked me, he thought I didn't really like him when I was actually very interested in him, but he didn't show me any interest back. So that began a very confusing, immature exchange of emotions between the two of us that I couldn't really even call a relationship because we were never really together. We had love/hate exchanges that were filled with frustration. During a rehearsal for the junior play that we were putting on in school, he was sitting in the auditorium with a couple other guys and a boom box because they were in charge of the music. I was in charge of taking tickets and handing out programs, so I was just meandering in the auditorium during the rehearsal. At some point, we ended up talking a few rows behind the other guys and had a heated argument. I don't even remember what it was about, but he said something that offended me, probably about me having sex with him because that was a big issue of contention between us. It was the classic "Guys give love to get sex, and girls give sex to get love," and neither one of us was willing to give first. Anyway, I slapped him across the face, not too lightly and not too hard, but it did get us some attention from a teacher who was positioned in the back of the auditorium. She took us out into the hall and gave us a lecture about our inappropriate behavior. We certainly didn't want to get into real trouble at school, so we apologized and promised to control our tempers in the future, and we did—in school, at least.

While I had this low-level violence occurring in my nonrelationship with my crush, I had a more serious incident with my father. On Thanksgiving, Mom made dinner for the family, and I invited Tina to join us. She and I really wanted to go out to Boto to meet up with our older crowd friends, but I had to appease Mom by having family dinner first. We finished our uneventful dinner, and then, I don't remember what my brother and I started arguing about, but we did. We were both pretty passionate about it apparently, because we each got pretty close to my dad's face and were complaining about each other. Before I realized the physical position that we were all in, my dad had backhanded my brother and me across our faces at the same time, hitting my brother first and then me. My brother got a bloody nose, and I got a bloody lip, which dripped down onto to my beautiful new white blouse that I had worn for the holiday. I was stunned, shocked, hurt, and embarrassed by this incident, which occurred right there in front of my friend. Of all the crazy, violent, and dysfunctional behavior I had witnessed in my home, my dad had never hit me in anger before. I had seen him physically abuse my brother, which was disturbing enough, but it hadn't happened to me until now. My head was reeling with this whole new level of something bad happening in my parents' home.

Since we had finished dinner, I asked my mom right away if I could leave with Tina, and she said yes. I remember talking to Tina about the incident on the way out to Boto, but I couldn't make sense of it. She just listened kindly as a friend, and I mulled it over in my mind for weeks, trying to understand my new reality. I knew that I had become more and more angry about all the crap that my parents had put me through, and I found it harder and harder to forgive and forget the way the rest of the family seemed to do. Some behavior just wasn't right, and it shouldn't be forgiven or forgotten; it should be corrected and stopped. I discovered that, however, when you're the only one in your environment who feels that way, nothing is going to change. I was taking my anger out verbally on my mother and my brother more and more all the time. I would say the worst things to them that I could think of, knowing what would hurt them the most. It was a case of hurt people hurting people. I had years of pain that started when I was seven years old with my second molestation and had built up year after year and incident after incident without any help or resolution of the things that happened to me. Now the anger was bursting out of me in ways that I couldn't control and that didn't help. They just made things worse, and I was becoming someone whom I not only hated, but loathed. I had no value and nothing to offer.

CHAPTER 55

"Leather and Lace"

(Stevie Nicks and Don Henley)

While I was still trying to process the incident with my dad, I walked down to Junior Mart to hang around while Tina was working one evening. The weather had been cold but clear when I walked there, but it had started raining, and I wasn't looking forward to the walk home. I told Tina that I was just going to stay there until it cleared up, or I got brave enough to get soaking wet, so I was shocked when her old boyfriend, Donnie, came in and walked to the counter to buy cigarettes, and Tina asked him to give me a ride to my house a couple blocks away. He agreed and asked if I was ready to go. I had my reservations, but I accepted his offer, said goodbye to Tina, and followed him out to his burgundy Trans Am, where he opened the passenger door and quickly got me out of the rain. He asked if I wanted to ride around town for a bit before going home, and I said yes. He was very pleasant and easy to talk to, and I didn't find him nearly as scary as his persona appeared to be. He was six feet, two inches, had a big, muscular build, and had an aura about him that said, "Don't mess with me," which was how my mom described my dad when she met him, so I hadn't expected him to be so friendly. After riding around for about thirty minutes, he took me home, and he asked if he could see me again. I told him that I would like that, so we made plans for our first date, and we quickly became a tentative couple in spite of the fact that I was sixteen years old, and he was twenty-five. I say tentative because I still had feelings for my crush, but that relationship wasn't going anywhere. I finally had to make a choice between the two of them one night when I agreed to go to a party with Donnie at one of the older crowd's homes, and my crush was there.

When we got to the party, my crush was leaning up against the sink in the kitchen. Donnie and I made our rounds saying hello to everyone, then went our separate ways, as was our habit. He usually talked with the older crowd and I with the younger. I got myself a drink and leaned against the counter in the kitchen, where my friends were gathered. Eventually, my crush made his way down to where I was standing, and he started talking to me in a low voice out the side of his mouth, and I responded the same so that nobody could hear what we were saying, but we weren't that close to each other. I don't remember exactly what we said, but I know we were expressing our frustrations with each other, and he was getting more and more angry. At some point, he moved close enough to stand arm to arm with me, and he started pinching my arm from behind his so nobody could see what he was doing. He would say something angry and pinch and twist my arm, then stop when I would respond. This happened several times, and eventually, after going to the restroom or something, we ended up on the other side of each other, where he started the pinching process again.

After a few times, I couldn't take it any longer, and I went outside and sat on the front porch, trying not to cry. Donnie came out a few minutes later and asked me what was going on. I told him that I needed to go home, and he agreed, so we got into his car and left. He started asking me about my relationship with my crush and wanted to know what was going on. When we were almost at my house, I told him to keep going, and we could talk a little more, so he drove up to the lake. We talked, and I cried all the way, and by the time we got to the first lookout point and stopped the car, I was ready to pull up my shirt sleeves and show him several bruises on each of my arms. He said he would go and whoop my crush's ass right now for doing that to me, but I pleaded with him not to. He told me that he loved me and really wanted us to be together, but he couldn't if I was going to let some other guy do something like to me, and I knew that I definitely was not and that I had to make a choice between the two of them.

Looking back years later, I realized that I wasn't just making a choice between two guys, but I was actually making a much bigger life choice. Donnie had been good to me while we were dating, and now he had professed his love for me, and deep in my heart, I knew that I could love him too and marry him, get out of my terrible home situation, and start a new life for myself. Of course, I didn't think all this consciously, but now I can look back and see it clearly. He was a grown man, who had actually been married previously, and I knew in my heart that he would take care of me. He showed me respect and admiration. He was safe. The alternative was trying to make a normal relationship with a high school boy who, although he told me that he cared about me and wanted to be with me and we had a powerful chemistry between us, he really brought me nothing but turmoil and potential violence, much like my current homelife.

Donnie got out of the car and walked around the lookout, and I thought long and hard, trying to make my very important decision, and I did. When he got back into the car, I told him that I didn't want to be with my crush but that I wanted to be with him. From that point on, we were together as a real couple, and I told him at some point that I loved him too. I did my best to forget about my crush, and I did, for a while. I don't remember exactly when Donnie and I got together, but by March 3, 1982, we were husband and wife. I also don't remember exactly how we decided on even getting married, but it happened. After all, I was already four years over Dad's "if you're not married by twelve-years-old, you're going to the old folks' home" rule. Ha!

It was one of those situations where we just knew that we were going to be together and get married, so we were ready to get on with it. Once Donnie asked my parents for their permission, which was required in the state of Arkansas as I was only sixteen years old, we set a date, and Donnie also asked my parents if he could just move into my bedroom since we were almost married. Mom and Dad loved Donnie, and although he was a very likable man, he wasn't the husband I believe most parents would have chosen for their daughter. First of all, I was only sixteen; he was twenty-five. I wasn't pregnant. We weren't even having sex. He had no job at the moment because he worked road construction and was always laid off in the winter and lived on unemployment benefits. He didn't have his own place to live and was currently sleeping on his parents' couch. He had no assets other than his car and the personal items that he could fit into it, and we had only been dating each other for about four months. I didn't even demand that my parents give me their permission, as my sister did, but they had no problem saying yes. My dad did make one demand himself—that I graduate from high school. Donnie and I both promised that I would.

Of course, at the time, I was very happy with their decision, but looking back, it makes me feel like I had absolutely no value or worth to my parents whatsoever, and they were happy to get rid of me. They've never given me a reason to believe otherwise either. The school in Murfreesboro didn't have a problem with me getting married either. While it was unheard of for a student to be married at the other two high schools I had attended in California and Washington, it wasn't that unusual here. It wasn't common, but people were certainly not shocked by the idea. The school even had a policy that a newlywed must take one month off from school after the marriage as a period of adjustment. This would allow for a honeymoon trip, moving in together as a married couple, etc., which didn't apply to me at all.

I loved Donnie, and I took our marriage very seriously. I intended to be married to him for the rest of my life, and I was dedicated to the oath that I made to him by the power of a justice of the peace in my parents' living room, wearing nice jeans and the same white blouse that I had managed to get the bloodstain out of, with my husband wearing the same, jeans and a button-down shirt. My parents, brother, sister, and brother-in-law were in attendance, although my sister was very upset that I didn't wear a dress to be married in. Two of our friends, whom I haven't mentioned up until now, were our official witnesses and pseudo best man and bridesmaid. There was also an old friend of Dad's from Aberdeen who was staying with my parents because he was helping Dad on the truck. His girlfriend was also on the truck with them, and she made Donnie and me the ugliest wedding cake that I've ever seen, but I did appreciate her efforts. Nobody from Donnie's family was in attendance, and in fact, from the time that Donnie had moved into my bedroom a few weeks earlier, I hadn't even been allowed to enter his parents' house at the mandate of his mother because we were living in sin. I never understood why Donnie was allowed to be in her home when he was living in sin with me, but I was the only one who was banned. In a show of solidarity, however, he refused to do so until I was also welcomed in their home. Because of this, we were definitely on the outs with all of Donnie's family, however. After we celebrated for a short time with this small group of people, we left for our honeymoon, which might have been a gift from my parents or the result of a collection put together by several people, possibly including Donnie. However it came to fruition, we spent one night at a cute little cabin at Lake Greeson, then returned to my bedroom at my parents' house to start our married life together.

We stayed at my parents' house for a few months until the weather warmed up. Donnie went back to work, and he was able to afford our own place. In the meantime, I had my month out of school and spent a great deal of that time suffering from and recovering from pneumonia with pleurisy. It was a miserable time, made even worse by getting sick from the antibiotics the doctor gave me to cure the infection. I finally recovered from my illness and was allowed to go back to school, where I discovered it had been a big mistake to be gone for one month. I couldn't have cared any less about attending school any longer, although I had enjoyed it before I got married. I tried to get my head back into the game and talked to Donnie, my mom, my friends, and school administrators about it, but there was no going back for me. I quit with only three weeks to go in my junior year. I kept it a secret from Donnie at first and then from my father, and when each of them found out, they expressed their disappointment, but I didn't care. My decision was firm, although I did ask the school if I could just take my finals and test out of each of my classes for that year and then start with my senior class in the fall. When they said that it wasn't possible, I started making plans to get my GED right away.

Before I could get that done, I had an accident while doing dishes at home by myself one day. I had my hand down inside a glass in a sink full of soapy water, rotating it around in the glass to get it clean when the glass broke and cut my hand pretty badly. When the soapy water suddenly became bloodred, I pulled my hand out and saw blood shooting out of the small artery on my hand above my index finger. My thumb was also bleeding at the base, but it was the shooting blood that got my attention. I went to the phone on the wall and called my sister. I told her that I hurt myself, needed stitches, and needed to go to the emergency room. She said she was feeding the baby at the moment, and I told her that it couldn't wait and that I had blood shooting out all over the place. She put me on hold for a moment to ask Wayne if he could take me since he was at home for lunch at the moment. She came back and said that yes, Wayne would be right over to take me to the ER. I hung up the phone and turned around to see almost the entire kitchen covered in blood, and I grabbed the dish towel that was hanging from the refrigerator handle and started wiping up all the blood I could see.

It was almost time for Tom to come home from school, and I didn't want him to think someone had been murdered in our kitchen. I was continuing to wipe up when Wayne came in and said something along the lines of "Holy shit!" when he saw all the blood, and I told him I was trying to clean it up. He said that wouldn't do any good if I didn't get my hand covered with something because it was shooting blood out. That hadn't occurred to me. I got a clean dish towel out of the drawer, and he wrapped it around my hand to stop the bleeding. I hurried to finish cleaning up the blood and finally drained the bloody water from the sink and cleaned it out, and I was ready to go. When we got to the hospital, I got five stitches in my hand and two in my thumb. It left a sensitive scar that I still have, and it was difficult trying to get things done with one hand for a while, but I'd been through much worse.

I was doing my best to be a good married lady even while still living in my parents' house. I had such a hard time with cooking, and I've still never learned to "cook for an army," like my mom and so many others do, so I was really put to the test when Dad came home off the road one evening along with Sam, whom he had picked up in Washington State. I'm not sure why Sam was on the road with Dad at that particular time, but it was so good to see him! I had made a meatloaf for dinner for Donnie, Tom, Mom, and me, and now I had to add two more portions. Along with the meatloaf was mashed potatoes and a couple of canned vegetables, and I didn't have the knowledge or ingredients to add anything else. My solution was to dish up a plate for each person using all the ingredients I had and portioning them appropriately. I was so worried that someone would ask for more, but I think everyone could see how hard I tried, and Sam was especially complimentary of my cooking, which didn't deserve it, I'm sure.

As soon as my hand was healed enough to write, I went down to the courthouse and took my GED tests, which I passed in the ninetieth percentile, and went back to the same courthouse soon after to get my driver's license. I was very good at taking care of business, and the next thing to accomplish was finding a place for Donnie and me to live.

CHAPTER 56

"Landslide"
(Fleetwood Mac)

Housing is very limited in Murfreesboro, as I mentioned earlier, so our choices were very small. Somebody told me about a furnished house that one of the wealthy women in town rented out, and they said it was small but very nice. I got in touch with the lady and made arrangements to meet her at the house, which was down at the far end of Second Street, which was the street that we lived on when we first moved to town. It was an adorable stucco house with a small living room, one bedroom directly to the right of the living room, a tiny eat-in kitchen directly off the rear of the living room, and an even tinier bathroom directly to the right of the kitchen. The kitchen and bathroom were uncomfortably small, but the whole place was furnished very nicely and had everything we needed, except for small items. I fell in love with the place and wanted it, and Donnie agreed, so we rented it and moved in with our meager belongings. I was so excited to buy dishes, linens, cookware, and everything else we needed in our new home.

It meant everything to me that I had my own place in the world, where I had some control over what happened around me and to me.

I hadn't realized how important that was to me. I decided that I was going to make a huge change in myself and learn to control my anger or, better yet, be grateful for everything I had instead of being angry about all the things that were wrong in my life. My home was my refuge and my safe place. Donnie was very agreeable at that time and pretty much let me do what I wanted. I wanted to please him and show him how much I loved him. I never wanted him to see the ugly, angry side of me, and he never did. It was going to be him and me against the world, and we were going to make a life that we were both happy about. He invited his friends over, ones that I knew but got to know better or hadn't met yet at all. I liked them, and they liked me. We had good times together at one another's homes, playing card games or watching TV together. Then I started trying to learn to cook for the first time, and I did okay at first but soon learned that Donnie didn't like what I wanted to cook and vice versa. I didn't care for meat, and that was Donnie's main focus. I also didn't know how to make a pot of beans or a pan of gravy. I became very discouraged and hated cooking for about the next ten years. It was always a point of contention between us. I was an excellent housekeeper and money manager. I showed him respect and was kind to his family and friends, but Donnie never acknowledged those things. He seemed to become increasingly disappointed in me as a wife. I guess that's to be expected when you marry a sixteen-year-old. We weren't able to bond sexually either. I had no experience, but I was enthusiastic in the beginning and relied on Donnie to guide our relationship sexually. Sadly, it never worked out between us, and I'll just leave it at that.

Donnie ended up becoming more and more oppressive, cold, and disrespectful to me, but he didn't cuss me, beat me, cheat on me, or have a drinking problem. He also worked hard at his job and brought his paycheck home to me every week, so according to a lot of people's standards, there was absolutely nothing for me to be unhappy about. I did take comfort in the fact that I was out of my parents' dysfunctional home and had a little more control over my own life now. That was detrimental to my survival. I don't know who I would have become had I not done that. My home with Donnie was dysfunctional in other ways, but eventually, I would triumph over that too and take the beautiful blessing that God had placed inside me.

EPILOGUE

"What a Wonderful World"

(Louis Armstrong)

I'm ending this story when I officially left my parents' house as a married woman at the age of sixteen, but there's so much more to tell, which I may do someday.

My parents continued to have a marriage of infidelity and potential violence for many more years. I won't say more because I don't want to give away their unlikely ending.

Dan continued to have a life so incredible that it's hard to believe it's true but in much different ways than he had before the car accident that almost killed him.

Sam continued to be an enigma, which was so extreme that he alienated many people in his life and created a great deal of pain for some who he left behind—as a consequence of his actions.

Patty managed to climb out of her grief to on top of the world for quite some time while pursuing her creative passions, only to later crash down to the lowest of the low in life until she managed to claw her way back up again, repeating that cycle several times and making two more beautiful children along the way.

Paula moved from Arkansas to rural Virginia in 1983, and her life has pretty much been exactly the same since then. She and Wayne have now been married for almost fifty years, have eight children, over twenty grandchildren, and live the devout life of fundamental Christians.

Tom Jr. has spent at least twenty years now acting out the same alienation as Sam and our uncle Dean before him, causing the same pain to some of us, although I won't speak for anyone else. He even left our country to become a citizen in another one. It used to hurt me a great deal, but now I try to focus on all the blessings that I have and not the things that I don't.

As for me, I am damn proud to say that I graduated with a Bachelor's degree from the University of Washington–Tacoma in 1997, have owned a few homes, had a successful and exciting career in several different fields, and married the man of my dreams twenty-two years ago, who also made me the proud Army wife of a now retired Sergeant Major. We've had a beautiful life with our two amazing daughters and two grandsons, along with our soldier family. I've explored this country and other parts of the world, and I hope to keep traveling and having adventures for as long as I can. Most importantly, I have received countless blessings from my Creator, Lord, and Savior, for which I am exceedingly grateful.

Printed in the USA
CPSIA information can be obtained
at www.ICGtesting.com
LVHW091300140924
790990LV00001B/80

9 798890 61926